Justice and Reverse Discrimination

Justice
and
Reverse Discrimination

Alan H. Goldman

Princeton University Press
Princeton, New Jersey

For Joan and my parents

CONTENTS

ACKNOWLEDGMENTS

I would like to thank first and foremost the three eminent philosophers who read the entire manuscript at earlier stages and offered criticisms and encouragement: Hugo Bedau, William Blackstone, and Thomas Nagel.

No philosopher writing on a topic so broadly addressed by others will have done his homework responsibly without owing a large debt of gratitude to his colleagues. Those whose articles had the greatest influence on the views to be presented here include James Nickel, Michael Bayles, George Sher, Robert Simon, and again Thomas Nagel. Probably none will agree entirely with my position. Others, I hope, are adequately acknowledged in the notes. Many readers will recognize my debt to John Rawls regarding the moral framework from which the study begins. Other theoretical sections draw in part from the work of Joel Feinberg.

Much of the first draft of this manuscript was written while I held a fellowship from the National Endowment for the Humanities at Tufts. I am grateful to the NEH for that opportunity.

Portions of my previously published articles have been reproduced here: "Justice and Hiring by Competence," *American Philosophical Quarterly*, 14 (1977); "Limits to the Justification of Reverse Discrimination," *Social Theory and Practice*, 3 (1975); "Reparations to Individuals or Groups?" *Analysis*, 35 (1975); "Rights, Utilities and Contracts," *Canadian Journal of Philosophy*, Sup. 3 (1977); "The Principle of Equal Opportunity," *Southern Journal of Philosophy*, 15 (1977); "Reverse Discrimination and the Future: A Reply to Irving Thalberg," *Philosophical Forum*, 11 (1974-1975); "Affirmative Action," *Philosophy & Public Affairs*, 5 (1976). I thank these journals for their permissions.

Finally I am grateful to Dayle Williams for typing the manuscript, to Gretchen Oberfranc of Princeton University Press for rendering the prose readable, to my wife Joan for criticisms and help with proofreading and preparation of the manuscript, and to my six-year-old son Michael for occasionally leaving me alone over the past two years to work on it.

Justice and Reverse Discrimination

ONE

Introduction

This book will present a sustained argument for a single coherent view on the question of preferential treatment for
members of minority groups and women. Arguments derived
from other philosophers and lawyers will be considered when
relevant to the development of this view, but I shall not attempt to provide a survey of possible positions on each facet of
the issue. Collections of articles representing different moral
viewpoints on the subject are available, but in the course of
writing several articles myself, I came to the conclusion that
the subject cannot be treated adequately in such limited
space. The issue is too complex, and the opposing claims too
plausible and initially compelling, to be sorted out in twenty
or thirty pages. Adequate development of a reasoned position
on so difficult a moral issue demands preliminary exploration
of such fundamental moral concepts as rights and their relation
to utilities, the value of and right to equality and equal opportunity, and the concept of adequate compensation for injury or
injustice.

That the issue demands such thorough treatment needs
little argument. Relations among races and between sexes,
assertions of individual rights, and demands for equality in
distributions of society's benefits—all of which figure prominently in this issue—constitute the fundamental social problems of our era. Thorough philosophical treatment is demanded not only because many persons' futures are at stake,
but also as a test of the fruitfulness of ethical theory itself. If
concrete social issues cannot be settled by thorough moral re-
flection that aims at consistency with settled moral convictions
and accepted principles, they can be settled only by political
muscle or in terms of shallow initial impressions. If normative
moral theory cannot be tested by implications regarding correct solutions to real issues, then it remains academic and in
all probability oversimplified. If moral philosophers do not

dirty their hands in the soil of social problems, their abstract principles remain without adequate grounding. In fact, the sterility of such supremely general principles as the principle of utility becomes apparent only when we see how many distinct and less general principles need to be developed before a coherent solution to a problem like the justice or injustice of reverse discrimination can be even suggested.

Our object here will be to decide in which situations and for which individuals preferential policies can be justified and in which situations they cannot. We may begin by defining reverse discrimination as preferential treatment for minority-group members or women in job hiring, school admissions, or training-program policies.[1] This definition will be improved throughout the initial chapters, as I examine the initial distributive rule for awarding positions, and as I distinguish among the various forms that preferential hiring and admissions policies can take. One form of preferential treatment that we will be considering attempts to correct for situations created by earlier treatment that departed from generally relevant criteria in an invidious way. Another form aims to create equal opportunities for those who presently have none. The question we must answer is: When can corrective preferential treatment of either form be justified and for whom. The question is a pressing one because preference is being given to many individuals under government pressure (affirmative action programs), and it is clear that the results of such pressure do not always accord with justice. While the realignment of political power that is taking place may be an improvement in distributing power to those who formerly lacked it, from a moral standpoint the policies that emerge from this realignment may not always be the best of available alternatives. The fact that different forms of preferential treatment are officially advocated in executive orders and put into practice under their threats makes a decision on their constitutionality by the courts (now partly decided as a result of the *Bakke* case) and on their justice by social philosophers even more crucial. While the opinions of social philosophers may be of less immediate practical consequence, and while philosophers have no exclusive insight into the correct verdict, we may presume that those in power will generally pursue a policy of whose justice they are convinced and that moral philosophers trained to analyze arguments in this and similar areas may be best equipped to do the persuading.

The recent Supreme Court decision in the well-known *Bakke* case did little to resolve this issue morally.[2] The decision found against only those programs of professional schools innocent of prior discrimination that aim at fixed quotas of minority representation. The legal status of the great majority of affirmative action programs that set goals for minority representation in education and employment was left unsettled. More important, it is questionable whether the *Bakke* decision, which prohibits programs that require fixed percentages of minority-group members in positions at professional schools but allows race to count as a positive qualification for admission, is morally consistent. If race (or sex?) is considered a qualification in itself, then a person otherwise better qualified can lose a position solely because of his or her race (or sex), independent of whether the person thus advanced actually suffered from discrimination in the past. If this policy is to be justified on grounds of the value of diversity in the classroom, as Justice Powell argued in his key opinion, why not use quotas to achieve a mix that is considered optimal? That there is by definition a difference in degree to which race is considered in these two methods cannot be maintained, since no program has ever called for filling a quota with applicants who otherwise lack minimally acceptable qualifications. A school can adjust this level of minimal acceptability by adjusting the size of its quota as easily as by adjusting the degree to which race is to count as a qualification.

Hence there is no moral distinction—or any basis for a legal distinction—between the two types of programs distinguished in the *Bakke* decision, and especially in the opinion of Justice Powell. The real moral distinction is between those programs that award preference according to race or sex and those that demand evidence of individual desert for preference. This difference was not seen as crucial in the *Bakke* opinions. That decision, like the decision on abortion in *Roe* v. *Wade*, seemed politically astute in aiming to satisfy as many of the competing interests as possible. However, if the Supreme Court is not to be one more majoritarian political institution in our society, decisions in which distinctions lack legal or philosophical basis deserve little praise for their political astuteness. We shall be concerned here with the moral rather than the legal issue. But if denial of equal protection of the laws under the Fourteenth Amendment includes denial of equal opportunity for social benefits through the operation of state regulations or programs, and if we interpret equal opportunity in the morally correct way, then these issues appear to coincide.

I shall argue that those most competent for the positions for which they apply have prima facie rights to those positions; that reverse discrimination is nevertheless justified in order to compensate specific past violations of these rights or denials of equal opportunity; that a policy of preference is justified as well in order to create equal opportunity in the future for the chronically deprived; that preference *cannot* be justified when directed indiscriminately at groups defined only by race or sex, in order merely to increase their percentage representation in various social positions; and that affirmative action programs are unjust to the extent that they encourage or directly mandate such group-oriented preferential policies. The position to be advocated here falls between that of those who call for preference for all women and members of minorities until percentage representations are proportionate to numbers of those seeking positions from various groups, and that of those who believe that any departure from "merit criteria" is unjust. My position differs from the compromise view represented in the *Bakke* decision in calling for individualization of criteria for preferential treatment. This can be accomplished even when aiming to correct only injustices connected with racial and sexual discrimination, as opposed to all economic or social handicaps. Given the extensive amount of past injustice to individuals still seeking positions—denial of jobs and promotions to most competent or potentially most competent women or blacks, denial of equal educational opportunity by forced attendance at segregated schools, etc.—and given the chronic social deprivation prevalent in many ghetto communities, the preferential policies advocated would need to be fairly widespread. My objection to present policies is not that they are preferential or involve reverse discrimination, but that they tend to benefit many (and in some cases mainly) individuals who do not deserve preference on either of the grounds to be defended.

Before pursuing and developing the main argument, I shall make clearer some initial definitions and distinctions, and say something about the methods to be used in arriving at a final verdict.

Initial Distinctions

For treatment to be preferential, it must employ criteria that depart from characteristics generally considered relevant to the award of the positions in question and from the rule stipulating these generally relevant characteristics. For example, race or sex are not generally considered relevant characteristics upon which to base appointments; when they are used as such, the decisions will be preferential toward some individuals and discriminatory against others. Chapter Two will be concerned with establishing a general rule for awarding positions in a just distributive social system. Justifying this rule from a moral standpoint will involve not only more precise definitions of first-order and reverse discrimination, but also a demonstration of their prima facie injustice. (The distinction between these forms of discrimination lies in the intent of the latter to compensate or prevent the former and in the individuals for whom the latter is therefore preferential.) All discrimination departs from criteria that are initially relevant from the point of view of justice, hence all is prima facie unjust. Obviously, no redeeming features of discrimination against minority-group members or women (first order) can override violation of the normally proper rule (rather, further injustices are involved, such as undeserved insult). The question is how can compensatory and other considerations override prima facie just criteria for award of positions in the case of reverse discrimination or preferential treatment of minority-group members. This question will occupy subsequent chapters.

One central distinction between the forms of preferential policies mentioned above pertains to their application to whole minority groups as opposed to their application to individuals. Preferential policies, as stipulated in official programs, now generally grant preference to members of broad groups defined by race or sex. Various rationales can be offered for stating the criteria for preferential treatment this broadly. For example: that the original first-order discrimination for which this policy attempts to atone was made on the basis of race and sex; that only programs that employ these broad criteria can create equality of opportunity and give a fair share of power to all women and blacks by granting them desirable positions of responsibility quickly; or that insuperable administrative difficulties are avoided by stating the policy in terms of such easily identifiable characteristics as race or sex. I shall argue against these rationales in the third and fourth chapters. As we shall see, most of the reasons given in justification of preferential treatment are also compelling reasons for defining criteria of eligibility more narrowly than by race or sex, in order to single out only certain individuals within minority groups for preference. For example, if the reason given for preference is past discrimination, then we should prefer individuals actually discriminated against in the past. If the justifying reason is to end the cycle of chronic economic and social deprivation, then only those who are so deprived should be preferred. The desirability of increasing representation of particular groups in particular professions is not judged in itself to be a compelling reason to override the prima facie rights of others to positions. The concept of group rights does apply in certain contexts, but not in this one.

An initial distinction must also be drawn between weak and strong forms of reverse discrimination, and among the forms of strong discrimination. Weak reverse discrimination occurs when a minority-group member is preferred only when as qualified as any other candidate for a position. Strong preference is shown in one of two ways: when a minority-group member is given a certain percentage advantage within the scale of competence requirements used in hiring or admissions (we may term this "handicapping"), or when certain places are reserved outright for such individuals (sometimes with the requirement that the individuals demonstrate a level of competence above a prescribed minimum). An example of the former would be to add a certain number of points to the standard test scores of minority candidates when comparing them with those of white male applicants to graduate schools; the latter could be illustrated by an order to increase minority membership in a union or police department to 20 percent, or to reserve places in a professional school for members of some group in proportion to their percentage of the local population. The latter, if accomplished without comparing the qualifications of minority applicants with those of others, is the strongest form of reverse discrimination possible. The policy of the University of Washington Law School, challenged by De Funis, apparently involved the former type of strong preference; that at issue in the *Bakke* case involved the latter type.

These last distinctions are more important when award of the position in question depends upon open-ended degrees of competence or excellence rather than a fixed level of competence. Thus the justification for preferential treatment in hiring unskilled laborers, where equal competence may be expected to be widespread and where political considerations therefore may be allowed to have more weight, may be different from the justification for preferential programs of hiring in the universities. When open-ended degrees of excellence are possible for positions (such as those of doctors or professors), preferential policies will tend toward strong rather than weak reverse discrimination, the latter being applicable only in cases in which applicants have equal qualifications. There also will be differences between preferential treatment in training programs or admissions to schools and preference at the level of hiring, resulting from differences in the availability of the positions and the social costs involved in filling them. If and when reverse discrimination is justified in such cases as hiring in universities, the applicability of a strong or only a weak form will have to be made clear in each instance.

Finally, there is an initial distinction to be drawn among the types of reasons for preferential policies, that is, justifications in terms of compensation for past harm (backward looking) and those in terms of creating equality of conditions or equality of opportunity (future looking). It can be argued that those groups or individuals against whom there has been unjust discrimination in the past are now owed compensation in kind, that is, jobs of the type formerly barred by discriminatory practices. It can also be argued that those who are culturally or economically deprived through no fault of their own cannot have equality of opportunity for themselves or their children without decent jobs to raise their standard of living and level of motivation. These different lines of argument can be combined in various ways: if either justification alone is accepted, the group for whom the preferential policy is advocated will be larger; if both justifications must apply, the group will be smaller. I shall examine backward-looking justifications in the third chapter and future-looking in the fourth; the preliminary issue of a generally just initial rule for hiring and admissions will be settled in Chapter Two.

Deductive Methodology

As the foregoing indicates, this book will be an exercise in applied social philosophy, as opposed to pure moral or social philosophy. In the latter discipline philosophers generally begin with clear-cut moral intuitions regarding specific situations or cases and work backwards to fully general moral principles implying these initial verdicts. For example, they might begin with intuitions that stealing is wrong but that stealing to save a life is permitted, or that it is worse to inflict harm than to refuse aid even when the results are the same. They then attempt to find as few general principles as possible—or, just as good, a method for generating principles or moral rules— that will generate such specific priorities. When the general principles clash with other strongly held intuitions on specific cases, this is normally grounds for altering the principles. Although it sometimes strikes beginning students as disappointing or circular, this method is particularly suited to ethics, since in this area we do not investigate a reality that is ultimately independent of subjective desires and judgments. While there are nevertheless criteria of rationality or consistency that can be critically applied, the goal of pure ethics remains that of "reflective equilibrium."[3] Our derived principles must accord with our specific intuitions and at the same time enable us to decide difficult or controversial cases.

At the level of application at which I shall be working here, we are involved with this second step toward reflective equilibrium. That is, we begin with certain general moral principles already derived, or with an assumed moral framework for generating principles, and use these to derive more specific social rules in the given social context. These more specific rules lead to a verdict on the specific difficult and complex issue at hand. Thus, in order to decide whether and when the policy of reverse discrimination is justified, we must have at hand a set of distributive and compensatory principles, or, preferably, a method or framework for generating them and the priorities among them. The moral framework I assume for generating rules and recognizing rights is a contractarian one.

There are different versions of contractarian morality. According to the strongest criterion of this type, social rules are considered to be just if they are capable of being rationally willed or freely accepted *by all from their respective social positions*. Just distributions of goods and burdens result from the operation of such rules. This is a most stringent requirement and is undoubtedly too strong to generate a full set of moral social institutions or rules. We must accept some rules that could not receive unanimous approval from all rational agents, regardless of differences in social or economic status and interests. That a rule could be willed by all rational agents from all social positions is therefore a sufficient, but not necessary, condition for it to qualify as a just rule for distribution of social goods and burdens. I shall refer to this test as the "strong criterion."

Weaker constraints of a contractarian type might be either of two types. First, as a criterion of the justness of given rules (or distributive arrangements generated through their operation), we might accept that they could be willed by all from an initial position of social equality.[4] Here we posit hypothetical equal agents and imagine how they would formulate a system of distributive rules according to which distinctions among them would later arise. We shall consider the resulting distributions fair if the differences among real individuals that are ignored or ruled out in the definition of the hypothetical contractors are differences that may be fairly ignored in the context at issue. The more distinctions among real individuals that are ruled out in our definition of hypothetical contractors, the more radically egalitarian our distributive rules will become. Rather than defining the contractors as equal, we can achieve the same effect, as Rawls does, by denying them knowledge of their real-life differences. The contractors to which I shall appeal in using my weaker criterion can be defined as ignorant of their social positions, race, and sex, but not necessarily of their natural endowments, such as intelligence or physical agility. My unwillingness to deny knowledge of the latter traits results from my uncertainty as to whether society has the right to nullify all natural differences among individuals, even those that are relevant to the performance of certain tasks and hence naturally useful to the individuals who possess them. If untalented or unintelligent individuals have no inherent claims upon the talents of others, and I do not see why they should, then it is not demanded, nor perhaps even permissible, that society nullify the distributive effects of these differences. Nor do I require ignorance in the contract situation of the structure of present society. Since we are not concerned with just relations among different societies at different times but with resolving a social problem in our own society, such ignorance is not necessary or helpful in finding principles to guide the search for a correct position. Initial differences in social positions of actual persons, on the other hand, are clearly irrelevant to later desert of positions or other distributive benefits, which is why we rule out knowledge of social position for the hypothetical contractors choosing just social principles. Likewise for race and sex. In any case, barring these characteristics from initial consideration in the choice of distributive rules (though not necessarily from considerations of compensation) is crucial to getting a grip on the issue at hand in a fair way.

Second, from an alternative weaker framework, we might accept rules and arrangements that are the outcomes of compromises, contracts, or exchanges—rather than of free unlimited choices among all possible alternatives—among individuals from various actual positions. Here we allow to stand all distributions arising from such unforced transactions.[5] The framework described in the previous paragraph is weaker than our strong criterion in that it drops the requirement that rules must operate to the maximal advantage of all in different actual social positions. The one described here is weaker still in that it drops the requirement that the rules or arrangements adopted must be acceptable to all, as opposed to all conceivable alternatives. Here compromises or outcomes of actual bargaining situations are acceptable. We intuitively accept as just some rules that could not maximize interests of individuals at all representative social positions in relation to all possible alternatives (rules that meet this strong test are uncontroversially acceptable). For example, a distributive principle may be required when no alternative will maximize the advantages of doctors and sanitation workers alike. The debate over a right to free and decent medical care is an illustration. Recognition of this right would benefit all but doctors, and so would be accepted if considered from an initial position of social equality in which contractors knew the various positions in their society (in which the chances of ending up a doctor are slight) but did not know which positions they were to occupy. The right to free medical care is not recognized through an actual agreement in our society, however, since doctors are powerful enough to effect lesser compromises.

A contractarian framework views the justice of distributions as a function of their being in some sense acceptable to or freely adopted in practice by all. If we consider the justice of such rights as that to free medical care to be determined by rules chosen by hypothetical agents before social positions are known, we will recognize such rights. If we consider the justice of such rights to be the outcome of compromises and exchanges (without physical force) between actual agents, we will not recognize them. The former is a liberal framework, the latter a libertarian one. The former begins from a presumption of social equality; the latter seeks to maximize free exchanges within an ongoing social system. In one sense my strong criterion is weaker than the libertarian one. Although the former demands that rules be freely willed in relation to abstractly possible alternatives by all from their various social positions (and not simply accepted by those in relatively weak positions because of their weakness), it demands acceptance only by *rational*, self-interested agents and not, for example, by actual individuals with irrational hatreds and biases. If we are going to use this criterion at all, this seems a minimal ideal constraint, obviously weaker than demanding acceptance only from hypothetically equal agents. Without it we cannot know whether actual agents could all agree to anything without coercion or forced compromise of some sort; probably they could not. On the other hand, since the libertarian is willing to accept the results of all "free exchanges" (even though the have-nots in reality may be forced into certain exchanges out of weakness alone, and through the operation of rules that they are powerless to alter), he need not demand rationality in these exchanges in order to arrive at an applicable criterion of just distributions. For him, those distributions that result from free transfers and exchanges are just, and acceptable rules reflect the unwillingness of individuals to restrict these freedoms, except to prevent direct harm.

Application of the Method to Reverse Discrimination

Most of the general rules I shall defend—for example, the principle of hiring by competence, or the principle of compensation holding that injured parties should be compensated in kind by those who injured them—meet the most stringent requirement of being capable of choice by all from their respective social positions. I shall argue in the second chapter that it appears to be in the interest of all in the long run, even of those less competent for certain desirable positions, that as a general rule the most competent should be hired to fill these positions. Likewise, I shall argue in the third chapter that a principle of compensation must be accepted by all, regardless of social position, if they are to be consistent and sincere in their adoption of any other (distributive) rules. What is not available as an alternative in a contractarian framework is a "rule" applying only to one's own case or except in one's own case, for this would not be a genuine rule at all. In the case of hiring, some alternatives would be: a rule for hiring the most competent universally, or except when overridden by other rules; a rule for hiring the most competent within certain areas of employment; one calling for randomization of selection procedures; or one allowing free choice by corporations, etc.

Where departures from the strong criterion of justice are necessary, I accept the liberal rather than the libertarian criterion, since, as I shall argue briefly, it better accords with our intuitions regarding a moral point of view. If recognition of the moral equality of others, implied in the recognition of their subjectivity, is part of what is involved in adopting a moral point of view, then rules forced upon the have-nots by the haves as necessary compromises, given their differences in power, cannot on those grounds alone be counted just. We intuitively think it unjust that the initial social advantages of some result in lifelong advantages and far greater shares of social benefits. Thus an example of a principle I use that meets the liberal but not the libertarian criterion is one stipulating a right to equal opportunity. Contractors ignorant of their social position, sex, and race would want to prohibit their own and their children's exclusion from achieving their long-term goals on grounds of race, sex, or social position. Even from considerations of self-interest, they would recognize that it is worse not to have a chance to achieve what one is willing to work for than it is to lack what one is not willing to work for. Actual agents in advantageous social positions, on the other hand, might not want (merely) equal opportunities forced upon them or their children.

Thus our moral framework will generate principles like hiring the most competent, compensating those who suffer from violations of distributive rules, and creating fair equality of opportunity for acquiring the benefits of unequal distributions. Some rules, such as hiring the competent, may be supported by several more general principles, some of which are implied by the strong framework and some by the liberal. This will be made clear in the course of the argument. The main problems, once these rules and principles are accepted, will be to establish priorities among them and to see their implications when considered together for the justification of reverse discrimination as a social policy. For example, does the right to compensation or that to equal opportunity take precedence over rights of individuals most competent for various positions? In what situations are the former to override, and how widespread a policy of preferential treatment can be justified on these grounds?

Primary attention must be paid to the questions of which specific individuals or groups deserve preferential treatment, in which contexts, and for which reasons. Policies will be evaluated in relation to all possible alternatives, for a fallacy in some political debates on the subject has been to ignore some feasible alternatives, and hence to argue for certain policies against only straw men (generally, a single policy will be urged against only some unjust status quo). The practical feasibility of considered policies in relation to scarce resources will have to be evaluated as well, for policies that may be justified in a period of expansion in the job market may not be acceptable in periods of high unemployment. Indeed, the entire question becomes pressing only when there is a scarcity of decent jobs (but given that unpleasant jobs also have low salaries, and that some must perform these tasks, this scarcity is uneliminable by expansion alone). I shall attempt to sort out the justice or injustice of hypothetical policies in various economic contexts in the next three chapters, ending with an evaluation of actual affirmative action programs in light of earlier conclusions.

One final word about the relationship of this contractarian moral framework to the specific issues of discrimination and reverse discrimination. A more specific variant of the notion of conditions or rules that are acceptable to all regardless of social positions can afford us a rough test of whether discrimination of either form is occurring in a given context. It can also, if applied honestly, help us to root out our own biases and interests in judging the morality of the practice in question. I shall call this device the "reversal test." The basic idea is to imagine role switches among the individuals in the situation. For our issue, these role switches involve race or sex. Applied as a test of whether discrimination is occurring, the test calls upon us to judge whether a white male with similar qualifications would have been given a position refused to a woman or black. To identify reverse discrimination, we ask whether a white male with similar qualifications would have been given the position granted to a minority-group member. As a method for rooting out biases in intuitive reactions toward instances of reverse discrimination, it calls upon us to judge whether a white male in similar circumstances (having been discriminated against in the past, or a member of a class discriminated against, being economically deprived, etc.) would deserve preferential treatment in the context in question.

Strong proponents of the policy of reverse discrimination might ardently object to this test because it ignores that in the present social context being a woman or a black may constitute an independent qualification in itself for a position. In a section of the next chapter on credentials and qualifications, I shall argue against this contention. In any case, when sex or race is a qualification, it can be built into the reversal test itself (being a white male would be a qualification if the situation were exactly reversed). More often, however, prior application of the test shows that these characteristics should not be counted as qualifications for positions, with few exceptions. For example, when it is claimed that women students learn better from women teachers and that this makes sex a qualification for teaching certain classes, we can ask whether the same reasoning would apply to white males learning from teachers of their race and sex and thus should be counted in favor of hiring such teachers. It might also be argued that the test, when applied at the level of job hiring, ignores that women and blacks, unlike white males, have been denied the opportunity to acquire qualifications at lower levels. Again, I do not think that this objection, while generally true, invalidates the test as applied for either purpose. As to the question of whether reverse discrimination is occurring, prior denial of opportunity to acquire qualifications at lower levels does not show that reverse discrimination does not occur when those with lower qualifications are now hired, although it may be relevant to its justification. As to the justification of reverse discrimination, denial of opportunity can again be built into the test (what if the white male had been denied opportunity in the past?).

Inductive Methodology

The principles to which I shall appeal, then, are those implied by the contractarian framework as described above, incorporating both the strong and the weaker liberal criterion for just principles. Just principles are those to which all actual agents could rationally agree, or those to which contractors ignorant of their social positions, race, and sex would agree. This framework captures our convictions on other, morally easier issues regarding distributions in our society. It is justified by implying just those distributions of burdens and benefits and more specific criteria for distributions that we confidently consider fair in specific cases. When addressing oneself to a difficult moral issue, it is also possible to appeal directly to clearer cases that appear analogous in morally relevant ways. We seek correct solutions to difficult issues by appealing either to principles or to analogous cases upon which we agree. We then see what solutions are deductively implied by the general principles, or how we should extend convictions on specific cases inductively by analogy. Since general principles in ethics are themselves induced from specific convictions, these two methods in moral reasoning are equivalent. At various points in the arguments to follow, I employ the more direct inductive method. For example, in order to see whether preferential treatment can be owed as compensation to whole minority groups, we shall examine other cases in which compensation clearly is owed to groups and point to analogies and disanalogies between these groups and those of minorities or women. The question of whether compensation can be owed by white males as a group is addressed in a similar way by analogy with other cases of group responsibility or liability.

The goal of both forms of moral reasoning is the achievement of maximum consistency in the set of our moral beliefs and decisions. Consistency demands that we give reasons for our judgments and apply those reasons to other cases in which the characteristics they cite are present. Conversely, if we judge two cases differently, we must be able to show morally relevant differences between them, that is, if one situation is judged differently from another because of some feature present in the first but not in the second, then this feature must make a moral difference in other classes of cases as well. Given these demands of consistency, the correct solution to the morally difficult case will be the solution that is most consistent with judgments in cases with similar morally relevant features, upon which there is agreement or firm convictions. Or it will be the solution that is implied by the set of principles or the general moral framework induced from those firm convictions. When persons disagree on some controversial issue, they can reason to the correct solution by beginning from shared convictions on other cases and finding the view that is implied by principles underlying those convictions, or the view that can be generalized from agreed cases with minimal morally relevant differences. This view will be the correct one in terms of their shared moral framework.

The claim that there are correct solutions (in the sense of "correct" just defined) to such complex issues as reverse discrimination does not beg any meta-ethical questions or run aground of relativist or subjectivist theses in meta-ethics. Given that this issue arises within the context of a single moral community or society, we may presuppose a broad base of agreement in moral judgment from which we can reason to the most consistent solution. This can be considered the correct or true verdict both by the subjectivist, who acknowledges no subjectively independent moral facts in the world, and by the objectivist or absolutist, who takes values to be objectively grounded. The subjectivist can simply assume a coherence criterion of truth in ethics, while the objectivist will take coherence with obviously true moral judgments to be a sign of correspondence to moral fact. Furthermore, even if value systems differ without any neutral or non-question-begging way to choose between them (even if relativism is true in this sense), this need not thwart our attempt to find the rationally preferred position on issues like reverse discrimination. Within a single moral community and within a context of broad agreement on specific judgments and principles, we may assume that when parties disagree on the rightness or wrongness of some specific practice they disagree upon relevant nonmoral facts, or, just as likely, one of the parties holds a view that is inconsistent with some principle it accepts or with some other judgment it is willing to make. The goal of moral reasoning is to eliminate these inconsistencies and hence to foster moral agreement.

In a pluralist, heterogeneous society there may be disagreement as well on some cases considered by the opposing parties to be easy or clear-cut. Then, too, people may feel more strongly about their opinions on difficult and controversial issues than about their views on easier, less interesting cases. But emotional attachment does not entail the right to be confident, and confidence may arise from thinking of an issue according to a certain model, while ignoring models derived from other, more closely analogous cases. While moral disagreement between members of the same society most likely will extend beyond the difficult case at issue, we ought to be willing, as long as there is a broad enough base of agreement with others in the shared community, to resolve disputes by finding solutions most in accord with those principles and judgments upon which we all agree. I do not expect that all will agree with the principles defended in this book, or with the view on reverse discrimination that follows from them. Inconsistencies may remain, or there may be other agreed-upon cases more closely analogous to facets of this issue or from which other principles or models might be induced. Argument toward the correct view proceeds by criticizing principles in terms of their specific implications, by showing that one's principles do not imply the view one initially holds, by showing morally relevant differences between cases thought to be analogous, or by producing more closely analogous cases upon which there is agreement and by which a different verdict is implied.

Such is the complexity of moral reasoning regarding social issues that involve conflicting claims of right and utility, and such is the challenge those issues present to moral reasoning.

If we accept this challenge, we can be confident that there are correct solutions to be found, even in complex and difficult cases like that of reverse discrimination. But of course this faith is empty if it does not prompt the careful chains of reasoning necessary to see our way through to those solutions.

TWO

Awarding Positions by Competence

The issue to be settled in this chapter is that of a general rule for hiring or awarding scarce desirable positions in society. In recent political debates on the subject of reverse discrimination or preferential hiring the principle of hiring by competence has seemed to remain sacrosanct, at least if one is to judge from the lip service paid to it by all sides of the discussion. Proponents of affirmative action at the level of hiring in universities go to great lengths to distinguish minority "goals" from quotas. While strict quotas for raising percentages of blacks and women employed by a fixed date, which would result in strong reverse discrimination, are acknowledged to be incompatible with the maintenance of strict competence standards, percentage goals for minorities are held to encourage minority hiring while maintaining existing standards. Some affirmative action supporters also argue that because minority-group members have suffered discrimination in the past, their real competence cannot be judged in terms of their "paper credentials," that some women and blacks who appear to have lower qualifications on paper (in terms of degrees, experience, etc.) may actually raise the general level of competence if hired and given the chance formerly denied them to develop and use their talents. Opponents of the policy, on the other hand, seem to feel that affirmative action programs in universities can be shown to be unjust by demonstrating that academic standards of excellence suffer and that the most qualified individuals fail to receive positions through pressure for reverse discrimination. They seem to believe the argument won if they can only show that affirmative action in practice violates the rule of hiring by competence.

Despite the apparent unanimity regarding hiring by competence in the context of this public debate, the principle has recently come under attack in more sophisticated philosophical circles from both the right and the left. Libertarians argue or imply that corporations or organizations with positions to fill can give them to whomever they choose, that society has no right to interfere in this free process. Corporations, like individuals, have the right to control their legitimately acquired assets and to disburse them to whomever they choose; the right to hire freely is part of this more general right. Egalitarians, on the other hand, hold the principle of hiring by competence to be unjust because it rewards initial social positions and purely native talents that individuals do not deserve and for which they can claim no responsibility. I shall argue here that these attacks are misguided.[1] In terms of the moral framework indicated in Chapter One, I hold that hiring the most competent probably meets the stringent criterion of justice by being in the interests of all in society in the long run (as opposed to alternative rules), and is hence capable of being willed as a distributive principle by all contractors regardless of social position.

Philosophical clarification regarding the issue of preferential hiring for minorities demands prior consideration of the justification of hiring by competence for two reasons. First, reverse discrimination, or first-order discrimination for that matter, can only be precisely defined relative to some rule for hiring that is held to be just. Discrimination, as the concept is used in this context, involves treating relevantly similar persons differently or relevantly different people the same. Any award of scarce goods or positions requires some differentiation among those individuals considered; such differentiation amounts to unjust discrimination only when the characteristics on the basis of which it is made are irrelevant to the rewards from a moral point of view. But to know whether discrimination is occurring in practice, we must first know what constitutes relevant distinctions in the area under consideration.[2] In our context this means knowing what rule should govern the award of positions. Second, unless some just distributive rule is violated by the practice of reverse discrimination, and unless certain people acquire at least prima facie *rights* to positions by satisfying the criteria stipulated in this rule, reverse

discrimination will never be seriously unjust. The question of
its morality would then be decided on utilitarian grounds,
which I hold to be largely irrelevant.

Thus I shall be concerned in this chapter with two central
questions: (1) Does society have the right to impose and enforce any rule of hiring against corporations with positions to
fill? (2) If the answer to (1) is affirmative, which principle for
awarding positions ought to be adopted from the point of view
of justice? I shall argue that society does have this right, both
to protect its own welfare as a consumer of goods and services
and to protect equal opportunity for its members. The principle of awarding positions by competence will be seen to satisfy
our strong criterion in all probability, and certainly to satisfy
the liberal criterion. Enforcement of this principle, it will be
argued, overrides rights of corporations to control their assets
by hiring whomever they please and is more just than seemingly egalitarian alternatives. Once the awarding of positions
on the basis of competence is accepted as a just initial rule, the
question for later chapters becomes that of deciding when
principles of compensation require departures from the distributive rule. But the general rule must be established
against possible alternatives before that question becomes relevant.

The Rule for Awarding Desirable Positions

The first question to be faced here is why one system of hiring
or awarding positions can be judged more just than another.
That is, why does the award of positions by corporations, as
opposed to the award of other benefits by private individuals,
involve considerations of justice rather than simply questions
of right and wrong. There are situations in which individuals
or corporations can make wrong, even overall morally wrong,
decisions without treating anyone unjustly or unfairly. I can
for instance be wrong in telling my friend he is a poor tennis
player without being unjust to him. To say that principles of
hiring are a matter of distributive social *justice* is to imply that
certain individuals acquire distributive *rights* to certain positions and that to refuse them these positions is to refuse to

grant them what is legitimately due them. Part of the reason that we do in fact recognize such rights is that one's career or social position affects the quality of one's life as much as any other single factor. Having attained a particular position through effort or work is for many a crucial ingredient in a sense of self-accomplishment, satisfaction, or self-respect, as it is a central element in the respect that one enjoys from the community. Of course one's occupation is not the only source of respect, pride, and satisfaction; other sources are perhaps morally more significant—for example, the ways in which one treats other persons. But it is of sufficient importance for individuals to be rightly concerned that opportunities to compete for and attain desirable positions be equal or fairly distributed.

It might be objected that those in our society who begin with social advantages for attaining desirable positions will not be concerned with such equality or fairness; in fact, they may well be concerned to prevent it. But certainly hypothetical contractors unaware of their initial social positions will be anxious to ensure their ability to work for desirable positions and to prevent the denial of these positions on capricious or arbitrary grounds. Barring individuals from achieving goals for which they have productively worked is to deprive them of an important source of satisfaction, a source that is somewhat independent of the other benefits attached to the desirable positions. Positions assigned in a totally capricious or arbitrary way could not rationally serve as sources of self-respect. It is the achievement of a goal for which one has worked that serves as this source. Therefore, if the attainment of self-respect and a sense of accomplishment is an important good; if the achievement of a position for which one has worked is a part of this good; if all contractors would wish to preserve the opportunity to pursue this good; and if the liberal contractual model provides a test of moral rules; then we have moral reason for creating some general rule for awarding desirable positions fairly. The rule would have to be such as to prevent the denial of opportunity to pursue and achieve these positions through effort and work. Acceptance of the rule would in turn create prima facie rights to positions for individuals who satisfy the criteria stipulated by it. At this point we can say that individuals would acquire rights not to be excluded on grounds other than those deemed acceptable as criteria by the rule. These rights would become ingredients in a general right to fair or equal opportunity.

Clearly, if any right to equal opportunity is to be recognized, we cannot allow jobs and positions in professional schools to be awarded capriciously, especially given the deep-seated prejudices known to exist in our society. An opportunity to compete with others and to be judged on the basis of one's performance, rather than on the basis of native factors alone, is a necessary condition for an equal opportunity to acquire all other goods. Since one's ability to acquire other social goods is a function mainly of one's job, equal opportunity for social goods does not exist without equal opportunity for decent jobs. While redistributive taxation, open housing, and integrated schools are advocated in the name of this right, they amount to little when jobs can be denied to those who have managed to acquire superior qualifications after escaping other forms of social deprivation. Thus the enforcement of some rule for hiring that is not based purely upon inborn or initial chance factors is the first prerequisite for equality of opportunity. Contractors ignorant of race, sex, and social position would want to ensure that effort and accomplishment play major roles in satisfying criteria for positions, not only because they will want to preserve the attainment of positions as a source of pride and self-respect, but also because they will recognize that it is worse to be prevented from attempting to achieve that for which one is willing to work than it is to lack that which one might not want to make efforts to acquire.[3] Moreover, the frustration of not being allowed to compete is greater than that of ultimately losing in competition. From the point of view of their own self-interest, then, and to prevent frustration, the contractors would want some rule stipulating initial rights to positions on the basis of criteria that give priority to effort, work, and achievement.

A critic might recognize that once we build the artificial constraints of equality into our contractual position via a Rawls-type "veil of ignorance," egalitarian rights like that to equal opportunity must emerge from it. But he might question once more our reason for building in these constraints. Here we are taken back to fundamental intuitions regarding the nature of morality itself. Part of the justification of the liberal moral framework is that recognition of moral equality among agents is central to a moral point of view. Placing the interests of all on the same level entails accepting only social rules that could be freely accepted by rational contractors defined as equal in certain respects. Although this framework creates a presumption of equality in distributions from which departures need to be justified, it is clear that such contractors would permit certain departures from strict equality. They would do so first in order to create incentives for individuals to develop their capacities and competencies, so as to be able to contribute more to the total pool of goods and services and to benefit all by so doing.[4] For these incentives to succeed, those who develop competence must be rewarded by being given those positions for which they are most competent.

Thus we have another reason why the rule of awarding positions to those most competent is just as an initial distributive rule, and why rights are created in relation to it. Inequalities are permissible in the first place partly to encourage individuals to be maximally productive. When individuals are encouraged in this way to direct their efforts toward maximal social productivity, differentials achieved in productivity or potential productivity cannot then be justly ignored. It would be possible to encourage productivity on the job by differential reward without initially assigning positions according to reasonable estimates of potential productivity. But this inconsistency would violate this purpose of differential rewards. Many positions require prior training, and we want people to train for positions in advance for the same reasons that we want them to perform competently in those positions. Contractors adopting rules by which to shape society would want to encourage efforts in early years toward attaining skills required for various positions, and the obvious inducement is the ultimate reward of the positions with their different pay scales. Once a rule for rewarding competence is adopted, it would be unjust not to reward those who satisfy its criteria. The rights that they acquire to positions for which they are most competent can then be seen as rights to have society fulfill its contractual obligations. The adoption of the rule results in contractual relations with those who work to satisfy its criteria: these individuals acquire the rights that their legitimate expectations to the positions be fulfilled.

To the fundamental presumption of equality, then, we must add limits to degrees of justified inequalities and means to ensure equal opportunity to attain the better shares of justified inequalities. The right to equal opportunity itself follows from the fundamental right to have one's interests counted on the same scale with those of others, since one's interests are not counted equally unless one is given an equal chance to satisfy those interests. According to the line of reasoning pursued here, this right is to be interpreted not as a right to equal or random chances to attain the better shares of justified inequalities, but as an equal chance to achieve those shares through work.

Thus, in addition to their desire to preserve their chances to succeed through effort, contractors would wish to adopt a rule giving initial rights to positions to those who best qualify in order to create a maximum pool of quality goods and services. This second reason relates not to those who will come to occupy the positions in question but to the public, to whom those in socially important positions are responsible for providing needed goods and services. Desirable positions, to which respect and high monetary reward attach, are generally positions of social responsibility, whose occupants have significant effects upon the satisfaction of social needs and demands. To have such positions of responsibility filled capriciously or arbitrarily results in sharply diminished utility to the public. This consideration motivates adoption of a rule for assigning positions by competence or potential competence. In fact, if we compare this general rule with any other fully general rule as a basis for assigning positions, it seems likely that its adoption would result not only in utility maximization across society, but also in a strong Pareto improvement, that is, in gains to all members of society in overall goods and services. Of course, some who might occupy desirable positions under some other rule will not do so under the rule that rewards competence or potential competence. But it seems probable that losses to these individuals will be more than offset—even for them—by gains in other goods and services derived from having individuals of maximum competence occupying those positions. It therefore seems likely that the rule for hiring the competent meets our strongest criterion for acceptability: it could be rationally willed by all actual members of society. Even if this weighing of goods is inaccurate, and even if some actual individuals would be willing to sacrifice quality and quantity of other goods and services in order to occupy desirable positions that they could not occupy according to criteria of competence, our weaker criterion is nevertheless satisfied by the adoption of this initial general rule as opposed to alternatives. Contractors ignorant of the positions they might come to occupy under different possible rules would certainly want to adopt the rule that maximizes the provision of quality goods and services to the community as a whole.

It is true that we have not barred knowledge of natural abilities from our hypothetical contractors. Those who know that they lack talents and are below average in mental abilities might therefore prefer rules that place less emphasis upon qualifications, the acquisition of which is greatly aided by talent or intelligence. But if we disallow advantages for acquiring qualifications deriving from initial social positions (as our contractors would), then those within a normal range of intelligence will recognize that attainment of qualifications for most positions will vary largely with the degree of effort made to acquire them. Given that a wide range of positions might be available as goals for individuals with normal capacities, given that all will suffer when unqualified persons occupy many positions, and given that special forms of compensation can be established for individuals with subnormal capacities, it is plausible that our contractors would all agree upon a rule with competence criteria. Few would prefer that positions requiring superior intelligence or talent for adequate performance be filled by individuals who lack those characteristics. Positions exist to satisfy social needs and demands. Even those individuals who lack the requisite potentials to attain such positions will recognize that there is little point to making one who could not defend clients a lawyer, or one who could not diagnose disease a doctor, or one who could not instruct a professor, or one who could not play an instrument well a musician, etc. They would recognize the rationality of a rule requiring qualifications, even if they felt that they might fare better under some alternative. Of course, only some positions require relative excellence. The rule for hiring unskilled labor might reasonably differ from the rule for awarding positions that call for special skills. The former might require hiring on a first-come or other random basis. But of primary interest here is a rule for awarding positions that offer above-average reward or respect.

A final consideration regarding award of these positions is that a person could derive only limited satisfaction from occupying a position in which he could not perform well. Increased monetary benefits to unqualified individuals who might gain positions under other rules would need to be weighed not only against decreased goods and services in general, but also against frustrations from trying to do jobs they could not really do.

Combining these two motivations behind the adoption of a rule for awarding desirable positions—the first of which calls for rewarding effort, or at least for permitting attainment of positions through effort and achievement, and the second of which calls for rewarding social productivity or potential productivity—we derive a rule for rewarding socially productive effort. Socially productive effort amounts to competent performance on a job or the attainment of qualifications for performing a job before one applies for it. There may be some question, however, as to the ease with which these two motivations can be combined. Even when we correct for advantages derived from initial social positions (which contractors ignorant of social position would want to do), productivity and achievement are not perfect measures of effort. Where these two criteria might conflict, I believe that the contractual model implies that productivity itself should normally serve as the basis for differential rewards, while estimates of potential productivity would become the criterion for award of positions. The contractors' motivation for rewarding effort appealed to effort as a measure of desire and to the fact that a lack of opportunity to acquire goods through effort frustrates desire more than does a lack of willingness to make efforts to acquire those goods. Given roughly equal natural abilities and correction for socially relative differences, however, productivity itself is some measure of effort and desire. While certainly not exact, it is questionable whether more exact measures could be institutionalized into social rules for differential rewards that could be applied fairly, consistently, and without excessive costs. Second, from the contractors' point of view, the prospect of unrewarded effort, representing frustrated desires for goods, would be more than offset by the prospect of increased goods and services made available by having maximally competent persons occupying various positions and being rewarded for producing at full capacity. Since awarding positions by competence rather than on some other basis entails increased goods and services for all society, it is difficult to see how contractors unaware of their initial or ultimate positions and interested in maximizing their prospective goods could choose any other principle.

For those in whom this outcome engenders suspicion of the acquisitive contractual framework as a criterion of just principles, we can argue inductively for the reward of productivity from convictions regarding simpler situations. There seem to be two sources of our intuition that productivity in itself merits reward. One is our feeling that individuals who contribute to the welfare of others by helping to satisfy their needs or interests deserve something in return. What they deserve is proportionate to how much they contribute. The second source of this intuition is our conviction that individuals deserve to keep what they themselves produce, and that they therefore deserve to keep their share of cooperatively produced products. Imagine that A and B agree to cooperate in some project. A works hard and accomplishes the project almost single-handedly, while B dawdles. Surely they do not deserve equal shares of the product. Now imagine that B does not dawdle but expends much effort in ways that do not contribute anything to the completion of the project, nor even seem intended to do so. Such effort does not alter our original opinion of the deserved shares of the reward. Only socially productive effort, or at least effort toward being productive, can count. Finally, imagine that B works as hard as A toward completing the project but is simply unable to contribute as much. Here our intuition may be altered somewhat; we might want to divide the final shares in some way between complete equality and perfect proportionality to contribution. We think it appropriate to reward such effort in itself, first in order to encourage socially productive effort in the future, and second in recognition that differences in actual contribution, given equal effort, are to some degree beyond the control of the individuals involved.

Both effort and actual contribution or production then seem independent basic sources of desert for social reward or benefit. But, as argued above, while we may often be able to measure effort independently of result in personal situations, it may not be possible to do so consistently in more impersonal social situations, which distributive rules must cover. This is the first reason why productivity must take precedence over effort in criteria for distribution of larger shares of social benefits (when inequalities are independently justifiable).[5] The second reason is simply that productivity, in addition to being a measure of effort and desire, is an independent source of desert. The intuitions that individuals deserve to keep what they themselves make or acquire through exchange, and that untalented persons have no initial claims upon those more talented, support productivity but not effort as a source of desert. To reward effort as opposed to contribution to the social product would require fundamental restrictions upon free exchange. Productivity—contribution to the satisfaction of social demand—is then naturally prominent in rules of social distribution (as opposed to redistribution). Of course, in sophisticated economies there are forces—political muscle, organization, etc.—that operate to effect reward out of proportion to contribution; and the operation of these forces may be morally acceptable on grounds of utility or efficiency. But certainly the reward of productivity is prominent as a source of the intuitive moral attraction of the free market itself as a distributor of benefits.

One might admit the preeminence of productivity as a criterion for reward and yet argue that it justly applies only to performance in jobs and not to awards of jobs and other positions themselves. But, as already indicated, there are two reasons why this would be inconsistent. First, the way to be socially productive in younger years *is* to work toward the attainment of qualifications for later positions. Second, if one ground for rewarding productivity is to encourage further productivity, so as to generate a larger pool of goods and services for all society, it would be self-defeating not to award positions by competence, which serves the same purpose. Thus our inductive support for rewarding productivity or competence is also support for awarding positions on the basis of competence or best estimates of competence.

In concluding this section, we may use another approach to support inductively the adoption of a rule for awarding positions generally by competence, an approach that is closer to the issue at hand. This is our conviction that first-order discrimination against minority-group members and women is not only wrong but seriously unjust, that is, in violation of their rights. Certainly our distributive principles ought to explain this conviction. Those who defend reverse discrimination by arguing that no one has prima facie rights to positions and that such rights therefore cannot be violated by the practice must be careful not to defend first-order discrimination on this ground as well. It certainly seems that if white males can never have distributive rights to positions, minority-group members can never have these rights either, and that if they can never have rights to positions, we cannot treat them unjustly in hiring practices. One possible way around this point is to counterargue that the rights violated by first-order discrimination are rights to equal consideration rather than to positions, or rights not to be invidiously insulted. Regarding the former suggestion, equal consideration amounts to nothing if there is no rule stipulating criteria for appointment or if one can be dismissed despite satisfying these criteria. Regarding the latter suggestion, I would imagine that most blacks care less about the opinions that whites may have of them than about getting decent jobs. Exclusion from positions is felt to be the most serious injustice, not the insults associated with exclusion, although the latter may add to the overall injustice of first-order discrimination.

The most plausible reason why first-order discriminatory practices are unjust is that they exclude individuals from social benefits or opportunities for benefits on grounds of unalterable characteristics unrelated to performance. Such practices would not be seriously unjust unless there were a rule that created rights to positions violated by the practices. But if such rights exist for minority-group members, then according to our reversal test, they must also exist for white males who satisfy the criteria stipulated by the rule. Of course, a rule that creates rights to positions would not necessarily require that competence be rewarded. For all that our argument has established so far, the rule might rather call for some fair random process for awarding positions. But the depth of our reaction to first-order discrimination indicates that this practice is unjust, not merely in relation to some abstractly possible rule, according to which *all* current hiring would be unjust, but rather in relation to a rule widely accepted and applied often to nonminority candidates for positions. This would be the rule for awarding positions according to competence or potential competence, which stipulates that it is most unjust when a woman or minority-group member is rejected at the level of hiring when most qualified, and that it is also unjust when individuals are denied the chance given others to attain qualifications. But this rule also demands that the most qualified white males as well must acquire initial or prima facie distributive rights to positions.

Thus both the contractual framework and inductive arguments by analogy from other cases imply that the most competent individuals have prima facie rights to positions. It is in the context of such rights that the debate over reverse discrimination takes form. Before deciding which other rights conflict with these in the present context, and which ought to override others, I want to consider in somewhat more detail the motivations for denying the existence of these prima facie rights and the question of how we decide who is most competent for various positions.

Rejection of Alternative Rules

The Libertarian Position

The libertarian denies that applicants for positions in private corporations could have rights to those positions. Such rights would conflict with the rights of the corporations to control their own assets or property and with the rights of their members to associate with whom they please. A corporation may be said to have a property right in the positions it chooses to fill by virtue of having legitimately acquired the assets with which to fund the positions. The freedom to control its own assets is empty unless it is free to disburse them as or to whom it chooses. Since present members of the corporation must associate with new appointees, the freedom to associate with whom one pleases may also be cited in support of the libertarian position here. A mandatory rule for hiring may force present members to work closely with others against their will, making their work unpleasant for them. And the friction created by this forced close association may be detrimental to the continued smooth operation of the company or organization. The corporation's property rights to control the disbursement of its assets and the right of free association of its members can then be held to imply a specific right of the corporation to hire whom it pleases without interference from society. The only rule that a libertarian would accept in this area would be one permitting private corporations to hire whomever they choose.

I argued in the previous section that rights to positions are recognized as part of a more general demand for equal opportunity, and as part of society's interest in generating a maximal pool of quality goods and services. Regarding the latter, the libertarian will ask how a social interest in more material goods and services can override recognized rights of individuals or private corporations within the society, such as the rights of property and free association. (Remember that the libertarian does not demand rational self-interest in contracts made or rules accepted. He accepts only actual contracts among actual individuals, not hypothetical contracts establishing rules among hypothetically rational or equal agents. Real individuals must be left free to make their own contracts and exchanges.) To determine a social interest is not necessarily to demonstrate the right of society or the state to further that interest, especially when individual or private corporation rights are apparently ignored in the process. For one principal purpose of recognizing individual rights within a system of social justice is to protect individuals from losses whenever utilitarian calculations run against them in particular cases.

Recognition of the right to property, for example, means that a person will not be dispossessed whenever another is in greater need, although such forced transfer would raise total or average utility in particular cases. The recognition of a right in relation to a certain interest determines in advance that the person whose right is at stake will take precedence over others with different and conflicting interests, even if the latter should seem greater in a given situation. Considerations of utilitarian balancing and maximization are not allowed to determine the relative priority of these interests. The rights to property and free association, it could therefore be argued, should not be overridden here by the social interest in maximizing goods and services. A private corporation with assets to disburse for jobs should be free to hire whomever it pleases, even when this results in lower efficiency in its production of goods and services. Efficiency cannot be permitted to override recognized rights, or our rights and freedoms would be fragile indeed. Thus while it may be in the interest of all, even of those in power in corporations, to have the most competent hired, the rights of free choice allow corporations to ignore this maximization of interest satisfaction.

As a counterargument, we might first state that, while utilities are not permitted to override rights once these are recognized, we do not recognize a prospective right when the consequences of accepting it are worse than the consequences of not recognizing it. Since the consequences of recognizing a right of corporations to hire whom they please are detrimental to the interests of individuals, we ought not to recognize this right.[6] But the libertarian might point here to other cases in which we recognize rights even when not doing so might

maximize utility for all. For example, even if there were some
proven scientific method of matching spouses that increased
their chances for happiness, we would undoubtedly continue
to recognize the right of individuals to choose their own
spouses.[7] Hence we cannot argue simply that when acceptance of a right lowers prospective welfare we ought not to recognize it. For the libertarian, freedom of choice normally takes
precedence over welfare considerations. Since we do recognize a right to property and the freedom to control and disburse legitimately acquired assets, and since this seems to entail a freedom to hire by choice, consistency appears to require
that we refuse to recognize rights of applicants to positions.

I would argue nevertheless that the libertarian misrepre-
sents here the way that rights are ordered, and that the analogy with choosing spouses is misleading. Regarding the latter,
aside from the difference in the interest that the public takes
in who occupies positions of responsibility as opposed to who
marries whom, there is a difference in the rights at stake. In
the case of one's right to choose a spouse, what is at stake is the
right over one's own person and body—perhaps the most fundamental of all rights. But in the case of hiring, what is at stake
is only a portion of corporations' right to control the disbursement of their assets. And we already recognize many exceptive clauses in rights to property, clauses that express the
priority of competing interests. My right to dispose of my
property as I please does not include a right to dispose of my
knife in an enemy's chest; my right to use my property according to my own wishes does not include a right to play my
stereo near my neighbor at deafening volumes; and my right
to spend my assets as I like does not allow me to buy nerve
gas, even if I keep it sealed in my basement vault. Which exceptive clauses are applied in the recognition of a particular
right depends upon the ranking of the particular values to be
embodied in the system. If there is to be any system of rights,
however, there must be an ordering of each in relation to the
others, and this means that there must be exceptive clauses
expressing these precedence relations. I can dispose of my
knife as I please, except in an adversary's chest, because the
rights to life and not to be assaulted take precedence over

rights to disposition of personal property, which therefore include this exceptive clause. Much political debate—and indeed, much of the debate over reverse discrimination as a social policy—concerns the recognition of new exceptive clauses in previously recognized rights when these appear to conflict. Since we recognize various exceptive clauses in property rights, and since a restriction on hiring practices removes only a small part of the right of corporations to control their own assets, it seems reasonable to accept this exceptive clause in the name of equal opportunity and public welfare. The same can be said of a restriction of rights to free association. We already recognize restrictions in public contexts in which access to important benefits is at stake—for example, access of minority-group members to privately owned restaurants, etc.

The libertarian will reply that freedoms, including those of disbursing property and associating with those of one's choice, may be limited only to prevent wrongful harm. A defender of this position undoubtedly would want to press the distinction between the interests of individuals in maximizing available goods and services, and any potential harm to them from the exercise of these freedoms on the part of corporations in hiring. He would grant that we cannot use our property in ways that directly harm other people, but he would allow total freedom short of this, including the freedom to ignore rational self-interest (to allow some to impose their conception of rational self-interest on others leads to repressive regimes, in his view). Nor will he recognize any such right as that to equal opportunity. He would hold that people have a right to what they have legitimately acquired and that no general right like that of equal opportunity should be recognized because it would involve violations of individuals' rights to their legitimately acquired property in excess of those permissible under the harm principle.

Let us, however, first consider the distinction in this context between preventing harm and maximizing welfare. I am not certain that this distinction can be maintained in relation to many positions of responsibility in society, such as those of pilots, doctors, lawyers, police, and even automobile, home, or toy manufacturers. Having relative incompetents in these positions entails not only losses in efficiency but also serious potential harm. Thus the harm principle itself, if it allows prevention of unnecessary risk or potential harm—which it must to be at all plausible—may require enforcement of a rule for hiring the most competent in many positions. With respect to a right to equal opportunity, which would include prima facie rights to positions as one facet, we argued in the previous section that this follows from the fundamental moral demand to accept the moral equality of others. In accepting the outcome of all "free" exchanges, even though these often result from the desperation of those who initially occupy lower positions, the libertarian fails to guarantee just distributive results. Rules or conditions that can be recognized only as the outcome of grudging transactions between haves and have-nots cannot be accepted as moral on that basis alone, since the haves may have inherited their advantages without deserving them and the have-nots may have begun where they are through no fault of their own. That some condition or distribution has been arrived at through transactions entered into "freely" by have-nots does not afford the same guarantee of its morality or fairness as when a distribution has been arrived at through the operation of a set of rules freely and rationally willed by those in the lower positions. Justice and morality demand placing the interests of all agents on the same scale, thereby limiting inequalities among them and granting them equal opportunity to satisfy those interests.

But are we not simply placing welfare considerations over freedoms, an ordering rejected by the libertarian? Have we arrived at a dead end in moral argument? This apparent impasse occurs because we have argued so far as though freedom is to be balanced against equality and welfare. But we can point out also that absolute liberty with respect to property and association may not result in the overall maximization of freedom that is apparently desired by the libertarian. For poverty and the lack of satisfaction of basic needs that poverty entails constitutes an impediment to freedom as well, that is, to the basic freedom to formulate and pursue a meaningful life plan and to control one's life as one desires. This is perhaps the most essential liberty of all; if it is denied through the opera-

tion of a social system that totally frustrates some so that others
may totally control their property, we can view this as an unwarranted conventional constraint upon liberty (property is
only protected and indeed created in the first place by the social system). It follows that a rule of hiring that results in more
goods and services for all, and especially for those whose freedom is compromised by want, can be adopted not only in the
name of welfare or utility but also to increase freedom. This
does not mean that every increase in welfare is to be counted
as an increase in freedom, or that despotic states with higher
GNP's are to be preferred, but only that no social system that
abandons those at the bottom to an enforced circle of dire poverty can be justified in the name of freedom. A free market
society with severe racial biases and no rule for hiring results
in that situation. Thus we again arrive at the conclusion that
society has the right to impose a rule for hiring against private
corporations, justified this time in the name of freedom. Restrictions upon the freedom of corporations to choose capriciously or invidiously in hiring are necessary to protect or
create more basic freedoms. Equality of opportunity is itself a
necessary condition for these most important and fundamental
freedoms.

That there must be an enforceable rule governing appointments to positions does not mean that the rule must be enforced in all situations—for example, in the cases of an individual's hiring someone for temporary help or a businessman's
giving a job to his son. The first distinction between the case of
a small business or individual and the large corporation is the
interest of the public in their products and services. If a small
business is the only source of a vital service or product in a
given area, it may be reasonable to demand competents in positions of responsibility. Otherwise, it may be unreasonable to
demand that the proprietor take the time and bear the cost of
advertising the positions, etc. This is especially clear in such
cases as my hiring someone for the afternoon to unload my
rented truck. The right of free association is also more central
in the case of a small business, and this may have been part of
the reasoning of Congress in applying nondiscriminatory regulations only to businesses with more than twenty-five employ-

ees. Since these differences are real, and since equality of opportunity and social welfare do not require that literally every position in society be open to all, but only a certain proportion of them, we may in applying these rationales establish a rule for hiring only for corporations over a certain size, recognizing that a precise demarcation will be somewhat arbitrary.

Thus the rights of individuals to equal opportunity and of the public to be spared potential harm justify enforcement of a rule that restricts the rights of larger corporations to control their assets by hiring or admitting whomever they choose. But is equal opportunity truly compatible with awarding positions by competence? We turn next to the objections of the egalitarian.

The Egalitarian Position

The egalitarian attempts to refute the above justification by arguing that those abilities relevant to awarding jobs on the basis of efficiency, that is, competence qualifications, are irrelevant from the point of view of justice. Because it rewards native talent and intelligence, the practice of awarding positions by competence is arbitrary from a moral point of view. Individuals deserve only those benefits they have earned. They have not earned their native advantages and so do not deserve those benefits, including good jobs, that flow from such advantages throughout their lives. A child born intelligent stands a far better chance than do other children of acquiring competence qualifications for desirable positions later in life; yet he cannot be said to deserve the better chance from the point of view of justice, nor therefore the job he eventually gets. Thus increments to social welfare from hiring by competence are a matter of social utility from which questions of justice must be separated. The egalitarian appears to have uncovered a conflict between the two criteria for a just rule for hiring that were advanced in the first section of this chapter. Maximization of utility through hiring by competence seems inconsistent with equality of opportunity in the deepest sense, and the egalitarian claims that considerations of equality take precedence over those of social utility.

In reply, I do not think that any such radical separation of analyses of justice and efficiency could accord with our intuitions regarding the former, as these are aroused by specific examples. Although we may not all be utilitarians, it seems we must grant that welfare does count at least as a positive consideration, and certainly at the extreme involved in this issue. I would argue, for example, that a practice or rule that generates a sum total of fifteen units of goods to be distributed in a hypothetical society of four individuals in shares of 4, 4, 4, and 3 is preferable from the point of view of justice to one that generates eight units to be distributed in shares of 2, 2, 2, and 2, despite the greater inequality of the former distribution. In other words, those who could have received four units under the first plan could legitimately claim injustice at having their shares reduced to equal the lowest share under the second (given no differences in desert among the individuals in the first and second situations).[8] If a claim of injustice or unfairness at having one's reward so reduced is justified, then aggregate utility in itself must be a consideration of distributive justice. Plans or rules that result in larger aggregates must be prima facie preferable. To deny this is perhaps to grant too large a moral force to the feelings of envy and pride. For even the person with the lowest share in our hypothetical case is better off under the first plan than under the second, except that others around him have more.

There may appear to be a complication here in that those with less relative (though more absolute) income may be in a worse position to bid for scarce goods. But the alternatives in relation to choices between hiring by competence and other rules may be taken to refer to goods available and not simply to income. The argument is that more goods will be available to all if competents occupy productive positions; this is what the egalitarian wrongly claims to be irrelevant to the choice of a just rule for hiring. Furthermore, the rule for awarding positions is itself independent of the degree of inequality of wealth and income throughout society. It is not as if the adoption of this rule increases inequalities between rich and poor. It affects not the relative positions themselves, but only who will occupy them. The egalitarian can press for equalization of pay scales and redistribution of wealth without altering the rule that determines who gets the better shares of justified inequalities. Unlike abandoning the practice of hiring by competence, the readjustment contemplated toward equalization of pay scales would perhaps not result in great losses of efficiency, but it would take massive coercion or drastic changes toward more social or altruistic attitudes on the part of businessmen and professionals.

Given that this demand for equalization is independent of the rule for awarding positions, a rule that creates a larger share of goods without affecting degrees of inequality certainly seems preferable to alternatives. But there remains the charge of injustice relating to reward of native talents. Since inequalities do exist in our society beyond those that might be justified as incentives or on grounds of differential productivity, it can be argued that it is crucial that the better shares not be assigned on morally arbitrary bases or on the basis of unearned native characteristics. An egalitarian could argue that although moving away from awarding positions by competence would not in itself result in a more equal distribution of goods, a more random process would at least equalize the chances of all individuals for acquiring the benefits of an unequal distribution. The point can be pressed that equal chances to unequal shares are fairer than unequal chances to unequal shares. The real question is whether the fact that native intelligence has some effect on the ability to acquire competence qualifications for many positions nullifies competence as a just basis for assigning positions.

To answer this challenge to our rule, we may question first whether the nullification of the effects of intelligence would itself be just, and second, whether there are alternative rules that do not also nullify factors that we consider to be intuitively plausible bases for differential rewards. Regarding the first counterquestion, the rights of individuals over their own bodies seem to indicate rights to what they can produce through the exercise and development of their capacities. The intuitions that one has this right to keep what one makes or contributes to a joint venture, and that the less intelligent have no initial right to the time or efforts of those more intelligent, in themselves appear to offset the claim that we should

nullify all effects of differences in intelligence in granting rewards. That an individual does not deserve something, or that
he can claim no responsibility for it, does not imply that he is
not entitled to it or to what he can obtain by using it, especially if the advantage in question is an inherent feature of the
individual. Furthermore, as we argued above, the justification
of inequalities as incentives to encourage maximal productivity also justifies the reward of competence independently of its
causal source.

Thus, even if society were able to nullify differential effects
of differences in intelligence without affecting other relevant
variables, it might not have the right to do so. The antecedent
of the previous sentence is also false. The failure of the egalitarian argument becomes more clear if we seriously consider
its alternative to hiring by competence as a general distributive principle. Presumably, the egalitarian would advocate
greater randomization in the process of sorting people for positions, in order to equalize the chances of all. The central question is whether a more random process would indeed be more
fair. The egalitarian's central complaint against hiring by competence is that it tends to reward initial differences for which
individuals can claim no responsibility. To be blessed with native intelligence is a matter of good fortune or chance. And the
rewarding of chance factors for which the agent can claim no
responsibility is morally arbitrary, whether the reward is jobs
or other benefits. But certainly a process of random selection
in the job market, aside from losses in efficiency, comes out
worse on this score. It was admitted that differences in competence for various positions constitute only imperfect barometers of prior efforts to acquire competence. But the acquisition
of qualifications for positions still represents the expenditure
of some effort in a socially desirable way; and the question is
whether it is more just to ignore socially productive effort altogether and make all reward a matter of pure chance, which
seems implausible or inconsistent if the only complaint against
hiring by competence is that it rewards chance factors to some
degree. The effect of randomization at any level is to negate
differences in previous efforts. If the cost of negating differences in native factors is to render all effort and productivity

negligible as measures of desert as well, it hardly seems worthwhile from the point of view of distributive justice. Even if the efforts of some are undeservedly doomed to failure, it still seems preferable to reward those who have made efforts and succeeded than to ignore effort entirely. If the complaint against the reward of native factors is that they are undeserved, then some other factors must be presupposed as entering into desert. Presumably, these will not consist in being lucky in some random selection, but rather in some such factor as socially productive effort. The question then becomes how to measure this in a social rule—and we are back to the argument that actual attainment of competence seems as fair a measure as can be fairly applied, if we correct for initial social differences.

In rewarding the attainment of competence we are *not* rewarding a native characteristic, although native characteristics enter as causal factors. Since the latter is the source of the egalitarian's complaint against our rule, his complaint can be seen to rest upon a false principle. This principle states that all causal antecedents of features that enter into criteria for desert must themselves be deserved. That it is false can be made clear by the example of a character like Soapy in the O'Henry story "The Cop and the Anthem." After an inspirational moment in church, Soapy vows to reform his ways and work hard from that moment on. If our character escapes Soapy's fate and fulfills his vow, we cannot say that he does not deserve the fruits of his labor simply because he did not deserve the inspirational moment that motivated it. By tracing back far enough we can always find causes for actions that create deserts that are themselves not deserved.

The real contrast, then, reduces to that between rewarding chance versus rewarding effort and social contribution; and it still seems that randomization in the award of positions, while it equalizes chances, is the worst possible choice by these criteria. Where there is no ulterior social purpose in the reward of some benefit than the distribution of some windfall good, and where no previous actions of the individuals in question can be seen to create differential rights or deserts to the goods, then a random process of distribution is fairest.

This follows from the presumption of equality of persons in a moral point of view. But when positions are assigned for socially productive purposes, and when individuals are therefore encouraged to direct their efforts toward fulfilling these purposes, past and potential productivity achieved through these efforts cannot be justly ignored. To avoid this unfair waste, positions might be assigned by some random process earlier in life. But the only relevant difference between this determination and the operation of original chance differences against which the egalitarian complains is that this assignment of positions would be more rigid and would involve losses in social utility as compared with more open competition for productive positions. Furthermore, randomization restricts the important liberty to pursue the career of one's choice. It might be assumed that randomization would increase this liberty for many, since it would allow all who wish to pursue a given position to do so merely by applying. But, as argued before, the meaningful pursuit of what one considers valuable and worth achieving involves effort and even struggle, and part of the enjoyment of reward is the feeling of success as a consequence of effort. Such real pursuit is rendered meaningless when positions are awarded by chance. Dignity or a sense of personal worth beyond the mere dignity of being human—often mentioned in egalitarian arguments—derives from a sense of having accomplished, not from winning by chance. An equal right to positions at all levels is bought at the expense of an equal chance to meaningful achievement through effort. Alternatives like randomization or assignment of positions proportionately to members of various groups in the population block this freedom to achieve.

Of course, in reality the egalitarian advocates randomization in the award of positions at higher levels only for those who can demonstrate a certain minimal level of competence. For him this represents a concession to efficiency rather than a consideration of justice, which is distinct. Thus arguments against this and other alternatives that purport to equalize chances for positions are well founded when they criticize such alternatives for nullifying variables that are indeed relevant to just distributions and for restricting individuals' freedom to pursue personal achievement. The egalitarian might reply, however, that a sense of dignity or achievement can be developed through performing well on a job rather than in the process of acquiring it, and that his system equalizes chances for the former type of achievement. But aside from the fact that this downgrades accomplishments culminating the first twenty-five years or so of a person's life, the sense of dignity or achievement of those who acquire positions through a random process most likely would not be appreciably enhanced. Could they be expected to perform well, having never found the need to do so earlier and possibly not having the capacity to do so? The prestige of the positions themselves and the self-respect that goes with them would soon diminish with the knowledge that they were attained by chance. Since prestige and self-respect are themselves sources of inequality, the egalitarian might welcome this change. But since not everyone seeks satisfaction through trying to attain a particular position, why deny this source to those who do? If all had equal chances to all positions, then none could pursue positions or feel any satisfaction at having achieved them. Furthermore, if competence were later demanded on the job, a series of firings and hirings would take place until competent people filled the positions, resulting in resentment among those who proved to be incompetent. If only those who achieved a certain level of competence through effort could apply for positions, moreover, why ignore all achievements beyond that level? (If several applicants are at or predicted to be at the same level of competence, then a random process of choosing does become prima facie proper.)

We do not want to reward purely native characteristics—to do so is generally unfair—but it is an empirical fact that there are few desirable positions in which successful performance demands only native talents. But despite all this argument, we may continue to be bothered by the inability of some people to acquire maximal qualifications for some positions no matter how hard they try. Some people simply do not have the native intelligence or talent, and any system of distributing positions in which efficiency is an important consideration will bar these individuals from certain desirable positions. If this seems sad or unfair, it is nevertheless a fact of life that cannot be justifiably improved by alternative rules of hiring. The point was made above that no matter how narrowly we construe the concept of justice and just reward, no one would seriously advocate randomization to fill the many positions crucial to social welfare and safety, which demand maximum competence. In general, those positions that stress or require excellence or intelligence are the ones that we would least want to open to a random process. Moreover, individuals have the best chance for satisfaction in positions that challenge without exceeding their capacities. This requires that applicants not be placed in positions for which they are not competent and, just as important, that applicants not be placed in positions for which they are overqualified and in which they are hence likely to become bored. From the viewpoints of both the public and the applicants, then, the egalitarian must appear like the skeptic regarding knowledge of the external world in the philosophy classroom when he attacks hiring by competence as an initial general rule, as someone not to be taken seriously in practice.

To say this is not to defend the present system of hiring in our society, for we have hired the most competent only within a very restricted initial class. Nor is it to defend the grossly unequal schedule of rewards that attaches to different positions. But if we lean toward egalitarianism, the only intelligent program is to press for compensatory programs where these are owed, for the creation of equal opportunity as far as possible, and for readjustment of pay scales, no matter how difficult to accomplish. The achievement of these reforms may well take priority over the further application of the rule to award all positions by competence. But if we are to have an initial distributive rule for awarding positions, a rule that creates prima facie rights to positions and prevents the denial of equal opportunity through invidious or capricious awards, it seems that it must be the rule of competence. There simply are no reasonable, practical alternatives.

Qualifications

No discussion of hiring by competence in the context of the debate on reverse discrimination would be complete without some clarification of the nature of competence qualifications and credentials for various positions. I said in my initial argument that a social rule for hiring could be justified in terms of universal increases in utility, and that hiring the most competent entails more goods and services for all. This must now be qualified, for the entailment holds only when competence is defined in terms of actual performance on the job. The problem of course is that in an actual hiring situation, future performance must be predicted on the basis of past achievements that are sometimes indirectly related to tasks required on the job. The question regarding the kinds of achievements or characteristics of applicants that should be made the basis of such predictions constitutes an independent issue in this context.

This complication does not affect my previous arguments or justification of hiring the competent, since the conclusion is still that we want to *aim* at universal increases in utility by having a rule calling upon us to hire the most competent, given the limits upon our ability to predict competence. Such practical limitations do not affect the adoption of ideal distributive rules of the level of specificity of the rule for hiring, just as at the most general level we are always called upon to do what is right, even though it may be difficult in complex situations to figure out what specific action is right. If we could never predict competence at all, then our distributive rules would be different, just as if we could never figure out what is right, we might have no morality at all. Happily, neither antecedent holds. The problem of qualifications in the context of reverse discrimination is that disagreements over which characteristics should be used to predict future competence can generate arguments over when discrimination and reverse discrimination occur in practice. It is therefore necessary to achieve some clarification regarding the nature of competence qualifications before we can know when arguments regarding the justice or injustice of reverse discrimination are to be applied. Without some settlement of this still preliminary issue, opponents of my later general position could always circumvent the arguments by claiming that what appears to be reverse discrimination according to a certain set of narrowly construed competence criteria actually satisfies the rule for

hiring the competent according to a broader and more reasonable set of qualification criteria. We want some guidelines for
deciding how far to accept such claims.

The necessary distinctions can be drawn more clearly in relation to a comparison between qualifying for a job and qualifying to win a prize in some athletic or scholarly contest.[9] In the
latter case there is a threefold distinction to be drawn among:
(1) credentials, in terms of which the outcome could be predicted in advance (in the case of a race, previous running
times; in the case of an essay competition, previous writing
samples); (2) qualifications or abilities (physical condition or
aptitude; composition skills); and (3) actual performance or
qualification for the prize as stipulated in the rules of the contest (crossing the finish line first; writing the best essay or one
judged best). The person with the best credentials may not be
the one currently in the best physical condition or with the
most aptitude, since the other contestants may have had bad
luck in the past or have improved greatly since their last contest. Similarly, the person with the best actual physical or
mental qualifications may not win the race or the essay competition, again owing to factors that we attribute to luck or
chance. In the former case he might trip or develop a cramp
despite his condition; in the latter he might happen to write
one bad essay or one that does not appeal to the judges. These
possibilities necessitate the distinctions. If the chance factors
did not exist, and if there were not a regularity to human (and
animal) performance nevertheless, enabling us to predict with
some reliability (2) from (1) and (3) from (2), there would be
neither horse racing nor reasonable social rules for hiring,
since similar distinctions can be drawn in the case of predicting job performance.

In the area of hiring, we can again distinguish among:
credentials—for example, previous test scores, academic records, or evaluations of performance on prior jobs; qualifications, that is, abilities or knowledge or skills needed on the
job; and actual performance on the job. (One apparent difference between the cases is that good or best performance on
the job will not be mechanically determinable by the application of a fixed set of rules. But this is not always the case with

contests either—for example, essay competitions.) While qualifications constitute the actual capacity to do well on the job, credentials are past achievements presented as evidence of this capacity, which is not testable until the future. It is important to note that when certain types of credentials do not prove predictive of real qualifications or performance, they are downgraded and other, more reliable ones are substituted (assuming that the motive is to satisfy the rules or make a true prediction). In the case of athletic contests and their prizes, the credentials to be used are obvious, that is, previous records from similar contests. When these prove unreliable in the case of a given individual or team, we simply lament their inconsistency and hold our bets, since there will generally be no more reliable barometers available. But in the case of hiring, applicants' credentials will usually reflect achievements different in kind from those required on the jobs in question; therefore more conscious efforts must be made to tailor credentials according to their predictive capacities regarding performance on particular jobs. And there's the rub.

Many who wish to have more women and minority-group members hired argue that credentials previously and still used for various categories of jobs are not "objective," that is, not predictive of real differentials in job performance, and that what appears to be reverse discrimination in favor of such individuals may actually satisfy the rule for hiring competents to a greater degree than do past and current practices. Again, this argument attempts to cut the ground from under the compensatory issues that we shall discuss later; for while we might show that real reverse discrimination has only limited justifiability, our arguments will be inapplicable if what seems to be preferential treatment really amounts only to the implementation of more objective or predictive systems of credentials.

Before assessing the validity of the various forms of this argument, we must examine a number of preliminary points. First, disputes over credentials are sometimes confounded with disputes over actual tasks to be performed on the job itself or over what abilities are required for performance on the job. For example, is scholarship or publication a legitimate part of the duties of a university teacher, and if so, how is it to be weighted against actual teaching ability? Is public relations part of the job of a policeman, or should courage, fairness, and physical ability constitute the only qualifications? These questions regarding relevant performance or qualifications for various jobs relate only indirectly, however, to the issue of reverse discrimination (it might be claimed or shown, for example, that women, although not as physically adept as males, tend to be better at police-community relations, or that statistically, women teachers happen to excel at teaching, although they are not as successful at publishing). In light of more urgent features of the line of argument under consideration, they need not occupy us further. It would be impossible for us in any case to discuss the nature of every relevant job.

Second, there is an important distinction to be made between acceptance of criteria or credentials that are fair or predictive in themselves but that historically have not been applied impartially or fairly, and acceptance of credentials or tests that are themselves unpredictive or unfair and discriminatory. Much discrimination has been caused by hiring officers who misapply or simply ignore criteria that are accepted as theoretically fair. While the application of merit criteria has perhaps been fairer historically in academia than elsewhere, that is, one's social class, accent, and ethnic or national origin has not mattered much (which partially explains the overrepresentation of Jews, who were long barred from other fields), this point must ring hollow to women or blacks, who have often been passed over because wrongly or biasedly assessed, or even when recognized as most competent. (The "old buddy" system of hiring among chairmen of academic departments has been unfair to many others as well.) Although violations in other sectors have been far more glaring, this is only to admit that discrimination has occurred and that fair rules have been ignored; it is not to say that we cannot easily detect such unfair practice in various areas, and reverse discrimination as well, by considering the rule and its current specification of relevant credentials. The argument under consideration here holds not only that the criteria or credentials currently accepted have not been applied fairly, but also that they are inherently discriminatory, that even when applied fairly or impartially they do not indicate future performance or allow us to identify real preferential treatment.

The more obvious forms of this argument make such claims as that tests for school admissions or jobs are totally irrelevant to future tasks, that they are intentionally biased against ,certain groups or individuals, or that they are ultimately shaped by the preconceptions of those in power in order to measure qualities considered important by them. An initial point to be made here is that in a truly competitive situation market pressures will militate against the use of irrelevant criteria or credentials. In a situation in which a corporation or institution survives only by satisfying social demands—for example, where many universities and colleges now compete for scarce funds, students, and recognition through the achievements of their faculty members—there will not be much room for intentional manipulation or rigging of credentials criteria; nor can they be as arbitrary as some have claimed. We have nevertheless seen that a partial market economy does not guarantee that the most competent are always hired even within the limits of predictability, that biases can alter motivations and color perceptions. Until recently, when the qualifications of certain individuals could simply be ignored, more subtle efforts to rig credentials criteria were unnecessary for the purposes of the racist or sexist. After the federal government and the courts began to be sensitive to such gross violations of law, there were undoubtedly attempts by unscrupulous hiring officers in some fields to overstress certain, mostly irrelevant deficiencies associated with minority-group members or women (such as physical strength for police) in order to continue to exclude them from employment. Now that such activities are being detected and monitored in those areas, it is probably easier once again to ignore fair criteria when discrimination can be gotten away with than to manipulate consideration of credentials.

Thus it still seems a good rule of thumb to apply the reversal test (see pp. 16-17) to detect either first-order or reverse discrimination. In a case of possible first-order discrimination, we can ask: If the candidate in question were white and male (if the person turned down is black or female), would he have gotten the job? If we want to detect reverse discrimination, we can ask the same question when the person hired is black or female. (Other variations are possible as well.) More subtle attacks on currently used credentials debate the applicability of this simple test. It may be argued first that in the current context being a minority-group member or woman should itself be considered a qualification for many positions, although it is not according to standard criteria. Or it may be claimed that members of such groups cannot be accurately judged according to standard credentials, since they have been denied the opportunity to acquire such credentials at lower levels in the educational system. Here it is claimed that present credentials will not measure the true potential of such individuals, who may prove more competent than rivals when hired through apparently preferential policies.

Let us consider first when sex or race should become a qualification. This may appear obviously true in a smaller number of cases, such as singing or acting roles or rest-room attendants (although in Europe attendants of the opposite sex fail to cause bladder problems). In such cases sex or race is generally conceded to be relevant. Attempts to press this line more broadly include such claims as that women or blacks teach some college courses more understandingly (for example, female psychology or black history); that female or minority-group students are more receptive to or more communicative with teachers of their own race or sex (in their roles as advisors as well as teachers); that persons living in ghetto communities feel more at ease with police of their own race; that minority-group members need lawyers of their own race or ethnic or national background, who know the community and can communicate better with clients and potential witnesses; that white students gain from having to learn in a mixed classroom because students of different races and backgrounds bring different viewpoints and accustom the whites to a mixed environment; and that women or minority-group members in positions of responsibility provide role models for students, and that this is required to create motivation, which is an essential ingredient of equal opportunity.

Some of these claims will be examined in more detail in the fourth chapter, when I consider future-looking justifications of reverse discrimination and the relation of purported utilitarian benefits to the rights of certain individuals to various positions. Here I shall offer some guidelines and some reasons why, in attempting to identify and justify preferential treatment, these arguments should for the most part be construed as narrowly as possible. There are two necessary and distinct considerations to be applied to claims such as these: first, are they factually accurate (on the basis of what empirical evidence are they advanced); and second, if they are empirically true, should they be morally accepted as creating qualification rights to jobs in accord with the rule for hiring the most competent. It is not at all clear, for example, that women students learn better from women teachers or men from men, nor that heterogeneous classrooms are more conducive to learning, although there may be other reasons for demanding them, at least at lower levels (in Sweden students of homogeneous backgrounds seem to learn no less than here). Nor must we suppose that women are better teachers of female psychology or blacks of black history (not only Europeans can teach Western history or Romance languages, few adolescent psychology courses could be taught by teen-agers, and not many toddlers could improve upon Piaget's theories, whatever we think of his experimental methods).

But more important than these empirical questions is whether race or sex should be given any moral weight for determining rights to various jobs. That they should be given little if any seems clear from another application of our reversal test, the exercise that calls upon us to switch the roles in the context in question. Suppose it were found that male students learn better from men or that white students learn better in all-white classrooms? Do we want to cater to such racist or sexist attitudes, and why on the part of women and blacks and not males and whites (unless we think it fair to let minorities exercise their baser attitudes for a while; but that does not constitute an acceptance of the argument under consideration)? It seems morally and pragmatically preferable from the point of view of women and minority-group members as well, since they may want to teach a variety of courses or work for Wall Street rather than ghetto law firms, to disallow such objectionable utility benefits from entering into consideration of qualifications. The rule for hiring the competent was justified in the first place partially in terms of the increases in social utility that would flow from it as opposed to alternatives. But these are universal increases that can be built into the formulation of the rules and the rights it determines; other, temporary increases for certain groups are prohibited by other rights that protect individuals.

Furthermore, according to our original argument justifying the social rule for hiring the most competent, an individual acquires a right to a position by satisfying the rule *through his own effort*. Insofar as we want to make competence some barometer of previous effort (and rewarding effort rather than chance was part of our justification for the rule as well), we shall not want to base competence qualifications on native characteristics. Considerations of universal utility may leave us unable or unwilling to rule out native intelligence, because it is difficult to separate its effects from those of effort and because ruling it out, even if possible, would almost destroy the idea of competence as the basis of hiring. But the same considerations do not apply to race or sex as qualifications for given positions, since they produce only limited and temporary utility. We want criteria that serve the public interest and toward which an individual can aim his efforts; and these must be applied consistently and with an attempt to guarantee equality of opportunity, so as to give maximum weight to choice and effort. Out of moral considerations then, and pragmatic ones regarding women and minority-group members as well, we should not consider race or sex as direct qualifications for positions.

For the same reason, and for reasons of clarity as well, it is better not to think of the policy of reverse discrimination, where justified, as creating new qualifications for jobs in terms of its justifications. We sometimes tend to think of qualifications for other types of benefits simply in terms of the overall purposes or justifications of the policies according to which the benefits are distributed. For example, wealth disqualifies one from a scholarship, and so having an income under a certain level can be considered one qualification for this benefit designed to remove economic handicaps. (There is a distinction here that I have not stressed between qualifying for entering a competition and qualifying to win it, but that is irrelevant in the case of jobs.) Although I have claimed that qualifications for jobs are to be recognized in relation to a general distributive rule for hiring the competent, this is not to say that this rule and the prima facie rights it creates (or rights subject to a limited number of exceptive clauses) cannot be overriden by considerations relating to other just rules, such as compensation for past harm or creation of greater equality of opportunity than empirically exists now. (If these rules were not also relevant to particular hiring decisions, the issue would be far simpler and this would be the final chapter of this book.) Numerous utilitarian justifications, such as increased social harmony, have been put forth to justify preferential policies for minorities, and they are at least intelligible and in need of evaluation. But if we think of race or sex (or poverty or past harm) as qualifications created through accepted justifications for preferential treatment, we might complete this circle of reasoning by arriving at the conclusion that what appears to be preferential is really not: reverse discrimination is really hiring the most qualified in terms of a comprehensive and just hiring policy. This reasoning obscures the identification of reverse discrimination and, perhaps more importantly, of first-order discrimination as well, and it disguises the nature of the justification for the former.

Therefore, rather than making race a qualification in order to atone for past discrimination, we should consider reverse discrimination as a way of honoring the right to compensation. And rather than making sex a qualification in order to help to restore women's self-respect, we might consider preferential hiring as a means to honor the right to self-respect and to help to make up for past affronts to that right. The latter language has the virtue of clarifying the special compensatory nature of the proposed policy and its relation to earlier violations of the general distributive rule, rather than obscuring the existence of preferential practices. While qualifications are defined relative to the distributive purposes of awarding jobs, I repeat that these must be general distributive goals and not shifting, special purposes; thus initial rights of individuals to jobs are conceived in terms of qualifications that all individuals can aim at acquiring, and discrimination of *both* types is to be defined and identified in terms of those rights.

Let us turn to the second form of the argument under consideration, namely, the claim that the true potential of women and minority-group members cannot be accurately assessed in terms of standard or "paper" credentials, since these will mask previous discriminatory practices that prevented the accumulation of impressive résumés. This version too seems inconsistent, especially if combined with a plea on behalf of the same individuals for compensation for past injury from discrimination. It seems that if past discrimination has been harmful, the handicaps will be real and not merely apparent, as reflected in misleading credentials. The opportunities denied will most likely be opportunities denied not only for acquiring credentials but also for acquiring real qualifications. That members of certain groups score lower on certain tests because of inferior prior education does not in itself prove the tests to be discriminatory; the question in this context is always whether the tests are predictive of future performance. Where lower scores are the result of poor education, the fault lies not in the present tests but in the past injustices. If the acquisition of necessary skills has been prevented or denied at lower levels, as reflected in the only tests available or suggested (if the plea is not for specifically different and more predictive tests but only for handicapping the scores of minority-group members or women on the same criteria), it is unlikely that such skills could suddenly appear without remedial help at the graduate level or on the job. At the higher levels it is hard to believe that educational deprivation, where it has occurred, has not resulted in a lack of requisite skills but only in the lack of ability to demonstrate them on tests, or that such abilities, which took years for those who had the opportunities to develop them, can be immediately acquired by others without special help. This of course is not to say that past denial of opportunity is not grounds for present compensatory measures, such as remedial programs, for those individuals injured through such unjust denial. Such apparently just measures, and the variations of them that are currently possible and available, will be evaluated in the next chapter. The point here is that the claim that credentials assessment is in itself biased or unpredictive in light of earlier discrimination is likely to be false, and again it overshadows the type of policy that ought to be advocated in light of such past injustice. It also obscures the nature of the possible justifications for remedial policies.

Sometimes the claim is made that tests or credentials criteria are racially or culturally biased even apart from discrimination or denial of opportunity at a lower level in the educational system. Reliance on such culture-bound tests is said to have the effect of excluding blacks or Spanish-speaking Americans from the higher professions, just as more overt or less subtle discrimination did in the past. But if the earlier injustices are claimed to be causally unrelated to the inability to compete on tests or to the acquisition of credentials now, this begins to sound racist; if not, then the arguments of the last paragraph apply. The causes of poor test performance will be hard to separate in practice, as the only relevant sample is the group of minority-group members who have had full educational opportunities. In the case of blacks, for example, this sample may be relatively small. In the absence of suggestions for more objective tests applied to all, tests more predictive of job performance, the claim that tests are culturally biased is indistinguishable in terms of its predictive consequences from the recognition that individuals in certain groups tend to be less qualified for certain positions on average than others. These same individuals seem to have a higher drop-out rate when accepted to graduate programs, despite test scores, confirming the predictive value of the tests.[10] (Nor, for example, should the fact that small differentials in medical school admissions tests fail to accurately predict relative success of doctors twenty years later cause us to dismiss the tests, given the extremely good credentials of all persons previously admitted to medical schools.) In light of past large-scale injustice in the educational system toward these individuals, and the unsupported racist implications of attributing the differences to other causes, blame should be placed upon the former and compensatory considerations applied.

If tests are culture-bound, graduate school and professional tasks may be as well, which is only to say that we live in a cultural setting in which certain types of conceptual skills are valued and required in certain professions. While culture-bound tests may not measure native intelligence, they may be the only reasonable barometers of qualifications for culture-bound tasks. But to suggest that individuals from certain racial or ethnic groups are incapable of acquiring these skills is a far more implausible claim, one rightly condemned as an expression of the essence of racism and as an excuse for empirically unfounded bias and injustice. In the unlikely event that this claim proved true on the average, justice might require vast changes in our entire social structure and hierarchy of jobs (in light of a deeper conflict between utility and equal opportunity than acknowledged in the last section); yet the claim that credentials are misleading would again be a far too weak and misleading way of expressing the problem. But in the present context the belief that prior massive injustice in the educational system (as well as extreme differences in economic levels) is at fault for present differences in credentials *and* qualifications should guide our search for a just policy.

Finally, the claim is sometimes made that differences in the credentials of women result not always from denial of educational opportunity or inherently unfair tests, but simply from unfair grading of women by male teachers. While this may occur occasionally—rare individual teachers may allow any irrational bias or neurotic dislike to influence their grading—it is equally plausible that some male teachers grade some of their female students less harshly than average. One implication of this version of the argument regarding evaluation of credentials should be that women previously hired in competitive situations, when their credentials were superior, should do better on the average than their male colleagues in professional life. If lower credentials mark equal qualifications, then equal credentials should indicate superior qualifications and predict superior performance. Here the empirical evidence is more relevant than a priori conjecture. While sufficient to dispel the myth that women tend to work less steadily in positions than do men, the available studies do not indicate relative overachievement either. One study of woman doctorates in America, for example, shows that in terms of scholarly achievement (as measured by books and articles), women do not compare favorably on the average.[11] This can be discounted by other variables, that is, the fact that relatively fewer women teach at large universities that have ample research facilities, possibly because of discrimination in hiring. Discrimination against women by journal editors and publishers might also be claimed, although there is no independent evidence for this conjecture. The essential point here is that when claims with empirical predictive consequences are made in this area, they should be held to exact evaluation of the evidence. Much prior discrimination was based upon absurd factual assumptions—for example, that blacks are lazy, or that women are unpredictable and unreliable. We must be careful not to base reverse discrimination upon opposite stereotypes of these same individuals as overly hardworking and overly qualified but held down at every step by unfair tests and biased grades.

Thus none of the above claims goes far toward justifying race or sex as a qualification for jobs or toward discounting credentials of minority-group members as inherently misleading indicators of qualifications. Certainly, problems arise from the conceptual gap between credentials and qualifications and between qualifications and performance. Presently accepted credentials that prove irrelevant or unpredictive should be changed or redesigned, not handicapped in favor of minority-group members. Nor need we place exclusive reliance upon "mechanical tests." It may be, for example, that given widespread past patterns of discrimination and economic deprivation, certain individuals who make it through college thereby demonstrate a higher motivational level than others; this can certainly be taken into account in predicting future performance. But it is important to note that this is a factor that can be applied to anyone from an economically deprived background; it is not equivalent to considering race or sex a qualification, or to judging the credentials of all women or minority-group members more leniently in assessing real qualifications.

While such nonmechanical criteria can be applied legitimately, it is in the interest of all candidates for positions generally that credentials considered be limited, standard, and publicized. For example, the personality of a prospective teacher might be taken into account in the extreme case that it might substantially affect his or her teaching ability, but in general, personality factors, as they relate to compatibility with colleagues, should be discounted in order to prevent both discrimination and unwarranted reverse discrimination. Standard criteria, such as degrees, publications, student ratings, etc., should be emphasized to ensure fair application of the rule for hiring. The same points apply to positions for which only a fixed level of competence rather than open-ended degrees of excellence are possible. The rule for hiring the competent must still be interpreted narrowly and applied impartially, the only difference being that more applicants will have equal qualifications according to this criterion and that positions will therefore be awarded more frequently on utilitarian grounds or by a random process.

Even if, contrary to all the above considerations, the criteria of credentials for some fields were found to be inherently discriminatory, this would only constitute a reason for finding more predictive or objective criteria and for compensating victims of past application of the unfair set, not for regarding race and sex as qualifications for hiring in the future. This can be made clearer in comparison with a hypothetical case. Suppose that at a school where women account for 50 percent of the enrollment only 10 percent of the persons on the dean's list are women, and that from this it is concluded that discrimination in grading or test designing has occurred. Surely we would not attempt to remedy this situation by insisting that being female is henceforth to be a qualification for the dean's list or that credentials of female students be more leniently evaluated on the same scale, since such moves would tend to destroy the notion of a dean's list as an indication of merit or achievement. Rather, we would insist that tests and other grading criteria be more fairly designed and applied and take steps to ensure this. Similarly, the idea of using race and sex as general qualifications for positions or of judging the credentials of individuals from certain groups more leniently than those of others in an attempt to apply the rule for hiring the most competent is self-defeating. If certain tests have on the average proved unpredictive of future performance by individuals in certain groups, there is no guarantee that keeping the same tests but grading them easier for all individuals of those groups will result in generally more competent people being chosen. Rather, more objective tests should be designed and applied to all. The feeling that at present the same tests cannot be applied fairly to all is a result of the past discrimination and economic deprivation that have handicapped some. But as argued above, the fact of discrimination and deprivation shows that compensatory programs are in order, not that the tests or credentials used are in themselves discriminatory or unpredictive of qualifications. Again, we should advocate reverse discrimination where justified and recognize the costs, not disguise them with misleading talk of native qualifications.

A significant part of the liberal trend in Western nations in the last two centuries has been the gradual elimination of native differences like race or sex as determinants of social roles and benefits. (That intelligence cannot be justly eliminated, however, shows the danger of oversimplification.) We have come to see common humanity as a sufficient reason to demand the satisfaction of basic human needs and, above that level, to distribute benefits more according to individual contributions and potential contributions to the public good. Progress has been slow and impatience warranted in the face of continuing injustice. But the current calls for reversing this trend are perhaps the most disturbing aspect of the debate over reverse discrimination, especially when the policies can be straightforwardly advocated for those individuals who deserve them for compensatory or equalizing reasons. The charge that certain credentials are unpredictive of true qualifications and performance on the job warrants attention and attempts to alter criteria of appointment so as to make them more predictive. This is especially important when present criteria, in addition to being unpredictive, tend to operate against members of groups that have suffered from overt forms of discrimination. But there remains a difference between criteria that individuals can attempt to satisfy through their own efforts, whether predictive or not, and those that count purely native characteristics as credentials in themselves. The latter, where avoidable, are not only inefficient but also unjust in denying equal opportunity.

The point of this section has been that the arguments to follow in favor of the policy of reverse discrimination should not be confused with appeals to abandon impersonal merit criteria regarding credentials and qualifications under the distributive rule for awarding positions. It is important here to separate distributive from compensatory considerations, although, as we shall see, the latter follow from the former.

THREE

Compensation and the Past

In opening this chapter, I shall briefly indicate once more
what was (and was not) established in the earlier sections of
the previous chapter. I maintained that society has the right to
enforce a rule for hiring the most competent in the name of
public welfare and to protect individuals from arbitrary denials
of equal opportunity. Individuals then acquire rights to various positions by satisfying the rule through their efforts. Although this rule was held to be superior to general distributive
alternatives, it is important at this point to recognize its limits.
First, it is applicable mainly to positions that call for open-
ended degrees of excellence. For other positions, qualifications above those minimally necessary for performance are
less relevant, and therefore more random methods of choosing
are fairest. Hence the rule is applicable principally for awarding positions in the professions, in graduate and professional
schools, and to some degree in undergraduate colleges. At
lower levels, educational opportunities should be equally provided to all. To defend this rule even in these areas is not to
defend the status quo or the system prevalent in our society,
for we have employed the merit system only partially within
business and the professions, and mainly in relation to a
privileged class of potential applicants.

Second, it is essential to realize as well that the rights
ideally created through the satisfaction of the rule, where
applicable, are prima facie; that is, they are subject to exceptive clauses for compensatory and distributive reasons relating
to the rule itself. The adoption of *any* distributive rule implies
that when violations occur, perpetrators are to be held liable
and victims compensated in order to keep distributions as consistent with the demands of the rule as possible. It would be
irrational, or perhaps even meaningless, for hypothetical
contractors to adopt a distributive rule without building in
stipulations regarding liability (not necessarily retribution or

punishment) and compensation for violations. If the results of violations are as a rule allowed to stand, then there cannot have been a sincere desire to distribute benefits according to the original principle. In the case of the principle of awarding positions by competence, compensatory considerations may entail specific suspensions of its further application until those who formerly deserved positions but were denied them are compensated in kind by being granted the positions as they open up. In this way, distribution of positions is kept as consistent as possible through time with the distribution that would have resulted from continuous application of the principle. Thus the apparent violations for compensatory reasons, rather than being truly inconsistent with the application of the rule for rewarding competence, are necessary to its maintenance.

Third, although the principle of rewarding competence with positions was held to be superior to general distributive alternatives from the point of view of justice, the distributive results of applying the rule are just only when advantages from initial social positions have been eliminated. In the absence of equal opportunity to acquire competence, its application can perpetuate injustice against those who begin with social disadvantages. We may therefore be justified in temporarily suspending specific applications of the rule if greater equality of opportunity can be created for the future by doing so. This can be seen to follow from the original justification of the rule in terms of utility *and* protection of equal opportunity. Such suspensions, if justified, will have to be limited in time and number, since indefinite suspension of a rule, for whatever reasons, cannot be seen to follow from its original adoption.

Given these qualifications, the importance of the distributive rule itself in the context of the issue under discussion might be questioned. If equality of opportunity has not existed in our society, and if compensation is owed for prior injustice in the form of rampant first-level discrimination, why emphasize prima facie rights to positions that are overridden by these considerations? The importance of these rights in the context of the later argument will be to show that the supposed utilitarian benefits to be gained from preferential policies are irrelevant to its justification. Because preferential treatment of some involves overriding the prima facie rights of others to positions, it is of utmost importance to decide exactly who deserves preference on grounds of compensation and equal opportunity. Granting preference to the undeserving is not merely inefficient, it is unjust.

The issue of preference as compensation will be examined in this chapter, and equal opportunity will be considered in Chapter Four. First, we require a principle to guide our judgment on reverse discrimination as compensation.[1]

The Principle of Compensation

The principle of compensation that governs paradigm cases in which compensation is owed is: *An individual harmed in violation of his rights should be restored by the perpetrator of the injury to the position he would have occupied, had the injury not occurred.* I distinguish compensation here from payment for services rendered, as well as from redistribution to lessen initial inequalities, although the term applies often in ordinary discourse to the latter two cases also. In the sense I intend, the term applies only where a specific injury has occurred to a particular person or persons as a result of a violation of rights. It is sometimes held that reverse discrimination as compensation for past injustices to women or blacks is analogous to special hiring considerations for veterans or the physically or mentally handicapped, and that those who recognize the justice of the latter should acquiesce to the former as well. In using the term *compensation* narrowly, I hope to draw attention to the differences between these cases. Special programs for veterans are best conceived as repayment for unpleasant services rendered by all veterans, while programs for the handicapped are more correctly justified on grounds of equal opportunity (see Chapter Four) than on grounds of compensation (I ignore here past discrimination against the handicapped).

The paradigm case to which the principle of compensation applies involves an intentional infliction of injury in violation of right, resulting in a measurable loss to the victim and benefit to the specifiable perpetrator. In this case it is clear that the guilty party ought to restore his ill-gotten benefit to the victim, plus any accruals to the original amount that might have occurred in the interim. As I indicated above, when such compensation interferes with further application of the distributive rule, it must nevertheless take precedence, despite the logical priority of the distributive rule, in order to approximate the distribution that would have occurred.

Deviations from this paradigm situation include the following cases. There may be no intent to harm, but merely negligence on the part of the individual at fault; or there may be no fault at all, the injury of one party by the other being the result of purely accidental and unforeseeable circumstances. It may be difficult to measure the loss; or losses to certain individuals may be indirect, via violation of the rights of others. There may be no benefit accruing to the injuring party; or it may be impossible for him to pay compensation or even to be located, as in most criminal cases. In clarifying the problem of those who deserve and those who are liable for the burdens of reverse discrimination, it will be necessary to consider some of these deviations and their implications regarding the application of the principle; we rarely deal with paradigm cases of injustice and liability in this area, which is one reason why it is such a thorny issue from the point of view of justice.

As implied above, the principle that victims of injustice generally should be compensated follows from the original adoption of the distributive rule that has been unjustly violated. The idea is to approximate those holdings that would have resulted from the continuous application of the distributive rule. The application of the compensatory rule, then, involves counterfactual reasoning, that is, reasoning about what would have been had no injury occurred. While this is not the place to attempt an explication of the metaphysics or epistemology of counterfactuals, the necessity of such reasoning in awarding compensation fairly has important implications for the justification and limitations of reverse discrimination. Once again it is crucial that the compensatory principle be capable of fair and consistent application in impersonal social contexts. Regarding the distributive rule for rewarding competence, the difficulty of measuring effort apart from productivity in such contexts was a reason for emphasizing the latter rather than the former in the rule. Similarly, for wrongs to be compensable, they must result in clear and measurable harms to the victims. Evidence for the truth of the relevant counterfactuals regarding injured parties can include reference to other individuals who were in similar positions at the time of the injuries and who have progressed normally. When harms are "remote, indirect or speculative,"[2] the relevant reference class cannot be specified narrowly enough. Nor can we be certain that in the interim other variables would not have affected the positions of those presumed indirectly harmed. When there is no clear answer to the relevant counterfactual, awards of compensation according to the rule will be inconsistent in practice and without firm basis. Unsubstantiated answers would result in unjust overriding of legitimate prima facie rights, reducing these to no rights at all. Hence the epistemological problem here limits just application of the compensatory principle to harms that are direct, clear, and measurable, a corollary long used in the law of torts—with important implications for our issue, as we shall see.

The goal of approximating distributions that would have obtained in the absence of harm to specific victims of injustice means that compensation is not made simply to restore the goods unjustly taken or denied, that is, to return them to the status quo ante, but to bring them to the level that they would have attained had there been no injustice in the first place. For example, a person formerly denied a position for which he or she was most qualified not only deserves a job now but also, at least, back pay as well. The question of compensation for victims of injustice is unproblematical when the loss is clear and measurable and when the offenders can be located and are able to pay. That this follows from the adoption of any distributive rules means that no independent justification need be given for this much of the compensatory principle: the same reasons that govern the initial adoption of the distributive rule, that render distributions according to it just, also make correction of its violations just. Distributive rules create rights of certain individuals to certain goods. To fail to add a principle of compensation is to imply that such rights are canceled through their violation, which is to imply that they are not

rights at all, which is inconsistent.[3] Thus while it was necessary in Chapter One to say something about the origin of distributive rules from a contractarian viewpoint, it is not necessary here to expand upon that framework in order to generate
a principle of compensation. Rational agents initially adopting
distributive rules must agree not to allow violations to stand
when they can be corrected by transferring goods from perpetrator to victim (although not all actual agents in a given society might agree, given that some could gain from unhin-
dered violation of just rules).

The general questions that remain prior to application of the
principle to our specific issue are, first, whether victims must
be compensated when perpetrators cannot be located or cannot pay, and, second, whether there is a value in making the
guilty or liable parties pay over and above the restoration of
the victim to his rightful state. In regard to the first question, a
positive answer would amount to a demand for mandatory insurance against loss from victimization or for state compensatory boards covering all injury. While there may be some
value to spreading the costs of injustice in this way, it does not
seem to be strictly demanded by considerations of justice. For
to spread the costs involves sacrifice on the part of innocent
third parties, and it does not seem that all victims of injustice
have the right to demand such a sacrifice from those unrelated
to the injustice (can I have a duty to compensate the wealthy
suburbanite victim of burglary?).

It may be thought that the idea of keeping distributions as
close as possible to what they would have been had no violations occurred *does* require spreading the costs of compensating victims, no matter how well off. Rationally, then, it would
appear that agents who initially adopt distributive rules would
also have to require universal compensation and not just restitution when the perpetrator could be located. The idea is that
a penny taken from each of one hundred people to restore a
dollar stolen from one man results in a distribution more
nearly approximating to that considered just under prior operation of the accepted distributive rules. One problem with
this, however, concerns its application to an actual society in
which distributions do not always result from the operation of

fair distributive rules. But, leaving this aside, I still do not believe the argument to be conclusive. For fair distributive rules
can result in fairly large inequalities in wealth and other
goods, and when restoring the wealthy victim requires contribution from those less well off, its justness does not follow
from the closer absolute approximation to the prior distribution. The penny to which the contributors are entitled according to the distributive rule may be as important to them as was
the dollar to the victim. While the original inequalities may
have been justified on grounds of universal utility as incentives, maintenance of these incentives does not require compensation here (given that violations are not extremely widespread). Therefore, to be rational I do not think we need or
necessarily would opt for a program of universal compensation
by unrelated third parties in cases when perpetrators cannot
be made to pay. On compensatory grounds alone, we need not
allow a universal right to compensation. That this is not demanded by justice does not mean that there is no obligation to
help those in need or those in need because of past injustice,
but such questions go beyond considerations of pure compensation and will occupy the next chapter.

As applied to the problem of reverse discrimination as compensation, the above point seems to imply that where perpetrators of the injustice for which compensation is claimed cannot be located or where unrelated third parties are concerned,
victims cannot demand that such parties (for example, young
white males) bear the burdens of the policy on compensatory
grounds alone. As we shall see in the sections to follow, however, the matter is more complicated than that. The relevance
of this implication will depend, I believe, upon the level at
which the injustice occurred, that is, whether at the job-hiring
level or in the educational system. There is one further complication or qualification to the above point regarding innocent
or unrelated parties, namely, that such individuals can sometimes benefit from injustices toward others, even though they
played no role in causing them. It is sometimes claimed, for
example, that white males who played no active role in discrimination against women and blacks nevertheless benefited
economically from their subjugation. Where such benefits can

be located and correlated with losses to the victims, the demand that distributions be kept as close as possible to those that would have resulted from the continuous operation of fair rules seems to call for transfers of the goods back to the victims. However, such transfers are in turn complicated by the expectations and life styles that may have developed from the apparently legitimate (certainly legitimate at the time in the eyes of the innocent beneficiaries) prior acquisition of the goods. We need say no more regarding such complex cases until we attempt to apply these considerations more specifically to the issue at hand in the sections to follow.

The question of whether there is moral value in making a perpetrator of injustice pay compensation in addition to the value of restitution calls for consideration of the different types of cases. In the easiest case, where the guilty party benefits from his act of injustice, it seems to me that the goal of maintaining distributions in line with the operation of the applicable distributive rule requires the culprit to relinquish his ill-gotten gains, even though in specific cases utility might be maximized by spreading the costs of compensation more widely. (The utilitarian might justify making the guilty pay in all such cases as a deterrent to further injustices, but this would probably not work in the case of unintentional or negligent fault.) In the case where no benefit is derived from the injustice, we must look to the distinction between intentional or grossly or unusually negligent fault versus nonintentional fault. Where the fault is intentional—when there is not only possible liability but also certain guilt—a retributivist (one who believes there is moral reason to punish those who violate moral law, beyond reformative and deterrent effects) would tend to hold the guilty party responsible for full compensation as well. A utilitarian might do the same for reasons of deterrence. The potential offender is less likely to violate the rights of others if he knows he will have to pay to compensate.

We must be careful, however, not to totally assimilate the notion of compensation to that of punishment. The two concepts are clearly distinct in law: first, in that punitive damages, when assigned in cases of malicious intent, are distinguished from compensatory damages; and second, because the so-called "benefit rule" holds that when an act violating a person's right results in accidental benefit to that person, the amount of benefit is to be subtracted from the harm in computing compensation owed, showing the principal aim to be restoration of the victim rather than punishment of the offender for the nature of his act. If the principal intent of compensation were the same as that of punishment, similar acts would require similar penalties, but such is not the case. The important implication of this distinction for our topic is the point made before: wrongs may be justly punished, but only measurable wrongful harms can be justly compensated.

Despite this distinction, I nevertheless believe that there is a retributive element to compensation as well. When an offender is intentionally at fault, I do not believe that he can legitimately complain of injustice if he is forced to pay an amount equal to fair compensation, even if that amount should go to some selected proxy for the victim rather than to the victim himself. An offender who violates the right of some person fails in his obligation or duty (since rights to goods imply correlative obligations on the part of others to grant, or at least not to deny, those goods), and he cannot complain if he is made to pay compensation equal in amount to that lost through his violation of duty. Forcing him to pay can be viewed as forcing him to fulfill his obligation or an equivalent one, and such a demand is not unjust. While I am not sure whether there is independent moral value to such payment, or whether it is *demanded* by justice when the offender derives no benefit from his act, this weaker point—the fact that forcing such payment is not unjust—will be important in the discussion to follow. In cases where payment is made to an actual victim rather than to a proxy, it can also be argued that if the fault is intentional, it is more just that the offender pay rather than unrelated third parties. This position places all the positive value of compensation in the restoration of the victim, but holds that sacrifices are better borne by the perpetrator than by those unrelated to his act.

In the remaining case of purely accidental damages there seems no reason, from the point of view of justice, why compensation for the victim must come from the other party, as opposed to institutions that spread the costs more widely. No-fault insurance for nonnegligent automobile accidents may be preferable not only from a cost-reducing or utilitarian view-point but also for reasons of justice, given that such accidents fall more or less randomly among a population of relevantly similar drivers. Such cases need not concern us further, since discrimination for which compensation in kind is demanded can rarely be viewed as purely accidental. While hiring officers and school board members may have been following widely prevalent practice in discriminating against blacks, for example, and while some may not even have seen themselves as treating anyone unjustly, given their biased views of the character of their victims, their acts were not accidental in the sense that someone's failure to be hired because his dossier was lost would be accidental. *Moral negligence* is perhaps the best characterization of the fault involved in such cases of discrimination without apparent intent.

The case in which we are primarily interested is then a case of intentional or negligent violation in which typically no benefit accrues to the offender. (There would be no benefit because discrimination tends to be inefficient as well as unjust, although the offender benefits in a stretched sense by getting what he wants—for example, nonassociation with minorities.) Since fault in these cases is typically intentional, the offenders cannot complain if made to pay an amount equal to damages caused, even if the actual victims derive no benefit from the payment; when victims themselves are paid, it is more just that compensation come from the offenders than from unrelated parties (or the state). Harms from unjust denials of positions or opportunities are direct and compensable; psychological traumas from association with victims are more indirect, speculative, and problematic.

The attraction of reverse discrimination as a means of compensation in the educational system, and especially at the level of job hiring, is that it constitutes compensation in kind; together with back pay, it comes as close as is literally possible to restoring to the victim what was previously denied him (one can never restore lost experience). When such literal restoration in kind can not be achieved (or should not for other reasons of justice), monetary compensation is accepted as second best. In regard to this alternative, when injury is clearly shown and liability determined, the difficulty of assigning monetary value to certain kinds of nonmonetary injury should never (and does not in court) bar payment of some compensation to be determined by the best comparative means available. Questions such as "How can you pay for the loss of an eye or for ten years of a person's life (when he should have had a decent job but did not)?" should not be taken to imply that no compensation, however token in effect in relation to actual injury, is owed. On the other hand, while all direct damages (that is, all damages that are the direct and foreseeable consequences of faulty behavior) are compensable despite difficulty of estimate, consequences that are remote, indirect, or speculative are generally to be dismissed, as argued above. For example, direct mental damages, such as mental anguish, loss of self-respect, or insult to the victim resulting from violations of his rights, should be compensated; but vicarious mental damages to persons other than those whose rights are violated seem too remote and speculative for liability to be imposed.

I have stated a principle of compensation and its general application to nonparadigm cases of the type we shall be considering. Crucial questions remain to be explored in relation to specific applications of reverse discrimination. Much recent philosophical debate on the issue has centered around the question of whether it can be just to treat a characteristic such as being black or being a woman as relevant in any hiring practice. My argument in the last section of the previous chapter showed that race or sex should generally be dismissed as a distributive qualification for jobs under the rule of hiring the competent. Whether such characteristics can constitute legitimate criteria for compensation, however, was left open. The practice of reverse discrimination has been defended by a number of different arguments: that the relevant characteristic is not being black, for example, but having been discriminated against because one is black;[4] that the only relevant characteristic is that of having been discriminated against (and not being black), and that therefore compensation is owed only to those discriminated against and not to the group of blacks;[5]

and finally, that being black is a morally relevant basis for hiring because in the past, discrimination was a general policy of society as a whole.[6] The outcome of this debate is simply that a characteristic morally irrelevant from the point of view of distributive justice may be relevant from the point of view of compensation. But the central questions remain: whether, when, and in what sense compensation can be owed to a *group* as a whole; whether women or minority groups like blacks qualify as the proper kind of group; whether compensation can be owed *by* a group as a whole; and whether white males constitute the proper kind of group to share such liability. These questions will occupy the next section; subsequent sections of this chapter will concern the distinction between levels at which discrimination occurs, insofar as that affects the type of compensation owed, and the question of strong versus weak reverse discrimination as compensation.

Groups or Individuals?

Group Desert

In what sense can a group of individuals be said to deserve compensation for past wrongs? The first sense in which this can be true involves the case in which each member of the group in question has been separately wronged to the same degree. This is often the case in class action lawsuits, as when a group of tenants sue a landlord because all were equally harmed by lack of services, etc. When harm has occurred to every member of a group individually in this way, we can say that the harm is distributive within the group. Such wrong dissolves without remainder into the separate harm to each individual, and to refer to group desert here in regard to compensation is shorthand for referring to the compensation owed separately to each member. A class action suit might be undertaken to save costs, but no one would be a party to such a suit who was not directly a victim of the wrongful act.

I do not believe that such distributive and equal harm can be claimed for members of the groups of women or blacks. Certainly not all members of these groups have been unjustly denied a job or a chance at a decent education—the type of harm that may call for reverse discrimination as compensation in kind. While each member of the past generation of blacks might be able to support such a claim—so gross was the injustice directed toward them—there are now at least a few blacks coming through the educational system who have not suffered this overt and glaring kind of denial. And among women graduating with advanced degrees, it is certainly not difficult to think of some who attended superior or exclusive schools at every level, who were never discouraged in their ambitions, etc. It may even be that every woman who has been working for some years at a job typically occupied by men has faced discrimination at some point, but this is certainly not true of every young woman just about to enter the job market, which is the subgroup most likely to benefit from present reverse discrimination policies.

To make any case at all for distributive harm to every member of such groups, it might be claimed that although not all have been denied a job or superior education, all have been at least indirectly harmed because such practices and the associated stereotypes caused them to suffer loss of ambition, self-respect, etc., and that preferring members of the group for positions of responsibility is the only means of compensating for such motivational damages. It also follows, according to this argument, that although the harm claimed here is distributive, in that all members of the group have been subjected to such unfair pressures, compensation in the form of reverse discrimination need not be universal in order to have a compensatory effect for each. Vicarious harm from the denial of opportunity to others, which is taken to reflect community attitudes, can be compensated by vicarious association with whichever members succeed in acquiring desirable positions. Reverse discrimination, which, like first-level discrimination, is directed only to some members of the group, can nevertheless compensate for the broader psychological harm caused by the attitudes manifested in the original injustice. It can operate to restore self-respect and motivation to all members of the group equally.

Several empirical assumptions or tacit premises in the above argument are open to serious question. Even assuming

that all women, to continue the example, have been subjected
to such pressures (though surely there are always some who
have been encouraged to seek careers by parents and teachers,
and who have not been seriously affected by injustices toward
others), those subtle pressures undoubtedly affect different
individuals in different ways and in several different ways can
fail to amount to harm. To assume distributive harm requires
an accepted model of what a woman or person should be (the
stereotype is something less), an assumption of unconscious
brainwashing and self-delusion rather than rational choice on
the part of those women who appear content in nonworking
roles, and an assumption that these pressures cause conform-
ity rather than, say, overachievement among all women who
are inclined to seek careers. Surely it is just as simple to find
numerous men who succumb to opposite social pressures by
working all their lives at jobs they hate in order to appear successful by those standards, or men who disintegrate into dere-
licts through failure to meet them. Are we going to suggest
that society owes these men something in the way of compensation, for example, the kind of support routinely available to
married nonworking women? They can no more be compensated by seeing other men in nonworking roles than can dis-
satisfied housewives by seeing other women get jobs that they
themselves did not even consider until too late. In both cases
acceptance of oneself may become psychologically more difficult rather than easier through such vicarious identification.

Even if we accept that women who have not pursued
careers have suffered motivational deprivation amounting to
harm, or even if we limit the group in question to women who
might desire careers but presently do not because of social
stereotyping, there is also an assumption here regarding the
intractability of motivations and the appropriateness of reverse
discrimination as the sole way of altering them through compensation. If discrimination were ended, and if work-ethic
pressures of self-support were applied to women as they have
been to men, the failure of many young women to pursue
careers would be more plausibly attributed to rational resistance than to the social injustice of the past. The question is
whether we have to go as far as reverse discrimination to

counter the psychological effects of past discrimination upon those toward whom it was never directed. Finally, in regard to the psychological effect of reverse discrimination itself, it is hard to see how the self-respect of many women, even of those who get jobs through the policy, can be restored if the jobs are granted preferentially and there is suspicion of lower competence of women on the job. The policy may then simply prolong the stereotype.

The conclusion to be drawn from the above points is that harm from social stereotyping or from injustice directed toward others with whom one is only distantly associated is that kind of "remote and speculative" harm that courts refuse, with good reason, to recognize in compensation cases. For at least some persons, self-respect is not tied to work at a job, and unjust practices against those who pursue careers might not be felt as harms by others who share some characteristic that was the basis for the discrimination. I do not mean to imply that in general no one can be treated unjustly by being denied something or a right to something just because he or she might not have wanted that thing in any case.[7] All those women who were denied the right to vote were treated unjustly, even if some of them might not have chosen to exercise that right and were not particularly concerned at not having it. And the fact that a particular slave is contented does not justify his being a slave. In the same way, it might be argued that even content nonworking women have been treated unjustly in that, if they had applied for various jobs, they would have been unjustly denied them.

Several distinctions weaken these analogies, however. First, an inferior status conferred by law is an injustice to the group singled out by that law in a way that private instances of injustice against certain members of the group may not be. Second, it seems to me that there is a difference between these cases in that the right to vote and the status of a free person are goods that any rational person would rather have than not (even if some do not exercise the right to vote and some slaves are content), while it might not be rational for everyone to desire a right to compete fairly for a job, as opposed to the availability of decent support without working. In that sense it can be maintained that those women who have chosen without pressure not to work have not been harmed, even given the assumption that they would have been unjustly denied jobs had they applied. Being Jewish, I may not have had a fair chance of making it to the top of many large corporations, if I had wanted to or had tried; but since I did not want to, I do not consider myself to have been harmed personally. Nor would I consider myself compensated in any way if Jews were given preferential treatment now by General Motors.

Third, even if we accept the above analogies, it may be that the case under question, like the case of the vote and the case of men who succumb to pressures to succeed in jobs that do not fit their particular characters, falls into the class of uncompensable harms (I pass over the century-old suggestion of forty acres and a mule for ex-slaves). How can we compensate the denial of the right to vote in the past—by granting two votes in the next election?[8] In what way should the reasonably content nonworking woman be compensated for the hypothetical denial of a career? It makes even less sense to talk of vicarious compensation for her through preferred treatment for some unrelated woman for some position that she neither knows nor cares about.

I suggested in the previous section that where injustices have occurred and specifiable distributive harms have resulted, inability to precisely equate monetary amounts should not bar payment of compensation. But there are some injustices so tenuously related to direct distributive harms or imbalances in individual cases that it seems irrational to try to compensate them now by further transfers of goods from otherwise deserving parties, especially given scarce resources. Thus we cannot justify reverse discrimination for a woman who was never discriminated against in the job market or in the educational system on the grounds that she must have nevertheless suffered vicariously from discrimination or on the grounds that compensating her will provide vicarious compensation for other women. The claim of universal distributive harm is false. If we shift from harms to wrongs, it is more likely that all women have been wronged at some time, even if only insulted, through the expression of discriminatory attitudes.

But as argued before, only wrongful harms require compensation. [9]

A further difficulty arises when indirect motivational pressures are allowed to count in claims for reverse discrimination as a means of compensation, namely, they open the door to seemingly irrelevant claims on behalf of other groups underrepresented in various job categories. When it is pointed out that Italians, Greeks, Poles, Irish, and Republicans, as well as women, are statistically underrepresented in academic departments at universities, the proper reply is that systematic discrimination was never practiced against the former individuals by department chairmen, and so no compensation can be owed in this area to members of those groups. But when appeal to motivational pressures is permitted, and when the patterns of customary roles and social stereotyping are admitted as harms for which reverse discrimination is owed as compensation, this reply becomes more problematic. It can then be counterargued that Italians, for example, have been stereotyped as barbers, opera singers, and underworld figures rather than as professors, that this stereotyping amounts to social brainwashing, and that Italians should be given preference for professorial jobs in order to counter it. One might also point out that the complaint of some women is that they have not simply been role typed, but typed into subservient roles. But we must be careful in characterizing some roles in a way their occupants would not accept (women working in lower paying jobs and kept from advancement constitute a different case). I do not think we should attribute to individuals those motivations they do not have, or blame "the system" for those they do, especially individuals who would not accept our model of what constitutes success in life. In any case, we cannot allow such arguments, even if their complex psychological premises are correct, and still keep a reasonable limit upon who is owed compensation.

As I have maintained, the case is totally different for those members of the groups in question who have been overtly discriminated against in the educational system or at the level of job hiring. Such individuals are clearly owed compensation, and reverse discrimination, at least for those in the latter category who are no longer as qualified as new applicants, seems fitting. But since we must draw the line at indirect psychological pressures, which affect different individuals in different ways and can plausibly be seen to harm only some members of the group, the claim of distributive harm to all members of the same group is implausible. Hence we can question the appropriateness of a policy directed indiscriminately toward an entire group, for it tends to benefit primarily those younger members arriving fresh at the job market with good credentials. Even discrimination against all group members would not have equal effects and so would not justify a policy of compensation directed randomly at the group as a whole. Reverse discrimination would still appear more appropriate for those overtly discriminated against, leaving vicarious compensation for vicarious harm, that is, harm from the violation of rights of others. (I have chosen purposely to speak of the group of women here and am less confident of the applicability of these arguments to blacks or Mexican-Americans, for example, who have been subject to far more disrespect and motivational pressure at every level. A policy of reverse discrimination for most of them can generally be justified on stronger grounds, although degrees of harm and hence priorities of compensation may still be distinguished. Furthermore, reverse discrimination is compensation in kind for a specific type of injury, not for such wrongs as discrimination in housing or police harassment. Discrimination in housing, for example, might be more suitably compensated by federally subsidized housing in formerly all-white neighborhoods.)

Is there then any other model of group harm and desert that could justify compensation for whole minorities or women as a group and further justify reverse discrimination as the means to such group compensation? To clarify the notion of nondistributive harm to a group—harm that cannot be exhaustively analyzed into separate and specific injury to each of the members separately compensable—it will be necessary to define a certain type of group that can be the recipient of such harm and thus the subject of such desert. As groups or social organizations are generally referred to by sociologists, their defining characteristic is actual interaction among members in relation to overall common purposes or practices. Members of such collectives occupy certain positions or play certain roles in the groups reciprocal to other roles, roles being reciprocal when their performances are mutually dependent.[10] Groups defined in this way can be the recipients of nondistributive harm, and compensation for injury or damages can be owed to the group as a whole in the strongest sense in which this is possible, first because injury to one member affecting his duties as a member harms all members, and second because many damages cannot be assigned separately to specific members but only to the group as a whole. Both these features of nondistributive harm are further specifications of its central feature: it cannot be analyzed into separate harm to each individual apart from his being a member of the group. Both characteristics of harm follow from the central feature of these groups, that is, the reciprocity of roles within them.

A paradigm example of this type of collective is an athletic team. An illustration of the first characteristic of nondistributive harm would be if members of one team deliberately broke the arm of their rivals' star in the midst of a crucial game. Here injury to one member of the group negatively affects the performance potential of the entire group and hence harms all its members, although the harm cannot be analyzed into separate injury to each individual apart from reference to the group. Compensation would then be owed to the team as a whole (with perhaps an additional amount for the player physically injured). If the team were forced to forfeit a game because of an unfair decision of the referees, we would have an example of the second characteristic of nondistributive harm, that is, an injustice to the group that cannot be more narrowly or differentially assigned to specific members. Here the injustice is not directed principally to one member but to the entire team at once, and again compensation is therefore owed to the group as a whole. Such compensation would normally and preferably take the form of some lump-sum payment (whether in money or some other good payable in this fashion—for example, a game in the standings of the league) to the entire organization, or of equal amounts to each of the members if no lump-sum payment is possible. Generally, it would not be fair to compensate some members more than others for this kind of non-distributive harm.

Compensation can be said to be owed in a weaker sense to a group when faulty action is directed toward some official organization, such as a corporation or a nation. In such cases the two features of nondistributive harm hold to lesser degrees; that is, there may be little interaction among some members of large organizations, and it may be possible to differentiate degrees of harm to different members. In order to award compensation there must be an official body toward which the action can be sensibly said to be directed (there is no intent to harm specific individuals except in their relation to the organization) and an organization that can receive compensation owed on behalf of all its members in their official capacities (for example, as citizens or stockholders). Thus, if some economic alliance unjustly imposes sanctions against American exports, compensation might be said to be owed to the United States. But when damages to subgroups or individuals within the larger organization can be distinguished, fairness calls for a type of compensation that will be reciprocal to the proportion of harm suffered by the different groups or individuals, such as favored treatment that would benefit just those American exporters formerly hurt most. An alternative would be internal proportionate disbursement of a lump sum paid as compensation to the organization. It would be unfair in the case of compensation for sanctions against exports if a lump sum were paid to the United States and then disbursed in a way that helped groups other than exporters. The latter might welcome the symbolic gesture of admitting the wrong and the probability that it would not recur, but they could still complain of the injustice of the policy of compensation in toto. Justice in all cases of harm, individual and group, distributive and nondistributive, calls for assigning damages as specifically as possible and reimbursing subgroups and individuals always in proportion to actual damages suffered under the unjust treatment or policy.

Keeping in mind our earlier arguments regarding distributive harm, are there any minority groups that meet the above criteria for groups deserving of compensation for nondistributive harm? There is one case, instructive for its contrast to others, of a group that meets all three criteria for our types of nondistributive damage and desert for compensation: Indian tribes whose treaties were violated by the federal government. Here we have collectives characterized by group practice or purpose and interaction of members, specific damages that cannot be assigned differentially within the group, and official bodies to receive compensation owed on behalf of all members, that is, tribal organizations recognized by members as responsible for internal disbursement of amounts received. Even here, however, to return to our specific topic, reverse discrimination in job hiring does not seem an appropriate type of compensation for the damages inflicted. In fact, it does not seem appropriate as compensation for any cases in which nondistributive harm is involved, since it cannot be paid in a lump sum to the group as a whole but must benefit separate members differentially. If membership in the group is to be the only criterion for consideration for preferential treatment—as it seemingly should be if the harm to be compensated is nondistributive among members—and if market considerations of competence are allowed to operate to choose specific members for various positions—as seemingly they must for reasons of efficiency—compensation will neither be equal among members nor proportional to damages. Thus, even when an entire group has been harmed nondistributively and is therefore owed compensation as a whole, reverse discrimination for the group does not seem called for. As we shall see, the problems facing a group policy from the point of view of justice are worse when harm to all members cannot be claimed.

With regard to groups other than Indians, blacks might be seen to meet the weakest of the above criteria for nondistributive harm, namely, the damages resulting from injustice directed at the group cannot be separately assigned to particular members. This might be the case in those geographical areas in which laws conferred a second-class citizenship in numerous important respects until recently. Here some kind of compensation seems owed to the entire group,[11] even though there was little or no interaction among many members, since attempts to specify harms to individuals would meet insuperable difficulties. Yet it is clear that all were substantially harmed. The chief difficulty here is the failure to meet the third criterion for nondistributive harm, or, more precisely, for nondistributive desert for compensation: the lack of any official body that represents all members of the group and that could act as the recipient of payment for all. Despite this difficulty, special aid might be specified for certain community projects and representative institutions—for example, colleges, businesses, etc.—with emphasis given to types of aid that would benefit large classes of blacks at once and thus approximate to general benefits. Here again reverse discrimination seems unsuitable as compensation for nondistributive harm, since it is by nature a distributive benefit working in favor of particular members differentially.

Women and other minority groups appear to me to satisfy none of the above criteria for nondistributive harm or desert for compensation, even though discrimination against their members has been widespread and even though specific laws operated against their interests in certain areas (for example, certain work protection and property laws in the case of women, and literacy tests for non-English-speaking minority-group members). The differences between these cases and that of blacks are that these laws operated only in scattered areas, harmed only certain interests (other laws operated to the benefit of women—for example, alimony and draft laws), and imposed injustices that did not always in themselves result in distributive imbalances in other goods and that therefore are not always clearly compensable. For these reasons the claim that the entire groups were seriously harmed is again implausible.

In none of these cases is this assessment intended to downplay the deep individual injustices that require differential compensation in kind (with regard to blacks and Indians, such compensation would be over and above that owed to groups in various areas). I am addressing myself in this section only to the question of whether reverse discrimination, as directed toward whole minority groups indiscriminately, is an appropriate response to the injustices against many of their members. The claim that *all* women and members of minority groups have been distributively or nondistributively harmed in a serious discriminatory fashion is not only implausible, but also the type of injustice that might be used as evidence to support this claim is not the type that requires reverse discrimination as compensation in kind.

Others have questioned the criteria that I have proposed for nondistributive harm and group compensation. As a weaker criterion for determining groups that could claim nondistributive harm, and hence compensation, we might simply accept the existence of mutual concern, cultural identification, and shared values and interests, rather than actual interaction and reciprocal roles among members. Even if harm has not occurred to all members of the relevant groups, we might be able to compensate, at least partially, those who have been harmed by granting preference to other members of the groups, if those members harmed identify with the interests of the other members and would prefer to see them, rather than outsiders, obtaining benefits. If each member prefers that benefits accrue to other members of his or her group rather than to outsiders, then benefits to any member might be said to benefit all, including those actually harmed through discrimination.[12] And if there is cultural and political identification as well, then all members benefit in the long run when those who become socially advanced help to further the cultural and political expression of the group.[13]

In replying to these arguments, we may take the points one at a time. In regard to the preferences of some persons that others be given special treatment and benefits, it is doubtful how much weight such third-party preferences should have against the rights of those for whom the benefits are directly at stake. Even if we do not find personal preferences for others of one's own race or sex morally objectionable (though we seem to do so in the case of white males), it does not seem that we should honor them in official policies by overriding rights of those directly involved in competition for positions by granting preferential consideration to others who do not deserve it on grounds of actual personal harm.[14] In regard to cultural identification, it certainly seems farfetched to think that individuals have rights to cultural production by others, or that to advance these others socially will increase their cultural expression (although this has been argued). That political benefits might accrue to some members of these groups if others are given preference for positions of influence is more plausible. But it is once again doubtful that at least some of these groups—for example, women—form cohesive political units with common interests or that those who gain positions through reverse discrimination will speak for those interests. Finally, and most important, it would seem obvious that those persons actually harmed, who therefore have rights to compensation, would prefer policies that direct preference toward themselves rather than toward other members of the groups with which they identify.

I am not condemning all preferential programs. But if such policies must be limited in scope, it is important to choose the most fair from among the possible alternatives. The fairest will be those that most directly accomplish their justifying aims, that is, those that attempt most directly to compensate individuals who themselves deserve it on grounds of actual prior discrimination or denial of equal opportunity.

The conclusion to be drawn from the above analyses of both distributive and nondistributive harm is that, with regard to groups that are defined only according to some shared characteristic, that have no official representative bodies, whose members have no formal interaction, and whose individual members may suffer harms from injustices that do not necessarily affect others, compensation can be owed only to the individual members who have been harmed and not to the groups as a whole. This seems especially clear when the injury in question is the unjust denial of a job or decent education; reverse discrimination is then intended as compensation in kind. Both injury and restitution here must be directed at individuals in any case, since hiring does not take place on a group basis.

The only questions to be decided are which individuals deserve the benefits, and should we trust compensation to chance or market conditions and forces. If someone is discriminated against for being Jewish, his injury is not mine (although I may feel threatened), and certainly I am not owed the compensation owed to him. When the policy in question is reverse discrimination in hiring, the attempt to apply it as compensation for whole minority groups, given only that such groups be defined in terms of some characteristic that was the basis for the unjust treatment of some members, will invariably result in injustices regarding the members who do or do not benefit, and in conceptual muddles regarding who owes what to whom.

Affirming that whole groups are owed the policy of reverse discrimination as compensation for past harm leads to further contradictions. One might say that all society owes preferential treatment to groups as a whole, while denying that it is owed separately by particular organizations to particular individuals who have been unjustly treated by them. Such a policy could be based on the belief that discrimination in the past has been so widespread that it would be arbitrary to single out certain corporations as guilty, given that no one in power could have been expected to have acted differently from standard practice and that others would have done the same. As we have already seen, however, it was not true that degrees of harm to individuals were indistinguishable; nor, as we shall see in the next section, should we construe degrees of guilt or liability as equal over all society. To argue in this way is to provide an excuse for wrongdoing that we would not want to allow. It would mean that a company or organization incurs no specific obligation to compensate damages when it treats individuals unjustly, as long as the practice is widespread. It would also mean that individuals who have actually been treated unjustly deserve no preference on compensatory grounds over those who have never suffered overt discrimination but who only happen to share the characteristic that was the basis for discrimination. This, as intimated above, is equally unacceptable.

The remaining possibility, if we are to affirm group desert despite the lack of an adequate model, is to claim that society has a duty to compensate groups as a whole that have suffered widespread discrimination in the past, and also that particular organizations guilty of unjustly denying jobs or admissions to particular qualified individuals incur debts to those individuals as well. A minor conceptual problem arises immediately in that this alternative implies that the latter individuals are owed reimbursement twice: once from society, as members of the group, and once from the particular organizations that treated them unjustly. If a fair monetary value were assigned to the compensation owed, they would be owed twice the fair amount, which is inconsistent. This may seem inconsequential to those unconcerned with logical niceties, and I myself am inclined to pass it off as hairsplitting, given that those persons would be satisfied if paid their due by anyone. The far more crucial point is that they are unlikely to get their just compensation at all if the policy is directed in any respect toward groups, given a limited or scarce number of jobs available, the tendency to advocate application of reverse discrimination only until minorities are proportionally represented in different job categories, and the operation of market factors in selecting members of the groups preferred for various positions. Analysis of this last factor, hinted at above, generates the most important point of this section—and perhaps of the book—and therefore deserves close attention.

It is clear that when preferential treatment is advocated for whole minority groups, the most competent members at each level will be chosen for admissions and hiring. This seems necessary to protect efficiency and to give them a reasonable chance at succeeding in their positions. Furthermore, if justice is linked to efficiency, as I claimed in the previous chapter, so that the most competent person has a prima facie right to a position for which he or she applies, there may seem nothing wrong with applying this distributive rule within the minority group singled out for preference. What *is* wrong is that the principle of compensation and the distributive principle of hiring the competent pull in opposite directions here. If the reason why minority-group members tend to be less qualified for various positions is to be found in prior patterns of discrimination, then those who are now most qualified will tend to be those who have been discriminated against least in the past. Thus a policy of preferential treatment directed toward groups as a whole will invert the ratio of past harm to present benefit, picking out just those individuals for present preference who least deserve compensation relative to other members. Those involved in university teaching have had a firsthand view of how such policies operate to give preference in hiring to women just coming to the job market from prestigious graduate schools—who just as likely were given preference at the prior level as well—and how middle-class minority-group members who have had a relatively easy time of it benefit more by admissions policies than others in the same group who have been severely oppressed in the past. As long as there are some members of these groups who have altogether escaped harm from previous injustice, they will be the ones benefiting from preference, while those who are owed compensation for actual injustices remain exactly where they are. Thus a policy that aims to accommodate the demands of both justice and efficiency results in losses of efficiency (when strong preference is given, others are more competent), as well as injustices to those minority-group members who deserve compensation but who are passed over, and to those white males who are presently most competent for the positions in question (the latter point will be discussed below).

One may still wonder how the distributive and compensatory principles could pull in such opposite directions, given the original conceptual link between them. If the notion of first-order discrimination involves the denial of a position to the most competent person on irrelevant (racial, sexual, ethnic) grounds, why should that person not generally continue to be the most competent and thus be the one to benefit, as well as the one to deserve to benefit, most from the policy relative to other members of his group? First, the model of discrimination stated here applies at the level of hiring and at higher levels in the educational system, where individuals attain rights to positions through having acquired maximal competence for them. But even at these stages at which the model is applicable, organizations given the choice and operating with criteria of efficiency will tend to prefer younger members who are just arriving at the level in question with continuously good prior credentials to older members who unjustly missed their chances previously. Thus, even those who were most competent in the past will tend to be passed over in favor of younger, presently more attractive candidates who never faced the injustice of discrimination. Second, the model ignores discrimination at lower levels in the educational system, where the right to an equal education is not dependent upon considerations of competence at all, but where discrimination inflicts especially deep disadvantages in acquiring competence for desirable positions higher up. When we take this lower-level injustice into account, it is clear that the injustice at each stage will compound that at the prior stage if preferential policies are directed at groups. When levels of injustice or discrimination are recognized, it becomes more apparent how such policies invert the ratio of past harm to present benefit.

It should be noticed that this last argument is relevant even if all members of a group have been harmed, since no one can deny that injustices and harms affect individuals differently. The question is still whether we want a policy that inverts the ratio of degree of harm to degree of benefit. The principle of compensation that justifies the policy calls rather for compensation proportionate to injury. Even if the middle-class black or woman graduate student may have had to struggle against psychological handicaps, although always accepted to the best schools, we cannot be true to the compensatory principle by creating a policy that benefits such individuals while leaving unaided those who have suffered more overt injustice and deprivation. The greater success of the former through preferential treatment may cause rationally heightened resentment. Some minority group members who have achieved high qualifications relative to other members of their group for certain positions may also have had to overcome greater obstacles (just as occasional white males have overcome economic obstacles derived from unjust distributive conditions). But if injustices in the educational system have led to real compensable harms and decreased opportunities, we would expect injustice to be generally proportionate to present disabilities of different individuals. In all cases, inquiries into actual personal backgrounds seem in order. When this is not done, the policy will tend to mask the real injustice rather than compensate it. While the present feeling seems to be that justice will have been done once women and minorities are proportionally represented in different job categories, at least in regard to upper-echelon or desirable jobs, to approach this goal through group policies will tend further to freeze where they are those who have been victims of the more severe injustices. (I will examine future-looking justification in the next chapter.)

Thus, if we want a policy that will compensate victims of injustice so as to approximate the distribution that would have held without prior injustices, we must compensate only those individuals who were direct victims of violations of fair distributive rules previously. Recent social and political debate has been so dominated by group thinking that the reaction, "Let them have a bigger slice of the pie for a change," seems inevitable. But such thinking is blind to the fact that the "them" getting a bigger slice tends to be comprised of different individuals from the "them" who got a smaller slice in the past. The call to remove the effects or vestiges of past discrimination should not be a call for statistical balance now, but for correction of the real effects of past deprivations upon those individuals who have been unjustly denied jobs or opportunities. When in the call for social compensatory policies there is no attempt to gauge present compensation to past injustice suffered (affirmative action, as we shall see, is perhaps not intended as such a policy), we must suspect that advocates are engaged in political maneuvers and that supporters are responding to those with enough political muscle to matter, rather than to the demands of justice. The advocacy of such policies in the name of compensatory justice resembles the waging of war in the name of peace, or the acceleration of arms building in order to be strong enough to reduce it (other arguments we have heard from Washington in recent years). Of course I would not suggest simply rewarding the least competent within each group, and this should not be the conclusion drawn from the above. I have suggested hiring those who have been discriminated against in the past at the level of job hiring; while not the least competent, they would still tend to be passed over in favor of younger applicants in the event that a group policy were pursued. Regarding injustice at lower levels, suggestions will be forthcoming in a later section.

Administrative Efficiency

In the last subsection I concentrated upon the injustice of group policies to those members of the groups who were discriminated against most in the past. Such policies may also be unjust to those white males presently most competent for the various positions in question. Before turning to an examination of this claim, however, there remains one further argument for group policies to be briefly evaluated, an argument that is not based upon notions of groups deserving compensation, as were the previous positions, and one that recognizes the possible injustices to individuals involved. This argument relies rather upon the distinction between justice under ideal circumstances and under the practical demands made upon the design of compensatory programs by considerations of administrative efficiency in actual social settings.[15]

The novelty of this argument lies in the shift from abstract or ideal principles of compensatory justice to the necessity of balancing claims in practice so as to maximize imperfect justice. Favored treatment for groups is justified by the greater administrative feasibility of such a program, as compared with the high cost and impracticality of administering compensatory justice on an individual basis. Thus, while there is only a high correlation between being black, for example, and having suffered discrimination and so being deserving of compensation, the balance of justice in practice favors preferential treatment for the whole group, even though such a policy will occasionally result in undeserved benefits. The only alternative policies seem to be: award of deserved compensation in the great majority of cases, with occasional undeserved benefit and hence injustice to white job applicants; or compensation on an individual basis, which would require demonstration of past injustice in court or before a special administrative body, so that the cost and difficulty of the operation would result in far fewer awards of deserved reparation. It is better, the argument holds, to award compensation that is deserved in *al-*

most all cases than to have a program that in practice would amount to almost no compensation at all; in effect, a policy that would not be accepted in an ideally just world becomes best in practice.

We may draw the distinction here between the justifying basis and the administrative basis for compensatory programs.[16] While the justifying basis appeals to past injustice directed toward individual members of the minority group in question (or to the creation of equal opportunity, with which we will be concerned later), the administrative basis appeals to such characteristics as race or sex in determining whether an individual should be awarded compensation in the form of reverse discrimination. The idea is to maximize in practice the satisfaction of rights to compensation. The appeal of characteristics like race or sex for determining potential beneficiaries is that these are readily identifiable, obviating the need for costly inquiry into personal backgrounds and thus directing the full resources of the program to genuine compensatory efforts. If the correlation between having such a characteristic (or being a member of the group defined by it) and having been discriminated against is fairly high, it seems that the relative administrative efficiency of a group policy will result in an overall maximization of rights satisfaction. This is a powerful argument in its favor. While the rights of certain individuals will be violated in the process of administering such a program—and this is admitted by this argument, as it was not by those considered earlier—the impracticality of administering more ideal alternatives would involve still more widespread violation or neglect of genuine rights to compensation. If individuals must come forth and prove prior discrimination, it is to be expected that many who really deserve compensation will not receive it; overall, in light of this difficulty, it seems more just to assume prior injustice to members of those groups that have been broadly discriminated against. If 80 percent of the compensations paid are deserved, that is, if eighty of one hundred individuals compensated actually suffered discrimination in the past, then the injustice of awarding compensation to twenty individuals who do not deserve it still seems preferable to awarding it in only half of the deserved cases and leaving forty individuals without satisfaction of their rights.

In reply, the first problem with the above argument is that each case of preferential treatment for a minority-group member or woman never discriminated against in the past involves not one injustice, but seemingly three: first, to the members of the same group really discriminated against, who are passed over for another preferred in their name; second, to the person most competent for the job, who has more right to it than the person preferred (though perhaps less right than a member of the group who was discriminated against); and third, to society or the public, which suffers from the loss of efficiency (the preferred candidate will not be maximally competent if hired through strong preferential policy). It can be argued, wrongly, as we shall see, that at least the first of the above injustices can be discounted, given that a group policy can have a broader scope with identical administrative costs and thus benefit more individuals who deserve it on compensatory grounds, along with those who may not deserve it. But this counterpoint already indicates that we cannot assume that the ratio of justice satisfaction to injustice involved will be the same or even approximate to the percentage of group members who actually suffered discrimination in the past. It would take a far higher correlation than 51 percent to justify the adoption of such a policy for administrative reasons, even if the percentage of deserving individuals who benefited from the policy approximated the percentage of group members who suffered past harm.

The far greater problem is that the percentage of deserving individuals who benefit under a group policy is not the same as the percentage of group members who were harmed in the past. What is overlooked here is the operation of the market criteria analyzed in the previous subsection and the inversion of the ratio of harm to benefit caused by it. That those who benefit most from preferential programs tend to deserve it least in relation to other members of the groups discriminated against does not imply in itself that these beneficiaries do not deserve preference in relation to white males.[17] But if we combine this premise with the premises that not all members of the groups have been harmed by denial of equal opportunity, and that relatively few of those harmed will actually benefit from preference, it does follow that beneficiaries will tend to be personally undeserving of special treatment. The practical results of the application of a group policy will depend upon the degree to which benefits reach those group members who were actually wronged in the past. But, as pointed out in the discussion of distributive and nondistributive harm, as long as there are some members of the group in question who have escaped harm, they will tend to be the ones who obtain desirable jobs through preferential policies. Thus, unless the correlation between past harm and group membership is extremely close to 100 percent, the market will continuously skim off the minority who do not deserve preference, and the percentage of undeserved benefit may be very high, depending upon the scope of the program and the conditions of the market for new openings in various fields.

In light of the problem of undeserved benefits and hence lack of deserved ones, a proponent of preferential policies directed toward groups might suggest that easily identifiable race criteria continue to be used for reasons of efficiency but that they be supplemented with other identifiable characteristics to raise the correlation. He might suggest that by adding criteria conjunctively we could raise the correlation between the justifying and administrative bases for the policy as high as we wish or as justice demands. For example, rather than direct a policy toward all blacks, we could direct it toward blacks from a certain geographical area and from families with incomes below a certain level. Of course, as we continue to add criteria, we pay with losses of efficiency in administration of the program, and when criteria demand verification by inquiry into personal backgrounds, one begins to wonder where efficiency is gained. (For women, I cannot think of any readily observable characteristics that could be added to increase the correlation.) In light of the market factor, the maximization of rights satisfaction would demand an extremely high correlation between the justifying and administrative bases of a policy. In order to establish such a high correlation for a specific group or to narrow specifications for group membership until

almost all those individuals who have been overtly discriminated against are included, and in order to determine for each
individual whether he or she belongs to the group so
specified, I imagine the steps needed would be as complex as
those involved in the immediate use of the justifying basis itself; that is, it would amount to administration of a program of
a case-by-case basis.

It also seems that the difficulties involved in establishing
past discrimination on the one hand and the ease of identifying
and verifying racial criteria on the other can be exaggerated.
For women, the latter problem does not exist—one is generally either male or female—but the problem of adding
criteria in order to narrow the group of women and raise the
correlation seems insuperable because discrimination has not
been limited to a particular readily identifiable class of
women. For blacks and other racial and ethnic groups the
problem could become very sticky if any attempt were made
to determine benefits by verifying claims of racial mix in one's
genetic tree. It can be claimed that such measures are not
necessary, since there has never been a rush of whites claiming benefits from minority programs. But difficulties could still
arise over percentage of minority blood needed to qualify.
Should we allow one-quarter Indian blood to qualify, or
perhaps to qualify for one-quarter of the benefits of a person
with pure Indian blood? This sounds silly, but the problem of
where to draw the line becomes important if criteria for preference are to be racial, and it does seem likely that a readily
identifiable black would have suffered more (though perhaps
not more psychologically) from discrimination than one who
looks white. There would also have to be a way of barring
newly immigrated Africans, Haitians, etc., if the justifying
basis for the policy were past harm from discrimination and
the administrative basis were racial characteristics. The apparent absurdity, however, of tailoring degree of compensation to degree of minority blood simply points up again the ir-
relevance of racial characteristics to the compensatory purpose: the degree of past injustice and harm alone is relevant.

With regard to the difficulty of proving past discrimination,
the establishment of administrative boards (like the Equal

Employment Opportunity Commission) with power to enforce decisions in such cases alleviates much of the cost and delay involved in the court system. Furthermore, certain general categories can be made applicable here that are sounder bases for inferring past discrimination against the individuals in question than are racial or sexual denominators. For example, if segregated schools are by nature unequal, as the Supreme Court decided in the *Brown* case, then showing that one was forced to attend such a school is evidence of past discrimination and grounds for compensatory treatment at the educational level (to be discussed below). It is certainly as easy to show this as that one has one-quarter Negro blood, and the former is certainly a firmer ground for compensation. To take an example at the hiring level, if it is shown that a company with regular openings for positions requiring only a fixed level of competence has in the past hired few or no minority-group members, then evidence of having applied for a job at that firm is evidence of past discrimination and grounds for being compensated with a position there, given that one is a member of a minority group (admittedly the latter must be established first in this case). The point of these examples is that one generally need not have detailed information regarding other applicants for the positions in question in order to make a case for compensation before a sympathetic board (where such information is routinely required, as under affirmative action programs, so much the better). There are types of evidence other than racial or sexual characteristics that are both fairer and sounder grounds for compensation and that are not insuperably difficult to demonstrate. Nor do these reduce to the other types of gross indicators mentioned above, such as level of income or area of residence. Where affirmative action programs exist in universities or corporations, there are certainly grounds for asking whether applicants believe themselves to have been victims of discrimination, rather than to judge that merely on the basis of race or sex.

A parallel case of a large-scale compensatory program is the German reparations to Jews for the horrors of concentration camps. Here claimants must show harm from having been inmates, or they must show themselves to be the survivors of inmates, the evidence for which is sometimes fragmentary but accepted anyway. This is not only a large-scale program administered on an individual basis, but also one in which the absurdity of doing otherwise is equally clear. Imagine that reparations were paid to Jews indiscriminately, or that there were some merit system for allotting reparations within the group—for example, how successful one has been despite persecution of members of the group elsewhere. Awards in the latter case would go to the wealthy native American Jew in Scarsdale, while former inmates would be told to wait their turn or to accept vicarious compensation. No one would support such a policy, even if all Jews, including the native American, suffered psychological anguish from knowledge of the existence of the camps. The policy would smack of inverse racism as well as individual injustice. (The Germans also make payments to the state of Israel, but this is to alleviate the costs borne by that country of settling refugees after the war and should not be interpreted as compensation to Jews indiscriminately or to their representative.) It is obvious that the difficulties of administering a program of compensation on an individual basis are more than offset by the advantages from the point of view of justice of avoiding these kinds of absurdity.

Finally, the argument for group policies on the basis of administrative efficiency fails to meet our reversal test.[18] Racists sometimes attempt to justify their discriminatory practices not by claiming that race alone justifies exclusion, but by appealing to supposed correlations between being black or female and having certain characteristics that are undesirable for employment. Of course the stereotypes implied in the premises of such arguments are false, and hence the arguments unsound. But suppose the more sophisticated racist or sexist could actually find specific correlations—an above-average chance of having a criminal record or certain conceptual deficiencies from inferior previous education, or in the case of women, lack of physical strength. Would he then be justified in arguing that because inquiry into personal histories is costly and time-consuming he can play it safe and hire no women or blacks? Personal injustices to competent blacks and women could not be rationalized in this way, and thus one can also maintain that individual injustices in the other direction cannot be justified on grounds of administrative ease. There are of course differences between the inclusionary and exclusionary motivations for the policies, between those that aim to compensate and those that merely discriminate, and the element of insult is not present in the compensatory policy as it is in the exclusionary one. Neither good intentions nor convenience, however, can excuse injustice.

From the point of view of justice there are important differences among policies that, on grounds of administrative ease or efficiency, employ statistical correlations between characteristics of applicants, which are considered as credentials, and actual qualifications for performance in positions. It is not necessarily objectionable, for example, for a professional school to refuse to consider candidates with grade point averages under 3.0, on the grounds that 80 percent of those admitted with averages below that level would fail to do well at the graduate level and that designing more extensive individualized tests, while perhaps more predictive, would involve prohibitive administrative costs. One might initially wonder why this is a morally acceptable argument, while the premise that 80 percent of the members of some minority group deserve compensation does not justify a policy based on ethnic or racial characteristics on grounds of administrative efficiency. Several differences between these cases were implied above. First, to find that 80 percent of the members of some group are unjustly disadvantaged does not mean that 80 percent of those given preference will individually deserve it, since the market operates to select candidates within the group; in the case of grade point averages, to judge that 80 percent of the applicants below some cutoff will not pass in graduate school does imply that 80 percent of those not considered do not merit consideration. Second, granting preference by race or sex alone is more like discriminating on the basis of race or sex—for example, like refusing to consider any woman for a position because 80 percent of women lack the physical strength necessary for it—than it is like using grade point averages as measures of qualifications.[19] Refusing to consider women on the basis of such a correlation is unjust because it bars some individuals from entering a competition at all on the basis of native features. Grade point averages, on the other hand, represent the outcomes of competitions that have more or less been announced in advance and toward which individuals can aim their efforts. (That those at a competitive disadvantage because of prior discrimination should be compensated is not at issue here.) Preference on the basis of native characteristics is more like the former case than the latter, since awards of positions on the basis of preference by race or sex, when individually undeserved, also bar others from competition or slant the competition unfairly against them. (This claim takes us to the question of group liability, however, which we shall address next.)

The plea of administrative difficulty and the immediate willingness to employ racial and sexual criteria must strike one again as evidence of the political nature of present compensatory programs. There are utilitarian as well as political gains to be made from the use of such readily visible characteristics as criteria for compensation, in that the effects of the program will be equally as visible. It is of more use and comfort to the politician when he can readily add up and show the percentages of group members who have benefited from his policy, and percentage results will be achieved more quickly when preferential treatment is indiscriminate among minority-group members. It is in light of such advantages that we must weigh pleas of administrative hardship or violations of privacy to minority-group members, such as the pleas that often issue from school administrative committees, which routinely make detailed inquiries into personal backgrounds anyway, including questions as to race, religion, etc. Such ad hominems perhaps have no place in a dispassionate philosophical evaluation, but it almost goes without saying that these advantages, like those of administrative efficiency, should not be allowed to override the demands of justice for the individuals involved.

Group Liability

When minority-group members are awarded positions through reverse discrimination, is there injustice to white male job applicants—specifically, to those most qualified for the positions?[20] In my view this matter can be intelligibly discussed only in the context of our previous discussion of deserved versus undeserved awards of compensation to minority-group members. In this subsection I shall consider the claims of white males in the case of compensation made through a group policy to individuals never discriminated against in the past. (The issue of deserved compensation is left for the next section.) My question here is whether, in addition to the injustice to the deserving minority-group members passed over, policies directed toward groups cause injustices to maximally qualified white males. For this discussion, our guiding precept from the analysis of the principle of compensation is that those guilty of violations of others' rights cannot complain of injustice to themselves when they are made to pay compensation, even if the benefits go to proxies for the victims rather than to the victims themselves. Thus, if there is a sense in which all white males are jointly guilty or liable for injustices to minorities in the past and present, none can claim injustice in being forced by a compensatory program to pay compensation in kind by giving up the job for which he is most competent, no matter who is actually awarded the job. The question is whether there is any sense in which all are so guilty or liable. To answer it requires an examination of collective guilt and of strict, vicarious, and collective liability, parallel to our earlier discussion of group desert. Such an examination has been lacking in the earlier debate. The standard reply to the claim that an unfair burden is being placed upon young white males has been that all white society shares the guilt for systematic discrimination and hence the liability for its compensation. We need to investigate this claim closely to see whether it accords with our established models of collective liability or guilt.

The first sense in which a group can be jointly responsible for injustice and hence liable for resulting injuries mirrors the clearest but most trivial sense of group desert, that is, the distributive sense in which the guilt of the group dissolves into that attaching to the separate acts or receptions of each of the members. The first way in which this can be true is when members are each guilty of the same type of action; to refer to their collective guilt is shorthand for referring to each separate action. An example of this would be a case of rape in which several men take part by separately attacking the victim. Each is guilty of the act of rape and would be guilty even if the others had not taken part as well. A second and related sense of collective guilt involves an act that is more literally a collective act, one whose description is not analytically equivalent to a description of the separate acts of the participants. An example of this is a bank robbery in which one member of the gang drives the getaway car, another keeps watch at the door, another waits at the hideout after planning the crime and organizing the gang, and a fourth holds a gun on the teller. The separate acts are not all of the same type, nor is the collective act one that could have been accomplished by a single agent, yet all are equally guilty, legally and morally, of the act of armed robbery. Here the guilt may still be considered distributive, in that each member played a direct causal role in bringing about the collective result; the criterion for the guilt of each is his actual contributory fault or personal causal role in the action itself. From a moral point of view, there is little difference between this and the first case with respect to the responsibility of each member of the group. In both cases, although the separate guilt of each is implied by the guilt of the collective, it may be possible to single out certain ringleaders. Where this can be done, it seems appropriate to assign guilt within the group proportionately even in these most obvious types of collective wrong.

It seems clear, however, that the purported guilt of all white males for injustices to minorities cannot fit either of these first two models. It cannot be claimed that each white male separately discriminated against a minority-group member at some time, nor that each directly causally contributed to such an act (as a member of a hiring or admissions board, for example). Most were never in a position to play such direct contributory roles as to be sensibly said to share in distributive guilt for such acts. If guilt in this case is to be distributive, it must be through some far weaker type of contributory fault. The only candidates would be those guilty of "sins of omission," of not having done anything to end injustices, or those guilty of "acquiescence" or participation in institutions or corporations that have engaged in discriminatory practices.

In a sense, even a random collection of individuals can be said to be guilty of an act of omission if they singly or together could have prevented some injustice of which they had knowledge and yet did nothing.[21] The neighbors who listened to Kitty Genovese's screams without even calling the police, or subway riders who placidly watch or ignore crimes occurring before them are cases in point. But we must be careful in attributing guilt of this type. Much depends upon the individuals' proximity to the crime, the ability to prevent it singly, or, if such ability is lacking, the opportunity to take collective preventive action. Furthermore, in order to assign guilt distributively to individuals in such cases there must be a reasonable expectation that a normally moral person would have taken preventive action in the circumstances in question. For a person to be guilty, his behavior must be substandard and constitute participation in the injustice through contribution or omission. *Substandard* here refers to moral standards. I do not take these, however, to be geographically relative, so that it is possible to blame a group of individuals for actions or omissions that are common practice in their region. Moral rules refer to those that would be agreed to by rational agents, and a normally moral person is one who for the most part adheres to such rules, whatever the time and place. Nevertheless, we cannot blame people for not being saints, heroes, or even unusually good samaritans, although we can assign blame to them in cases in which they could reasonably have prevented crimes that occurred in their immediate vicinity.

If we take a harder line here and attempt to hold people responsible for remote injustices to which even symbolic resistance would involve sacrifice and risk, we would have to hold blacks responsible for injustice to Indians and Indians for injustices to blacks, as well as whites for all the injustices in the country or the world. The danger in that line is not merely that it is unrealistic, but that it also blurs degrees of guilt and can be used as an excuse by the real perpetrators of injustice. It is a true cliché that when everyone is guilty, no one is guilty. There are degrees of guilt for given injustices. Or, perhaps more precisely said, acts that constitute participation in injustices or crimes through actual contribution or omission are substandard to different degrees, and the agents guilty of these different acts are not all equally blameworthy. A witness to a murder is neither guilty of the murder nor as blameworthy as the murderer, even if he could have prevented the act. Similarly, a white male who in order to support himself applies for a job in a corporation that has discriminated against minorities in the past is not himself guilty of the discrimination, although he "acquiesces" in the institution. And just as a group policy tends to invert the ratio of past harm to present benefit, so it may cause additional injustice by inverting the ratio of past guilt to present burden, placing the bulk of the latter upon individuals who were apparently guilty at most of sins of omission. This holds no matter how hard a line we take on these sins. But of course it is not even true that all whites were guilty of apathy in this respect—the present generation of young white males generally filling the job market includes those who took part in the civil rights activities of the sixties, sometimes at their own sacrifice and risk.

Another sense in which a group can be said to participate in guilt for the acts of individuals appears to be nondistributive. In one way this new criterion for guilt is weaker than that for participation through omission or acquiescence, and in another way it is stronger. It is weaker in that for the individual to share in this type of guilt, the crime need not be in his physical proximity, and he need not even know of its occurrence. It is stronger in that he can nevertheless be said to play a contributory role in the crime, not merely one of omission. I am referring to the situation in which a practice or an attitude is common and self-reinforcing among a group of individuals, creating pressures to conform. Such practices or attitudes render certain faulty or criminal actions practically inevitable. Although these are actually committed only by certain members of the group, other members can then be claimed to share the blame morally. One example of a practice of this sort would be a party at which all guests drink heavily and then drive home. If one of them causes an accident that would have been caused by any of the others had they been there, all are morally at fault.[22] An example involving shared attitudes is the racism that apparently dominated the thinking of many soldiers in Viet Nam. The attitude of "just another gook" has been seen by some to have made incidents like that at My Lai inevitable, and if this is the case, there may be a sense in which all who shared and fostered the attitude share some of the blame for such atrocities. This example seems particularly pertinent to the case before us, since it can be plausibly claimed that the rampant racist and sexist attitudes among white male society made discriminatory acts inevitable. Those who shared and advertised those attitudes share the moral guilt for such acts as well, first, because they would have acted in the same way had they had the power to do so, and second, because the atmosphere they fostered placed pressure upon those who were in power to act as they did.

But it is a far cry from acceptance of the above to the claim that no white males can complain of discrimination against themselves in cases when the beneficiaries do not deserve preference. Several factors make this step in the argument impermissible. For one thing, even if all share the moral blame in that all share to some degree the attitudes behind the culpable actions and would probably have acted in the same ways had they been faced with the same decisions, moral culpability here does not seem reasonable grounds for legal liability. It would certainly be a dangerous precedent if we were to begin holding people legally liable for their attitudes or for what they might have done in hypothetical circumstances, rather than only for their actual deeds. Second, the paradigm cases of such shared guilt involve close-knit collectives with common practices and reinforcing attitudes amounting to peer pressure to conform, that is, collectives with group solidarity and loyalty. A corporation or even a small town might fit that description, but white society is an amorphous collection, and the pressures exerted within it as a whole can easily be exaggerated in assigning guilt or excusing it for those who commit racist acts. Such pressures might mitigate punishment of the actual offenders, but not nullify the demand for just compensation or their liability for paying it. Third, it is again not true

that all white males are racists or sexists, even of the unconscious or "visceral" type,[23] although it is understandable that
those who have been victimized by holders of these attitudes
may believe so. Again, the above model fails to establish a
sense in which all white males indiscriminately can be said to
share the guilt for past injustices, and it still seems that those
just entering the job market tend to have less of a share than
others, if they share guilt at all.

At this point it can and should be pointed out that we are
not necessarily assigning guilt, but liability, and that while
guilt generally implies liability (as limited by the "ought implies can" precept regarding ability to pay), the converse need
not be true. Having unwittingly benefited from acts of injustice may create a liability to compensate them, at least to the
degree of relinquishing the undeserved benefits, but it does
not generally imply any guilt for the acts. (The former clause
as well may be mitigated by recognition of legitimate expectations, although these may count for little against rights to
compensation, if there is no other means for it; we need not
consider these complications just yet.)

The argument here is that the inferior economic and social
level of minorities is the result of centuries of discrimination
and worse, out of which much wealth for the entire white
community was created. Such universal benefit would imply
universal liability, even if not guilt. But was there universal
benefit to white males from injustices to minorities in the
past? Economists do not seem to agree even as to the long-
term economic effects of slavery. Given that discrimination,
by definition, entails inefficiency, it is not at all clear that the
majority group as a whole benefits from it. While the person
who undeservedly acquires a job or place in school benefits
from the individual act of discrimination, the public as a whole
suffers a loss of efficiency. How these gains and losses balance
out for the average white male in terms of positions, goods,
and services depends, I suspect, upon the extent of the discrimination, the chances that he would have had a job without
it, and other complex matters that I leave to economic histo-
rians to untangle. The empirical claim that the average white
male has benefited from the history of discrimination is cer-

tainly debatable and yet to be decided. In addition, it is relevant to this argument that white job applicants are not average in wealth, prior benefits, etc.; most have little or no resources at the time of application for their first position in graduate school or in the job market, and most have not attended exclusive schools. It is difficult for these men to see how, up to that point, they have benefited from previous discrimination (many may be only second- or third-generation Americans, whose parents had no easy road themselves). Certainly, they did not benefit to a degree that warrants that they pay by forfeiting their jobs to arbitrary proxies for real past victims. (The possible present and future benefits that these white males may derive from discrimination are discussed below.)

Another possibly relevant difference between guilt and liability is that in certain conditions the latter is transferrable or assignable without fault (or benefit), whereas the former is not transferrable and presupposes fault. Is there any model of strict or vicarious liability that is relevant to our topic? The answer is yes, regarding our broad topic for both strict and vicarious liability, but not in ways that would allow us to assign liability indiscriminately to all white males. Strict liability (assigned without demonstration of fault, that is, substandard, malicious, or negligent behavior) is generally applied when it is desirable to take extreme precautions against certain injustices or injuries. In such cases we may announce in advance that parties will be liable to compensate victims, while removing the burden for proof of fault from claimants and prosecutors. This involves gains in utility not only by securing compensation for victims, but also by encouraging extra precaution, and it serves as a means of allowing necessary and profitable enterprises that involve unusual risks to the public. We can therefore imagine rational agents agreeing to rules for holding agents strictly liable in these cases, and there are such laws at present. The concept has limited applicability to moral questions, but it is relevant to our topic in that to prevent future discrimination, it seems permissible to serve notice that corporations will be strictly liable to compensate victims, not only with jobs, but also with full back pay and credit toward promotion. This removes the burden of proof for showing intention of harm, negligence, etc., expresses society's impatience with continuing injustice of this type, and protects potential victims from unintentional oversight as well as malicious intent. However, needless to say, the concept is not relevant to the question of the collective liability of white males.

Various types of vicarious liability, that is, liability transferred from actual agents to proxies for them, are justified on grounds of general utility and maximization of rights satisfaction, and would therefore be recognized by rational agents as exceptive clauses to the right to be held responsible only for one's own actions. Parents, for example, may be held liable for the acts of their children. This is partly because *someone* must be held liable to protect the rights of potential victims to compensation (this differs from holding the parents punishable). Parents are the most likely candidates here, in that they may be indirectly causally related to the faulty acts of their children through negligent supervision or upbringing. Application or announcement of vicarious liability in this case may also have the deterrent effect of encouraging more diligence on their part. Examples more to our point are those of the liability of official bodies, such as corporations or governments, for the actions of their official representatives, and, within such bodies, the responsibility of superiors for those under them. When an individual acts in an official capacity, the nature of his action is transformed (a soldier who kills an enemy soldier in a war is not guilty of murder), and responsibility for the action is borne not only by him, but also by his superiors (if there are any and if he acts under official policy) or by the body in whose name he acts.

The obvious relevance of these last examples for our topic is that when a hiring or admissions officer pursues a discriminatory policy, whether the policy is exclusively his own or not, the corporation or institution he represents continues to bear the liability for compensation, even when that officer no longer holds that position and a different policy is pursued. Liability may even be transferred, when necessary, from one part of an institution to another; with respect to our topic, when an individual is discriminated against by a school on a low level in the educational system, one higher up may assume or be assigned the liability for compensation. The reason why we allow, and in fact insist upon, such transfers is that the rights of the victims to compensation seem the paramount considerations in such cases. Even though, as we said at the beginning, they have no right to demand payment from totally unrelated third parties, it is appropriate to attempt to find parties systematically or officially tied to the specific perpetrators. Knowledge of such transferability of liability also encourages parts or members of these systems to police other members to ensure compliance with law, if not the demands of justice.

Cases of vicarious collective liability, which might also be called nondistributive liability, again generally involve close-knit organizations with common practices or purposes and in which roles are reciprocally related. In the case of an athletic team an example would be the forfeiture of a game if one or several team members cheated. There are, it is true, minor examples in which collective nondistributive liability has perhaps justifiably been assigned to less closely knit groups when individual perpetrators cannot be specified, as when a teacher punishes a whole class for mischief that occurred in his absence. But as the severity of the punishment or seriousness of the debt increases, such collective assignment becomes morally more problematic; and in any case, justice generally demands in this area, as it did in the area of desert, as specific an assignment as possible. If the teacher could locate the guilty party, it would be wrong for him to hold the whole class liable out of convenience, even if the liability were not for punishment but to pay for a broken window. There again seems no way to extend the examples of justified vicarious liability to a case for the joint liability of all white males for compensation of discrimination, so that none could complain of additional injustices to themselves from undeserved awards made according to group policies.

One may nevertheless wish to stretch such examples of vicarious liability as the above into an argument for an obligation of all white males to bear the burden of reverse discrimination for minorities. It was held that when individuals act in official capacities, responsibility for their actions is generally borne by those whom they represent. In a democratic society the government is the representative of the people, and they must share the obligation to pay the government's debts. If, therefore, the government, as well as private corporations, has incurred an obligation to compensate minorities, the burdens for such compensation must fall upon all members of society. As argued above, however, the government can only be said to have an obligation to compensate groups (as opposed to an obligation to enforce compensation of individuals by individuals) when it has treated them unjustly as a whole through legal actions or discriminatory laws. We said that cases could be made on these grounds for Indians and blacks but not for reverse discrimination as the form of compensation. When compensation is owed by governments to whole groups, it should be of a type that benefits members equally, and it can be added here that payment for it should ideally be made from general funds so as to spread the burdens equitably. Reverse discrimination meets neither of these criteria for just group policies.

Some obligations of governments must be filled in ways that necessarily place unequal burdens on citizens. Drafts in time of war are good examples. Given that a war is just or defensive, young males (or perhaps it should be young persons of either sex if we are not to discriminate) cannot seriously complain of the unequal burden placed upon them, although it is a difficult one indeed. There is simply no other way to pursue the required course of action. But this example is not analogous to our case, since, as I have already argued, the government does not owe reverse discrimination to groups. Whereas the whole society is responsible for the burdens of just wars, our question here is precisely whether the whole (white male) society is liable for injustices to minorities, and it simply begs the question to try to press the analogy. Reverse discrimination is not compensation in kind for the injustices to Indians of broken treaties, nor, as I will argue below, can reverse discrimination in hiring be compensation in kind for denial through law of equal education, as in segregation. When specific agencies or institutions of government discriminate against individuals in ways that require reverse discrimination as compensation in kind, such compensation ought to be granted by the agencies in question (or the closest proxies for them, as with schools on a higher level) to the individuals in question. No case has been made for liability of the government as a whole in this area or of the entire society it represents.

Thus the attempt to assign liability to white males indiscriminately fails, and it seems that cases of undeserved compensation through group policies (it is important to keep in mind that these are the only cases I am considering in this section) involve serious injustices to white males who never participated in past discrimination against minorities. If the claim that these individuals cannot complain of injustice to themselves rests upon the possibility of justifiably holding them liable for compensating past injustices, it must be dismissed. That much has been established in the section to this point.

But can it be maintained that the way we have been looking at the matter has been all wrong, that white males cannot legitimately claim injustices to themselves through group policies, even though they are not liable for compensation at all? This argument holds rather that such policies do not require white males to give up as compensation to minorities anything to which they are otherwise entitled. What is being relinquished is only an unfair *present* advantage, to which they have no right in any case. It is not that they have benefited in the past from discrimination, and so owe reverse discrimination to the victims or proxies for the victims; it is rather that the present group of white male job applicants stands to benefit from their present unfair advantage, which is maintained by the continued lack of maximally qualified minority-group candidates who could acquire positions. And the latter is attributable to past and present discrimination.[24] Since no one advocates reverse discrimination as a group policy beyond proportionate representation of women and minorities in various job and graduate school categories, all that white males are being asked to relinquish is their continuing unfair monopoly on these desirable positions. Expectations based upon ongoing or even past injustice must count for little if they amount to a plea for its continuation.

Those white males who will be losing jobs through the

group policy of reverse discrimination, this argument continues, are precisely those marginally qualified ones who would not have acquired the positions in question if women and minorities had been proportionally represented from the beginning, that is, if no prior discrimination had occurred. Since the percentage results of such policies approximate what we estimate the proportions of groups would have been in various categories had fair distributive rules been followed from the beginning, and since those white males losing jobs are most likely the ones who would not have had the jobs, how can these individuals seriously complain of injustice? We are not ending competition for them, nor even really slanting it against them, as we would be if we hired minorities almost exclusively, as we used to hire white males exclusively. We are only making the competition fair. The policy places white males as a group in no worse a position than they deserve to be according to fair distributive rules, independently of any compensation for past injustice. It is not necessary to hold them liable for such compensation because they are not being asked to pay it. If white males were truly to make amends to women and minorities in different fields, they would have to accept as small a proportion of those fields as was formerly held by the suppressed groups, and this would mean virtually all men losing their jobs. But this is not being asked or seriously considered. For white males to complain is therefore tantamount to their demanding a continued unfair advantage or disproportionate share of the market.

This argument may appear more powerful than those regarding liability. In fact, it appears conclusive as long as we confine our thinking to groups and group percentages. But the problem with it, as with others in the area, is that concentrating exclusively upon group statistics masks the effects of policies on those qualified individuals who actually apply for jobs and who therefore have their own rights and deserts to those jobs. First, even the group percentages used in the above argument in themselves appear less fair when we consider the proper groups, that is, young white males and women and minority-group members just entering the job market, rather than the entire work-force membership of such groups. For it is primarily the former who are affected by the policy, and yet the percentages are usually measured in terms of the latter. If one's goal is to raise the percentage of women in a certain category to 40 percent, the tendency will be for one to hire a far higher percentage of women over a certain period and a far lower percentage of white males. Thus older white males will continue to be overrepresented, older women and minority-group members underrepresented, young white males underrepresented, and young members of groups given preferential treatment overrepresented. Overly broad identification of groups and percentages is misleading with regard to the treatment of present job applicants. One must be careful when arguing in this area not to include within the same group figure subgroups that have opposite purposes and receive opposite treatment in relation to the policy advocated. The group of white males is just such a conglomeration, consisting of those entrenched in power, who have nothing to lose, and those with no power, who are likely to be victimized through group policies.

Second, even if the percentages were accurate and applied to the relevant groups rather than to the larger irrelevant groups, they cannot be straightforwardly applied to individual cases in order to argue, as I did above, that those white males losing jobs (which they would have obtained but for the policy) are just the ones who would not have had jobs under continuous application of fair distributive rules. It may be that many have worked to acquire roughly the level of qualifications that they were led to believe would guarantee success in acquiring positions. It may also be that had the competition been stiffer from the beginning, these individuals would have been more highly motivated and would still have prevailed through greater effort. We can still maintain that they have no right to restricted competition now, since that would amount to a plea for continuing injustice. That they have no such right means that they cannot complain of the effects of active recruitment policies or remedial programs to stiffen the competition. But reverse discrimination is not simply stiffening or broadening the competition: it is changing the rules of the game. Even if we are only handicapping the credentials of others through the preferential policy, rather than reserving places outright for them, what we are doing is changing the rules midstream for the white male applicants. In our discussion in the previous chapter of legitimate expectations and rights created in practice, we said that even when rules are altered in the direction of greater justice, those caught in the middle, whose expectations are thwarted and who were not previously personally involved in the injustice, may be owed compensation in the name of fairness. Thus, even ignoring the above counterargument and the one to follow, we may be creating a moral infinite regress of compensations owed through the group policy. If, on the other hand, we are reserving places outright rather than handicapping within a fixed limit, we are not slanting the competition against certain job applicants but ending the competition for them entirely, which is *not* the position they would have been in under any reasonable distributive system.

Third, and most important, when group policies award preferential treatment to those never discriminated against in the past, any talk of percentages, even if limited to relevant groups, blinds one to the relative rights of the specific job applicants in question—and these are the only rights relevant to the cases in point. A familiar analogy will make this clearer. Suppose you enter a race, run fastest of all entrants, and cross the finish line first. Suppose that instead of awarding first place to you, the prize is given to the person who came in fourth because he shares some characteristic (unrelated to running) with others who may be faster runners than you, or would be if given the training (the person who came in fourth *was* given the training). Is it true that you cannot complain of injustice in this case because someone else might or would have won the race if he had entered, and might or would have entered if training had been available and he had been encouraged to train and enter? To take a stronger but less analogous case, even if there were another specific individual who would have won but was unfairly barred from entering, and if you had nothing at all to do with this injustice but took part in the race yourself in good faith, you could certainly complain of injustice to you *relative to the person who came in fourth*. While life is not a race, and applying for jobs is not exactly analogous either, the parallels between this case and the argument above regarding group policies appear to me to be strong enough to destroy the latter. Applicants for jobs acquire prima facie rights to the positions in question by being most competent relative to other applicants. If none of these applicants individually has either compensatory claims or liability (or claims of other types to be discussed in the next chapter), the most competent among them ought to be chosen and can complain if another applicant is chosen. This holds whether or not there are other people who have stronger claims but who did not apply. In fact, even were such a person to have actually applied, say a woman really discriminated against in the past, the most competent male would still have a complaint if some other woman without compensatory claims were hired over himself and the first woman. The person who comes in second, as well as the one who comes in first according to fair rules of the contest, is treated unjustly if the one who comes in fourth is awarded the prize for no justifiable reason.

It is often pointed out, correctly, that white males in any case cannot complain of the same type or degree of injustice as that suffered by women and minorities through discrimination in the past. Certainly the degree of systematic exclusion from positions and exercise of rights was far greater in the latter case than loss of jobs: members of these groups were systematically excluded from all positions of power and from common social benefits to which they had a clear moral right. No one contemplates denying to white males equal education at lower levels, police protection, protection of the court system, or the right to vote. No matter what policies are instituted, white males will not suffer as many minority-group members have been suffering for years. Furthermore, even if we consider only the denial on irrelevant grounds of a job for which one is best qualified, the intent and hence the effect of such a denial is different in the case of the white male from that of the woman and certainly the black. Most of those who advocate reverse discrimination as a group policy do so in good faith and with a (myopic) eye toward justice. The intent of such policies is inclusive rather than exclusive: to bring the races and sexes together and to affirm their equality, rather than to keep them apart. Such policies do not stigmatize anyone; they are not coupled with an attitude of insult and contempt toward those who lose out through their operation. White males are not denied jobs because they are white males but because of the desire to place more women and minority-group members in decent positions. Thus the psychological as well as systematic effects of reverse discrimination do not approximate those of first-level discrimination upon those individuals denied their rights.

But the point must still be made that the lesser extent and degree of injustice in reverse discrimination as a group policy does not mean that rights are not being violated in its practice or that we need not take these rights seriously. Their denial still entails material harm great enough to merit compensation in kind and so to create the problem of infinite regress (of which more will be said below) in the present context. It was argued at one point in the *DeFunis* case that inclusive benefits are distinct from the point of view of justice from exclusive policies, that the difference in intent between reverse discrimination and first-level discrimination does entail that the former violates no rights and involves no injustice.[25] The appeal is to a clever analogy. We are asked to compare a trust fund scholarship at a university to be used for the descendants of John Hancock with one to be used for the benefit of anyone but these descendants. Clearly, the former might be not unjustly accepted and administered by the university, whereas the latter ought to be rejected. The distinction between these cases, involving the element of gratuitous insult, is the same as that between the different types of discrimination, and it is implied that the distinctions from the point of view of justice might be entirely parallel as well.

But while these distinctions regarding degrees of insult or stigmatization are parallel, the argument ignores crucial distinctions between the scholarship and job cases that destroy the overall analogy regarding justice. These differences concern the number and types of rights involved. While the only right to be protected in the scholarship case is the right not to be insulted or abused in public, there are more fundamental rights involved in awarding jobs or desirable positions. No one has a right to a scholarship paid from a specific person's holdings or estate, and that person can generally donate his charity where he likes; but as we showed in the last chapter, individuals do acquire rights to positions, and institutions ought not to be permitted to grant them as they choose. Thus no one can complain if a scholarship is donated for a specific purpose (except possibly the donor's children, if they then cannot afford college), no matter how eccentric, as long as the element of insult is lacking, whereas individuals who deserve jobs or positions in schools can claim injustice at not being granted them. Regarding the latter cases, the positive intent of a policy is largely irrelevant in determining whether the rights of its victims are violated. That a policy is sincerely considered just by its designers and administrators does not make it so, any more than the actions of a sincere bigot are excused by his sincerity. The moral reformer can occasionally be as dangerous as the defender of the status quo, even if his motives are purer.

The conclusions of this section are: (1) minority groups as a whole cannot be said to deserve reverse discrimination as compensation; (2) when policies are directed toward such groups indiscriminately, market factors tend to invert the ratio of past harm to present benefit and that of past guilt or liability to present burden; (3) white males as a whole cannot be justifiably held liable for the injustices and harms of past discrimination; (4) when group policies result in unjustified awards to individuals, there is injustice to minority-group members and women owed compensation but passed over, as well as to those white males most competent for the positions in question.

These arguments are more pressing in the current type of economic market, with its acute scarcities, especially of jobs. A happy long-range solution to many of these problems in terms of rights satisfaction would be an expansion of opportunities in education and jobs (shifts of resources to education and service-related areas with technological improvement) and substantial reduction of inequalities in pay scales. Open admissions in colleges have already eased the pressure of competing claims at that level. But as long as there are differences in qualities of education available, and as long as there are more as well as less agreeable jobs to be performed (certainly a long-range prospect that is probably not desirable in any case to eliminate), philosophers and, more important, legislators and judges will be faced with the difficult task of weighing these competing claims and apparent as well as real rights.

Strong or Weak Reverse Discrimination?

If the arguments of the last section appear conservative in orientation in relation to presently advocated programs, those of this section should appear to lean in the other direction. I shall argue ultimately that in certain circumstances, namely, for all those individuals discriminated against in the past in hiring or promotion, reverse discrimination of the strongest type is owed by the institutions responsible, if those individuals are not still the most competent for the positions in question, which will often be the case. This position will at first appear problematic in relation to what we said in the last section regarding the rights of most competent white males to the positions for which they apply. It appears that we have conflicting principles and conflicting rights here, leading directly to a moral dilemma in which the satisfaction of one set of rights involves the denial of another set that on the surface appears as compelling.

On the one side we have a principle determining a prima facie right of the most competent to the job in question, and, as part of the principle of compensation, we have the claim that injured parties have no right on compensatory grounds alone to demand restitution from innocent or unrelated third parties. Since, as we argued in the last section, white males just applying for jobs tend to fit that category, how can we now demand that they lose jobs for which they are most competent in order to compensate even those who have actually been discriminated against? The former, it can be argued, had nothing to do with the original injustice to those persons and should not be made to bear the burden of repaying them. The principle that innocent parties owe no such restitution in general on compensatory grounds (I ignore need in this chapter) was argued for above, and I will not repeat the whole argument here. But it seems that all the reasoning of the last section relating to the injustice to white males when undeserving individuals are given preferential treatment can be applied here as well in light of that principle. The conclusion appears to be that only weak reverse discrimination can be granted to those individuals discriminated against in the past, that is, they can only be compensated with a job when no one has a stronger claim on grounds of competence.

On the other hand, we have the right to compensation of actual victims of past discrimination, which distinguishes the cases considered here from those examined in the last section. If only weak reverse discrimination is granted, and the jobs in question are of the type for which exact ties in qualifications are rare (how often does one choose among white males for a new member of a philosophy department in a completely random way because of no differentiating factors?), these rights will go unsatisfied, and their recognition through the admission that weak reverse discrimination is owed will remain token. Although we said that victims have no right to demand compensation from innocent parties (again leaving need aside), this principle is not unproblematically applicable here in defending the right of the white male. For he is not being asked to pay from his present holdings, to give up anything that is already his. Rather, we are overriding his right with another, refusing to apply the distributive rule further, in terms of which his right is recognized, until legitimate compensatory demands are met. And we also maintained that compensatory demands generally take precedence over distributive demands for further benefits, in order to keep distributions through the passage of time approximating to the temporal distribution of benefits that would have occurred without violations. These considerations seem to override those of the last paragraph and lean the verdict toward past victims when such cases arise. But before concluding the case in favor of strong reverse discrimination as compensation when necessary for those individuals formerly denied jobs unjustly, we should build up the case on the other side as strongly as possible, and we have not yet done so.

It can further be argued against strong reverse discrimination that no one is in fact owed such treatment as compensation, according to the dictum that compensation ought to be exactly reciprocal to injury, that is, compensation in kind. If this is applied literally to the question before us, it might appear that even a victim of past discrimination is owed compensation in the form of a job only when he is as qualified as any other candidate and not when others are more qualified. After all, the individual in question only suffered an injustice by being denied a job when he was as qualified as any other applicant. If he was not as qualified, then no injury occurred according to our original distributive principle. And if he needed to be most qualified to deserve a job, how can he now demand one when there are others with better credentials? This line of reasoning is faulty on two counts. First, the shift in time reference makes it less likely that the individual will remain most desirable on independent grounds, but it is unfair to hold this against him, since he should have had the experience on the job in the interim. Second, the injustice that occurred to him consisted of his being denied a job when more qualified than all others, and so it can equally be held that compensation in kind demands his now being given a job when less qualified.

Let us return from this overly semantic second thrust to the more serious matter of the rights of most qualified white males to positions. The above argument in favor of the strong version appeals to the claim that compensatory rights generally are to take precedence over further applications of distributive rules when their demands upon scarce resources or benefits conflict. But the application of this precept to the question before us seems no less problematic than the relevance of the principle that compensation cannot be demanded from innocents. The reason is that the rights of the white males being overridden or denied are of exactly the same type as the rights formerly denied to victims of the original discrimination, and it is not clear on the surface why similar compensation should not be owed this second class of individuals. In a tight market for desirable positions, a person may have only one opportunity to attain the type of position he both wants and for which he is most qualified, and if denial in the case of the minority candidate is grounds for compensating him, how can we deny the same right to compensation to the white male, when his denial seems exactly the same (ignoring the added element of insult in the former case, which seems irrelevant to the question of reverse discrimination as compensation)? This will appear to the new victim as a preference for minorities that is simply arbitrary.

We might agree that compensation will be owed to the white males in question but hold that victims of past discrimination ought nevertheless to be compensated first. But to admit this is to lead directly to the regress hinted at before, which seems totally unacceptable. A progression of compensations and new damages would be established until no jobs were being awarded on the basis of merit or competence, as they all should be according to our original distributive principle. The idea behind the adoption by rational agents of compensatory rules as necessary addenda to their distributive rules is that violations of the latter are not to be encouraged or allowed to stand. The enforcement of compensation discourages further violations and corrects the former ones, so as to maximize adherence to distributive rules and most closely approximate the distributions that would result from their constant application. In light of the subordinate or logically dependent role of the rule of compensation, it seems clear that a practice that results in an infinite regress of damages until no awards are made on the basis of the distributive principle could not be justified on grounds of original and limited violation of the principle. If we want to reestablish the distributive rule as the basis for awarding benefits in the area under its governance, would it not be better to allow a limited number of past violations to stand, so that all future awards can be made on its basis, than to generate a sequence such that few or no awards will ever be made on its basis again? The specter of all future positions in graduate school and jobs being doled out in flip-flop fashion to members of groups first given unfair advantage and then discriminated against, although ludicrous (can we imagine a black suing in ten years because discrimi-

nated against in favor of a white on compensatory grounds?),
seems the logical consequence of attempting to honor all
rights here.

Thus it seems that our earlier claim that award of compensation takes precedence over continued distribution must be
amended when such compensation involves denial of distributive rights identical to those rights originally denied. This
change appears to be necessary in order to avoid the infinite
regress. It therefore seems again that compensation in the
form of reverse discrimination must be granted only with jobs
for which the applicants are maximally qualified, that is, weak
reverse discrimination. We cannot ignore the claims of the
most competent white male without being arbitrary, and we
cannot recognize his claim along with that to compensation by
past victims, as shown above. This completes the case for the
most qualified applicant against less qualified past victims of
discrimination.

As indicated earlier, there is an important distinction between jobs requiring excellence or open-ended degrees of
competence and those requiring only a fixed or minimal level
of competence. The distinction relates to the usefulness or
applicability of weak reverse discrimination as compensation
for past injustice. In the latter category—for example, jobs involving relatively unskilled labor—numerous applicants with
equal credentials are to be expected, and those who were once
qualified are likely to remain so. Thus the application of weak
reverse discrimination should result in jobs for those who deserve them on compensatory grounds. But when infinite or
open-ended degrees of excellence are possible in a certain job
category, ties in real qualifications and even in credentials are
likely to be rare. In these cases a policy of weak reverse discrimination either will encourage administrators with the
power to do so to practice their own policy of strong reverse
discrimination, or it will amount to ignoring the rights of past
victims to compensation when the passage of time has made
them relatively less desirable candidates. Many desirable positions, especially in the professions, are of this type, and it is
in these areas that we seem once again left with a dilemma
from the point of view of justice. If we acknowledge the rights

both of white males to positions for which they are most competent and of past victims of discrimination to compensation in kind, we create the infinite regress described above. But if we recognize the rights of either of these groups while ignoring those of the other, it seems we are simply being morally arbitrary. Since we did not claim for the white male that his right was stronger than that of the past victim, but only seemingly identical, acceptance of his position leaves us in this quandary. But there is something more to be said on the other side, something that I take to be conclusive on this question.

The dilemma can and must be resolved in favor of the past victims of discrimination in the following way. First, it is relevant that once a person has legitimately acquired a position, he does not lose his right to continue occupying it if someone else with slightly better qualifications becomes available. This has limits and varies from job to job to some degree, and certainly if the person is performing incompetently, there is a right to dismiss him. Other variables affecting the legitimate degree of entrenchment include the condition and level of operating efficiency of the corporation or institution in which the job is held; if there is general inefficiency or competitive disadvantage, an overall effort to replace key personnel with others more efficient may be required. The reason we do not accept a general practice of firing those already in positions when more attractive younger candidates come along, however, is that the utility or efficiency that might be gained by such a practice would be more than offset by losses in job security. The prospect of having to defend one's job constantly by proving superiority to any other possible candidate would be too unsettling for most of us. Thus rational agents concerned for their security would not agree to such a rule. Seniority rules in various job categories protect those who have occupied positions longest against layoffs relative to less senior holders of the same jobs. While these have some rationale along the same line of reasoning, it is far less controversial that holders of positions be given a presumption of continuing in them against the claims of outsiders who would like to occupy them if they were available. It is perfectly obvious that when a position is occupied, it is generally not considered available, so long as its occupant is performing up to reasonable expectations according to the criteria by which he was hired. Considerations of the utility of job security justify this universal recognition.

The right of one who occupies a position over a period of time to continue in it has relevance for the resolution of our dilemma in that it is the model that should in fact be applied to the competing claims of the past victim versus those of the presently most qualified white male. In the argument to this point, we have considered both individuals as new applicants arriving on the scene without seniority differentials in the corporations or institutions to which they apply. Since according to the continuous application of the relevant distributive rule the past victim of discrimination should have been occupying a position in the organization from the time at which he first applied, we should consider that he has been so occupying it when we weigh his rights against those of new applicants. In fact, no opening should be thought to exist in the present at all, so that there is nothing for which the white male can legitimately apply. The rule for hiring competents of course applies only when jobs are available, and no right is acquired until there is a position for which the person applies. But here the place in question belongs to the past victim of discrimination, as it should have belonged to him from the beginning, and so the new applicant must wait for the next genuine opening. At that time he should be given the same consideration as minority candidates who were not discriminated against in the past and are not owed positions. In order to have any reason for not granting genuine past victims the positions they deserved in the first place and continue to deserve, the corporation in question would have to demonstrate that these individuals would have been replaced in the interim.

It is true that when one individual or organization owes compensation to another, the compensation must be paid from assets legitimately held by the person who is liable. If I owe you ten dollars but don't have it, I am not justified in stealing it from someone else in order to repay you. I have argued also that positions in corporations are not to be considered as their property to be disposed of as they please. It then may appear analogous to the case of owed money to conclude that, even if a corporation owes a position to an individual because it discriminated against him or her in the past, if another, more competent individual has a present right to that position, then the corporation is not justified in denying that right in order to pay its debt.[26] This type of analogy or model in the background is what made the demand for strong reverse discrimination problematic, even where seemingly owed. But crucial disanalogies were implied in the previous argument. In the case of stealing to repay one's debt, the victim of such theft already possesses this money; moreover, his right to it contains no exceptive clause regarding paying the debts of others. In the case of the presently most competent applicant for a position, on the other hand, a *further* application of the distributive rule is required to grant it to him, and his right to it does or should contain an exceptive clause calling for payments of compensation before further applications of the rule. In this case the position is not the corporation's to be granted as it pleases, because it should have been and continue to be occupied by the previously most competent applicant.

Levels of Discrimination and Compensation

I have now justified the strongest type of reverse discrimination in jobs as compensation in kind for those actually discriminated against at the levels of hiring and promotion. Despite the complications of the previous section, this is theoretically the easiest claim to establish. Much discrimination takes place prior to this level in the educational system, and there the passage in time between injury and contemplated compensation makes the issues more complex. Discrimination at this level takes many forms, from forced attendance at inferior and de facto segregated schools to more subtle assignment to curricula involving lower expectations—for example, the direction of female students into home economics curricula. Where such assignment or tracking is forced upon or suggested to naive children, it demands compensation to equalize opportunity. But if someone is treated unjustly at the elementary school level—by being forced to attend an in-

ferior segregated school, for example—we cannot ten years
later grant him literal compensation in kind by enrolling him
at an unusually good elementary school. It is obvious that
higher-level schools or training or professional programs must
assume the responsibility or be assigned the liability for restitution. But the question of what kind of compensation is
owed, of what constitutes fair restitution—whether handicapping credentials in graduate programs or at the hiring level
would be fair, for example—is difficult for several reasons.

Once again it seems that we must compare the claims of the
past victims with those of the persons best qualified at present
to fill various positions. This time, however, the argument that
resolved the issue in the last section in favor of past victims is
not available to silence the claims of other applicants. It is not
possible to argue that since the past victim was denied a position identical to the one being disputed, he continues to have
a right to that position, as if he had occupied it all along. The
right of a person to continue at a position he already has and in
which he is performing competently is irrelevant here because
the position denied, that is, at an adequate elementary school,
differs from the one at the higher level that is in dispute. Thus
the options here may at first seem even more unpalatable regarding the satisfaction of conflicting rights than those in the
earlier, less complex case. On the other hand, options that
were not available as compensation in kind for denied jobs are
available for restoring denied educational opportunity and
satisfying all rights involved. It is not necessary always to override rights in compensating lower-level denials. The irrele-
vance of the final argument of the last section (that positions
should not be considered available at all when owed as compensation), while making compensation for denial of educational opportunity theoretically more complex, is balanced by
the availability of more practicable alternatives.

Since compensation in kind for denial of educational opportunity calls for reparatory efforts at the educational level if possible, the happiest solution lies in expansion and equalization
of opportunities, which can be more easily accomplished in
the educational system than in the job market. Where the system itself can be expanded, educating or training those who

have been unjustly denied equal opportunity to acquire task competence is less likely to prevent that opportunity in the present for other potentially qualified individuals. Thus compensation at this level in the form of granting education or training to those who have been denied it may not have to constitute reverse discrimination at all. Nevertheless, if an institution is simply expanded through open admissions to allow students to enter without proper training, and if no adequate special remedial programs are instituted at the same time, there will be serious problems with maintaining standards, with meeting the needs of better-trained students, and with placing extraordinary pressures upon the formerly victimized applicants. Furthermore, the possibilities of expansion reach limits in graduate and professional schools, where the size of classes should be limited by the potential job markets for graduates. We cannot, for example, justifiably continue to expand doctoral programs in light of legitimate demands of women and minorities, given the present situation in the academic job market. Access to professional training programs amounts to little if there are no jobs waiting at the end of the line.

Where expansion is not possible or not desirable, where applicants must compete for a fixed number of desirable higher-level places, are we justified in handicapping the credentials of those formerly discriminated against at lower levels in the educational system? Although this might seem parallel to strong preferential treatment in the form of jobs for those previously victimized, the shift in educational levels involved in the passage of time distinguishes this case. The idea behind handicapping is that the candidate is given credit for having credentials that we expect he might have had if he had been given an equal chance at acquiring them. Its attempted justification again derives from the general principle that the purpose of compensation is to restore the victim to the level at which he would have been had no violation of fair distributive principles (here equality of opportunity) occurred.

One problem here is the application of the general principle to individual cases—the difficulty of judging where a given individual might have been or what he would have done if . . .

—which is especially acute when the deprivations occurred early in life. A more serious problem from the point of view of justice is that to handicap according to such predictions amounts (or will certainly seem to the presently most qualified candidates to amount) to rewarding hypothetical but unproven effort and contribution to the same degree as the real past efforts and accomplishments of the other candidates. To those in the latter category who are turned away, this will appear worse than arbitrary preference among individuals with equal rights or claims. What someone might have accomplished if he had been encouraged to make the effort and had been afforded the facilities is not, after all, the same as what another actually has accomplished. The former drew no sweat and forecasts no payoff to the public. This is not to say that the life of the former victim was not worse in other respects; but positions are to reward effort, contribution, and potential contribution, not prior amount of suffering.

Another problem with handicapping credentials as compensation for discrimination in education, then, is the potential loss in efficiency or utility to the public. In the case of strong reverse discrimination for those who were denied jobs for which they were most qualified, these losses will likely be minimal, since the individuals were most qualified at some time in the recent past and so are unlikely to be incompetent now. But when handicapping is contemplated—for positions in medical school for students inadequately prepared, for example—the potential losses in public welfare may be serious. It is sometimes argued, as in the *DeFunis* case, that the public will not suffer from handicapping as long as it is restricted to the educational level, as long as standards are maintained within the schools, and as long as only fully qualified persons graduate. Efficiency can be maintained at the job level, despite preferential admissions to professional training programs, if rigorous standards are upheld in the school system and if those who graduate have been made to compete favorably.

This may be true in theory—although potentially more qualified individuals will have been turned down—but it is difficult to uphold the last clause in practice. First, the pressure on those persons whose handicapped credentials admit them into highly competitive situations is likely to be enormous, and the letdown of being accepted and then flunked out because of inadequate preparation could be psychologically devastating. It can be replied that the choice of accepting such compensation is theirs to make, and we should give them the opportunity of making it rather than patronizingly protecting them from such pressures. But the question is whether it is possible to offer a more attractive choice than that between competition when underprepared or nothing. Second, enormous pressure is also placed upon teachers, who are sensitive to the burdens of such students but must at the same time attempt to accommodate the demands of those better trained at lower levels (I speak here from personal experience). The temptation is strong to give passing grades for work not previously acceptable, thereby lowering standards, since grades naturally become geared to expectations. It is easier to lower one's expectations than to attempt to teach other students as usual and at the same time undertake the large-scale special remedial help that may be necessary. Thus there are likely to be people graduating from schools who would not have passed but for their teachers' knowledge of their prior handicap, the desire to reward effort at present, and the unreasonableness of expecting greater ability on their part to compete against better trained students. When such is the case, the public must expect to pay a price in welfare later.

Although disutilities do not generally override rights—here rights to compensation for past injustice—the utilities and disutilities listed above with respect to handicapping illustrate again a conflict between the distributive rule for assigning positions (stipulated partly in terms of such considerations) and the compensatory rule applicable when violations to the distributive principle occur. Fortunately, it is not necessary to devote more space to weighing the conflicting claims, rights, and principles, for there is an alternative that seems preferable to handicapping credentials or reserving places for those discriminated against at lower levels in education: adequately funded remedial programs to afford opportunities to obtain the training previously denied. Just as discrimination at the education level calls for correction at that level if possible, rather than through reverse discrimination in hiring, and just as the former policy involves less injustice to other applicants and less inefficiency, so the denial of opportunity to acquire basic qualifications at lower levels calls for granting that opportunity through sufficiently endowed special remedial programs, rather than for reverse discrimination by colleges and graduate schools. Reverse discrimination is required as compensation in kind at the level at which the original injustice occurred: if a maximally qualified minority candidate was denied entrance to graduate school, then the arguments of the last section apply, and he should be admitted now, whether still most qualified or not. But if injustice occurs at a lower level, remedial programs are more appropriate than reverse discrimination for admissions to more advanced curricula.

When such remedial programs are instituted and admissions to regular programs are continued on the basis of relative qualifications, other candidates for admission cannot legitimately complain. No one has a right to limited or restricted competition, and remedial programs for those who were previously discriminated against in education only stiffen the competition by allowing them to compete fairly. Unlike reverse discrimination, this type of policy leaves white males in the relative position they deserve, even when lowering their opportunities in relation to the status quo. It simply removes unfair advantages. Of course, as argued in previous sections, admission to such remedial programs cannot be simply on the basis of race or sex, but only on the basis of prior injustice suffered. Again, this should not be inordinately difficult to demonstrate, given the availability of school records and the applicability of broad categories mentioned earlier (for example, having attended a particular school or a school in a particular area). Admission to the programs must be preferential for those individuals formerly discriminated against (assuming limited resources), as opposed to those who simply missed earlier opportunities they now regret having passed up. A final advantage of this type of policy accrues to the public, since such remedial programs can only increase efficiency by stiffening competition, rather than decreasing it by admitting those

underqualified to jobs or scarce positions in school through a
policy of reverse discrimination.

Despite these significant advantages and the prima facie
preferability of remediation over reverse discrimination, given
the level on which compensation must be made for past discrimination on a lower level, we can imagine objections from
all those with opposing interests on the issue. For example,
white male candidates for particular positions might argue that
while they themselves have no right to unfair restriction of
competition, the remedial programs may exceed corrections
for past handicaps, thereby producing results that would approximate those of reverse discrimination. The question
seems to be where to draw the line in the training afforded at
the remedial stage. If training is continued until a certain percentage of those enrolled are guaranteed success in pursuing
regular positions, where is the difference from reserving this
number of places outright? There is, it is true, a great difference in efficiency, or in likely gains versus losses to the public
in social welfare later on, but this is not a distinction relevant
to the relative positions of white male candidates. It seems
that we respect their rights to fair competition only if we provide remedial training so far but no farther. We want to gear
the degree of remediation for minority candidates to the degree of unjustly imposed past disadvantage; yet it seems impossible to measure the latter except in terms of present disadvantage. And it is certainly impracticable to try to tailor
remedial programs individually in proportion to varying degrees of past injustice suffered. From a practical view, we
must attempt to train all those enrolled equally, to the point
that they can compete favorably for regular positions. But here
is where the objection from other candidates arises.

The objection, however, entirely misses the purpose and
nature of sound remedial programs. Competition and grading
practices within them should be as demanding and selective in
results as were regular rating systems at lower levels for majority candidates. These are not to be programs of individual
tutoring, which spoon-feed those enrolled until they attain a
certain level no matter what. Rather, they are meant to approximate the affording of competitive opportunities formerly

denied unjustly. Thus those who graduate from such curricula should have met rigorous grading and competition to the same degree that white males had to meet them earlier, and in this sense they are to be fully equal in terms of present qualifications and past obstacles. The difference is that greater efforts to motivate and impart basic study skills may be required in general in these programs in comparison with those required in regular schools at lower levels, since these factors are more difficult to acquire later in life. But aside from this distinction, to the degree that remedial programs are administered competitively and rigorously, and to the degree that they thereby approximate competitive obstacles successfully overcome by white males at lower levels, the latter have no legitimate complaint regarding increased numbers of candidates qualified for various positions. I am not claiming that this is how remedial programs are now run; their resources and results are at present so minimal that no one can claim general comparable or competitive qualifications of those who graduate. I claim only that this is how they ought to operate if no one is to have legitimate complaints against them.

Even if remedial programs are run in the way I have suggested, objections may still arise from the other side, that is, from those who were discriminated against in the past and who are offered this policy as compensation. It seems they can argue that in offering only this, we would not be satisfying the principle that compensation is to restore victims of past injustice to the level at which they would have been had no violations to fair distributive principles occurred. It is clear that had many of these individuals not been discriminated against earlier by being forced into inferior programs involving lower than average expectations, they would now have desirable jobs or be progressing toward them at a normal pace in the regular advanced school system. This is the level to which they should now be immediately restored; yet we are contemplating only a program that offers years of remedial study, duplicating the experiences that should have been afforded in the first place. This is equivalent to restoration of the status quo ante for these individuals, not to restoration to the positions they would have rightfully occupied at present. What are we doing to compensate the unjustly lost years? First, we must offer adequate monetary support in the form of scholarships and living stipends. We cannot require those in remedial programs to continue to support themselves independently when they are at a stage at which they would normally have jobs. To offer adequate support is at least to offer more than a return to the status quo ante. There seems no way to go beyond this, however, short of reverse discrimination for regular positions; and again, given shifts in levels from discrimination to compensation, preferential treatment of that type would amount to rewarding accomplishments that might have been on a par with those that were actually achieved by others. Monetary compensation, plus the chance to seize opportunities formerly denied, seem the limit of justifiable restitution for denials lower in the educational system.

If the purpose of remedial programs is to restore to truly competitive status those who are inadequately prepared for desirable positions, and if at the same time they are to grant adequate monetary support for those enrolled for the period that may be required to accomplish this goal, they are going to be far more expensive than the type of token summer programs attempted for the most part until now. Whereas I earlier argued that remedial compensation would be less costly to the public than reverse discrimination in terms of efficiency or goods and services, the total costs of the former may now appear greater than indicated and the earlier claim questionable. I still believe that long-range utility and public welfare lie on the side of remedial programs, although more sophisticated economic analysis than I can bring to bear is necessary to settle this issue. But in any case, our concern here is not with cost minimization in compensatory policy, but rather with maximization of rights satisfaction. From among the feasible alternatives we must choose the policy that will involve the fewest continued injustices to all involved. Surely the resources of the federal government render our preferred policy in these cases feasible, given the desire to implement it. The distributive rule for awarding positions is designed in part to ensure maximum quality goods and services in the long run, but nothing further is implied in it regarding ceiling costs for justified compensatory programs when violations occur. Once the distributive rule is in effect, the expectations and rights of individuals created through it become paramount considerations relative to further calculations of utility.

I have now justified strong reverse discrimination for those discriminated against at the level of job hiring and graduate school admissions, and I have suggested well-funded remedial programs as the best solution to the problem of compensation for injustice lower in the educational system. But some victims of discriminatory injustice or unequal opportunity have still been left out of the picture entirely, and there are others for whom remedial programs will not work. Before considering the latter class, I turn to another group of individuals who constitute one of the most difficult classes of cases. These are persons who were never overtly discriminated against either in school or when applying for jobs but who never even reached the stage of applying for desirable positions for reasons relating to various types of discriminatory injustice. Some, intimidated by knowledge of injustice to other members of their race or sex, may not have applied for desired positions from the conviction that they would not have been considered seriously or fairly. Undoubtedly, the number of women who never applied for jobs as pilots, although they would have liked such jobs, exceeds the number of those who were routinely turned down after applying. Others may not have known of positions that remained unadvertised or unannounced. In all such cases it seems reasonable to think that people who never reached the stage of applying for places they very much would have wanted were injured at least to the degree of those who, in order to be unjustly rejected, had to have the positive psychological attitude necessary to apply. If the degree of harm to the former individuals was indeed as great, can we justify compensation to those actually discriminated against while ignoring their equally demoralized counterparts? It is true that harm to the latter was indirect, via direct injustice to others, but this seemingly does not prevent the degree of injury from being as great. And since the harm still derives ultimately from injustice, and since compensation for injury is meant to be proportionate to degree of harm, it seems that we cannot justly ignore individuals injured in a way that prevented their ever being in a position to receive direct discriminatory treatment.

The problem here, however, relates to the *kind* of injury, not to its degree, and to the type of compensation that might be fitting. Reverse discrimination for jobs does not constitute compensation in kind here, since only the *one* person most qualified deserves a particular position, or preference for it later if he or she is rejected unjustly. There is no way of knowing whether a person who never applied would have been the one to deserve a given position, not only over all those who did apply for it, but also over all other persons who did not apply. Hence there is no way of knowing whether reverse discrimination at the level of job hiring is owed according to the principle of restoration to rightful position. In any case, one can acquire a right to a position according to the distributive rule only if one applies for it: the rule stipulates hiring the most competent among all *applicants*. Equality of opportunity demands full public notice or advertisement of places, but when this is violated, it is usually impossible to judge which of the nonapplicants might have deserved the position. Thus, while it may seem in the abstract as if it makes little difference from the point of view of compensatory justice whether a person actually applies for a position or is too intimidated or uninformed to apply, the injuries received in these two classes of cases do differ in kind, so that one is directly compensable through award of a position later, while the other is not. As we saw earlier, only certain kinds of harms are compensable at all, and reverse discrimination is a relevant form of compensation only for a narrow class of injustices. Nor do remedial programs seem relevant here, since we are speaking of a group of individuals never discriminated against in the educational system either.

Although those indirectly harmed may suffer more psychologically, I have already argued at length that purely psychological harm is not compensable through the policy in question. I shall not repeat those arguments, but one central point was that if we take seriously psychological harm derived from unfortunate or unjust social stereotyping, we must also seriously consider the prospect of compensation for all the Willy Lomans among the harried white male population. Also of relevance here is the point regarding the reward of real effort and accomplishment, as opposed to hypothetical and unproven achievement. Those who actually applied for jobs or places in school are likely also to be the ones who actually made efforts to acquire the requisite qualifications. Such enterprising members of minorities, if denied positions for which they were sufficiently qualified, are owed more in the way of comparable jobs than others with the same educational opportunities who never pursued positions they might have. With an end to first-order discrimination, the latter, if they choose to, can apply for positions they never bothered applying for before. Others previously influenced into inferior programs are owed remedial opportunities, as established in the prior argument.

There will nevertheless still remain others to whom remedial training may be owed but for whom it will not work. Still difficult cases are those in which a person has been unjustly denied the opportunity to acquire qualifications for a particular position and is no longer able to acquire them even with remediation—for example, because of age. Where such cases occur, various factors must be weighed in deciding whether simply to award the job to the person not maximally qualified. These include responsibility and importance of the job to society, the candidate's qualifications or lack of them, past damages to him, importance in the job of skills no longer attainable, benefits or attractiveness of the job, and level of scarcity of the type of position in question. In those cases in which the job carries heavy responsibility and there are others more qualified in important ways, fair monetary compensation is probably the best alternative, if damages from unjust denial of equal opportunity can be shown. To take the obvious case of a surgeon, no one would advocate awarding a position to an unqualified candidate on grounds of discrimination in denial of admission to medical school, even if the individual in question has clearly been discriminated against and can no longer afford to spend years studying. Measurement of damages in monetary terms for such lost opportunities are difficult and may seem callous, but of course the courts make that sort of determination all the time. Differences in average earning capacities for those at different levels in education or training are useful guides for such purposes. In the case of a desk job in a government office, on the other hand, denial of adequate training in the past may be grounds for simply awarding and training on the job if prior training is no longer feasible for a particular individual and there are numerous positions available. When positions are scarce, actual achievements and claims of those better qualified will again become relevant. But while actual effort is to count more than hypothetical effort, individuals cannot be penalized for having been barred from making efforts. It would take too much space to attempt to order these considerations, even if I had a clear idea of how to do so, but the number of cases in this category, that is, those who cannot enter remedial programs offered with adequate support, is likely to be small enough that a list of relevant considerations like that suggested above should suffice for our purposes.

Finally, in a section on denial of equal opportunity we must mention a group of individuals for whom opportunity will not be equal even when discrimination ends in the educational system and even when schools make special efforts on their behalf. For children in certain communities and certain home environments, well-intentioned remedial programs may again prove insufficient. For them, however, it is not a question of compensating past denials in the school system, but of creating equal opportunity through other means. Thus, at this point we shift from backward- to future-looking justifications for preferential policies, including reverse discrimination, and we arrive at the topic for the next chapter. Before proceeding to additional justifications, we may summarize the major conclusions of this chapter.

(1) It was held that rational contractors must add a principle of compensation to their distributive rules. (2) Relevant sections of our principle of compensation, as applied to paradigm and deviant cases, included: (a) that victims ought to be restored to the level at which they would have been had no violations occurred; (b) that perpetrators cannot complain if made

to pay an amount equal to fair compensation, even if this should go to proxies for the real victims; (c) that victims cannot demand, as their right, compensation from unrelated or innocent third parties. (3) When applied to the problem at hand, these principles were found to imply that reverse discrimination can be justified for individuals formerly discriminated against, but only at the same level at which the injustice occurred. (4) Reverse discrimination directed at whole minority groups indiscriminately was found to involve injustice to certain members of those groups and to white males most qualified for various positions. (5) Such injustice was likely to be widespread, owing to market factors, and it therefore could not be overridden for reasons of administrative efficiency. (6) For individuals discriminated against, strong reverse discrimination was held justifiable under the principle that individuals rightly occupying positions are granted a presumption of continuing in them. (7) When compensation involves a shift between the level at which the discrimination took place and the level at which the compensation should logically be granted, as in the denial of equal opportunity at lower levels in the educational system, well-supported remedial programs were preferred as a compensatory policy over reverse discrimination in order to maintain efficiency, provide compensation in kind, and reward real achievement and real and potential social contribution.

FOUR

Equal Opportunity and the Future

Utility and Rights

Having justified reverse discrimination as compensation for past injustice in certain cases, I turn to the question of additional justification that looks not to the past but to the future benefits presumed to flow from adoption of preferential policies. Most future-looking arguments on the subject have been utilitarian arguments, those that look to long- or short-range benefits in public welfare—for example, social harmony among races—or to gains in satisfaction of interests among members of specific institutions for which the policy is advocated—for example, utility to students from diversity among classmates. As indicated earlier, two distinct questions must be posed: Are the utilities or interest satisfactions claimed real, and do they outweigh related disutilities? And, if overall gains in utility or interest satisfaction are projected from the specific policies advocated, should these gains be paramount considerations?

Utilities and Disutilities

Let us begin in this subsection by considering some of the claims made for the utility of such policies and by attempting to weigh gains and losses. Although it is impossible to consider all utilitarian claims, as there is a wide divergence in their specificity, a sampling should indicate how the winds of utility blow in many directions on the issue.

The most general utility cited in defense of reverse discrimination for random members of minority groups is the gradual easing of tensions among races and between the sexes. Reverse discrimination is believed to achieve integration of minority-group members into the mainstream of American life more quickly than would otherwise be possible. As members of different minority groups become more evenly spread among the social and economic strata, sharp divisions along these lines among different groups, which without doubt cause antagonisms, will disappear. And when members of particular racial and ethnic groups are no longer clustered at the bottom of the economic and social scales, both envy and paternalism between minorities and whites, as well as their acute group consciousness, should gradually diminish.

A more extreme version of this utilitarian argument for the policy as directed toward certain whole minority groups can be put in the form of a threat: when members of these groups experience the frustration of exclusion from the mainstream of social and economic life, they will take action outside the normal legal and political channels to make their interests felt. The most effective way of intruding upon the complacency of those in power is violence. If property damage and personal injuries are to be avoided, such exclusion and alienation must end, and decent jobs constitute one important positive step toward avoiding further disutilities (to put it mildly) on both sides. Whether phrased in terms of the utility of social harmony or the disutility of strife, this first utilitarian argument advocates group reverse discrimination as a means of integrating members of minority groups with those who are at present socially and economically privileged.

Other broad·utilitarian arguments for reverse discrimination involve the concept of *role models*, which we encountered earlier in the section in Chapter Two on qualifications. Minority-group members who obtain jobs through the policy serve as models for others in the type of position in question. The first way in which this can be effective again relates directly to relations among races and between the sexes. Since invidious stereotyping maintains prejudice and hence continued discrimination, the idea is that as minority-group members and women are given jobs and seen to function in them as well as white males, the assumption made by those in power that members of such groups are incompetent will eventually be overcome. This will enable more members of minorities to obtain jobs on their own and will also hasten harmony among groups, as described in the previous paragraph. Second, individuals who initially acquire jobs through the policy can serve as models for younger members of their group, creating motivations formerly lacking. What motivates young people to aim for a certain profession is often association or acquaintance with someone admired in that position, and the visibility of minority-group members in various areas formerly dominated by white males can only hasten integration of additional members, with the aforementioned gains in social utility. Whether young members of such groups have *rights* to be provided with such role models can be temporarily ignored in this section on utilities. But it should be noted that for role models to be at all effective, the most competent members of the groups in question must be the beneficiaries of the preferential treatment. Incompetents do not make inspiring models. As we saw in the previous chapter, however, hiring the most competent minority-group member runs counter to the probable order of rights to compensation among members of those groups, and hence violates rights of white males to positions.

Before considering conflicts between utilities and rights in more detail, let us consider purely utilitarian counterarguments to this first set of claims, that is, the disutilities possibly attached to the attempt to integrate minority-group members and women into formerly exclusive social and economic strata through reverse discrimination. Will preferential treatment for minorities really foster integration and social harmony, either directly through jobs given or indirectly through persons in such jobs serving as examples to end stereotyping and to motivate the young? The answers to both disjuncts are at least doubtful, given that others know that the treatment *is* preferential. First, the method of integration contemplated may cause more friction and resentment than that inevitable from residual bigotry, owing to the feeling that certain members of certain minorities received an undeserved break denied to members of other groups. Although the long-range effect of economic and social integration will undoubtedly be a reduction of racial tension, the interesting utilitarian question is one concerning the means of achieving this goal: reverse discrimination, which might achieve the proportionate mix faster, may yet be slower in bringing the desired harmony. Second, with regard to the effectiveness of role models, to the degree that reverse discrimination places less than maximally competent persons in various positions, it may prolong the stereotypes rather than dispel them, and further discourage potential achievers rather than motivate them. If minority-group students sense that their teachers of the same race or sex tend to be less qualified than average, they will surely not take them as models to be emulated. Knowledge that discrimination is no longer tolerated might be more effective as motivation, and nondiscrimination would provide sounder, if somewhat fewer, role models.

The general inefficiency of reverse discrimination to the public must be counted as an additional disutility. Some have argued that bringing minorities up to proportionate mix in various job categories would fully engage their talents, as they have not been used before, and thus increase efficiency. But such group thinking again masks inefficiency. By definition, discrimination of any form is inefficient in itself in terms of goods and services projected. Discrimination in favor of a certain group of individuals in the present cannot make up in efficiency for discrimination in favor of a different group of individuals in the past. Finally, on the side of disutility, general knowledge that preferential treatment is granted may unfairly stigmatize those members of the groups who receive it, especially those who could have obtained their positions without it, placing an additional burden on them to impress others with their competence and possibly creating unwarranted self-doubts.

The question of the psychological effect of reverse discrimination on minority-group members themselves, which is relevant to any forward-looking or utilitarian argument on the use of role models, is a controversial one, again indicating the difficulty of accurately weighing the utilities and disutilities of the policy. Evidence against believing that minority-group members themselves feel stigmatized or patronized by the policy is the fact that most representative spokesmen for such groups—for example, those who filed briefs in the *DeFunis* and *Bakke* cases—have argued in favor of preferential treatment. We may take this evidence initially at its face value. On the other hand, most such spokesmen seem to view the alternatives as acceptance of preferential treatment when offered or a continuation of the status quo, with its subtle and not so subtle forms of first-order discrimination. Faced with these alternatives, the choice is clear, and the support of many minority-group members for preferential policies may derive from their conviction that first-order discrimination cannot end without them. Within the narrow range of choices available to minority leaders, and with their limited power, any sign in public policy of a changing social and moral consciousness on the part of those in the white male power structure would probably be avidly supported, at least officially. Nevertheless, I have been comparing reverse discrimination with all possible alternatives from the point of view of justice and now utility (I shall speak more directly to the claim that first-order discrimination cannot be ended without reverse discrimination in a later section on affirmative action). If offered the alternative of effective enforcement of nondiscrimination, with compensation as described in the last chapter, it is not clear that minority-group spokesmen would continue to view reverse discrimination for whole groups as preferable in terms of utilitarian consequences.

On the other side also is the personal testimony of some of the recipients of such treatment—for example, the experience of one black law student:

> Traditionally, first-year law students are supposed to be afraid, or at least awed; but our fear was compounded by the uncommunicated realization that perhaps we were not authentic law students and the uneasy suspicion that our classmates knew that we were not, and like certain members of the faculty, had developed paternalistic attitudes toward us.[1]

To the extent that minority-group members view reverse discrimination as something owed them by society, they will most likely not feel as the individual quoted, just as veterans do not feel stigmatized when they receive preferential treatment. But in accord with recognition of the arguments of the last chapter, this is likely to be the case only for those actually discriminated against in the past.

At issue here as well is the effect of the policy upon the attitudes of non-minority-group members. I have already mentioned the danger of backlash hatred and additional resentment, but the above quotation points also to a negative effect upon the attitudes of even the well intentioned. Without proof that all applicants have been subjected to the same rigorous tests, existing biases or invidious suspicions of inferiority will be that much more difficult to dispel. Many psychologists of education believe, with some positive evidence, that teachers' anticipations of students' limitations tend to be self-fulfilling. To anticipate limitations tends to reinforce them when they do exist and to introduce them when they do not. Thus any policy that fosters or reinforces the belief that minority members per se require preferential treatment to compete favorably, regardless of their past or present home or economic environments, may be doubly dangerous in terms of its consequences, and may even backfire in its attempt to motivate younger members of such groups. (Preferential treatment more narrowly specified, that is, not directed indiscriminately to all members of minorities, need not have the same attitudinal consequences.) One black educator opposed to the policy on these grounds writes:

> What all the arguments and campaigns for quotas are really saying, loud and clear, is that black people just don't have it, and that they will have to be given something in order to have something. The devastating impact of this message on black people—particularly black young people—will outweigh any few extra jobs that may result from this strategy.[2]

Thus for each of the projected utilities associated with the integration of minorities into the mainstream of economic and social life, there are possible disutilities connected with reverse discrimination for all or any members of such groups that make it at least questionable that such a policy is the best means to achieve that highly desirable goal.

Narrower utilitarian arguments refer to advantages of having minorities proportionately represented within specific institutions or job categories, or of having professionals in specific communities or geographical areas. For example, students are said to learn better in an atmosphere of diversity. Such diversity in the student body can result in radically different points of view brought to bear on different subject matters, which is supposed to be conducive to the discovery of new truths about them. Second, part of what should be learned in school is the ability to live in one's society, to understand its problems, and to contribute toward their solution; in a pluralistic society like ours, this can be best imparted and absorbed in a pluralistic classroom. Thus these claims point to utilitarian advantages to all, and not just to minority-group members, from achieving racial mix and a proportionate number of females in the school system. Related arguments point to the advantages of having minority-group members in certain professions. For example, claims are made that as teachers, they are more sensitive to certain subject matters, that students of their race or sex are more open and learn more readily from them, that minority doctors or lawyers are more likely to serve in poorer ghetto areas where they are badly needed, and that minority lawyers are better able to serve clients of their race or national origin, given their knowledge of the communities or of other languages, where that is relevant.

Once again, some of these claims can be challenged on purely utilitarian grounds, some being stronger or weaker than others. Is it true that one learns better in a racially, ethnically, or sexually mixed atmosphere? Do students in Sweden then learn less than those in New York? Belief that people of different races or sexes per se bring to bear different perspectives or perceptions depends upon the assumption that perceptions are programmed by race or sex, and this begins to sound racist or sexist. Perhaps the weaker assumption is that in our society persons of different races or sexes tend to be from different social or cultural backgrounds and that these affect their perceptions. This seems more true for races than sexes, and if it is the basis of the argument, it should be made clear that we are after social and cultural mix rather than racial or sexual diversity. Perhaps the inference is only from the premise that persons of different races or sexes tend to have different interests in our society and that interests affect perceptions. While this may at present be true for some subject matters, such as applied ethics or politics, where views may at least initially be legitimately colored by interests, the assumption must be false for other subjects, such as mathematics. This counterargument is not meant to call into question the fact that all have a right to an equal education, at least at the lower levels, or that for minority-group members the satisfaction of this right at present seems to require racially mixed schools; I am only indicating that utilitarian claims in this area can be exaggerated or false. Furthermore, the advantage of learning to live in a pluralistic society is of more relevance to the lower levels of the educational system than to the higher, where close attention to specific and technical subject matters becomes paramount over broad social benefits of education to the students.

Similar questions can be raised regarding some of the other utilitarian claims cited above. Do students learn better from members of their own race, sex, or ethnic backgrounds? The influx of European intellectuals during and after the Second World War raised the level of teaching and learning at various universities, although the backgrounds of such teachers were very different from those of their students. Are minority-group lawyers and doctors needed for their communities? It is certainly true that some communities are in dire need of more professional services. But to fill these needs, benefits and incentives can be granted to those who pledge to serve a certain time in these areas, without basing such advantages upon race or relying upon the likelihood that minority-group members will serve there. We can resist using a racial basis on purely utilitarian grounds, again having to do with backlash resentment and the creation of even more acute group consciousness (additional reasons why we should avoid such bases for advantages will be given in the next subsection). It also seems unfair to minority-group members themselves to demand or expect them to make the monetary sacrifices involved in serving poorer communities to a disproportionate degree. Finally, knowledge of another language may constitute a standard qualification for certain types of service and ought to be considered a qualification for certain professional schools. But again, this need not be based upon race or even national or ethnic origin. And if it is a qualification, the question of reverse discrimination need not arise in relation to it.

These questions or challenges to utilitarian claims are not intended to defeat them decisively. In fact, I find it extremely difficult to predict the social consequences of large-scale group reverse discrimination. This nevertheless does not prevent my writing a book on the subject, since I do not believe that the justice of the issue is to be decided on purely utilitarian grounds like those to which the above arguments appeal. More important than the question of whether the utilities involved outweigh the disutilities is the question of whether they ought to be allowed to outweigh the relevant rights of individuals to the positions at issue, or whether utilities ought to be considered at all in relation to those rights. These questions are complicated, as we have already seen, by the fact that certain rights may be defined or recognized in the first place in relation to considerations of welfare. Let us turn to examine these relations in more detail.

Rights

I briefly discussed the nature of rights when establishing the specific rights of most competent individuals to various positions. At this point, in pondering the weight to be assigned to the above utilitarian arguments, we require a more precise definition of rights and a more explicit exposition of their relation to utilities and interests. The definition I propose, incorporating standard clauses,[3] is:

A person has a right to x (to do y) $=_{df}$
(1) it is generally not wrong for him to have x (to do y);
(2) if he claims x (desires to do y), then it is wrong for others to take or withhold x (prevent him from doing y)
(3) society ought to protect his claim to x (freedom to do y) through law.

The first clause states that a person's right to x (to do y) *in itself* means that it is generally not wrong for him to have x (to do y). This implies that certain considerations normally rele-

vant to whether it is right for him to have an object or perform
an action—for example, the interest of others in the object or
consequences of the action—will not be relevant in the context or for the type of object or action stipulated in the recognition of the right. It also means that he need not await the per-
mission or consent or benevolence of others to take or hold x
(or do y). He is justified in having it, and no further justification normally need be given. The hypothetical form of the
second criterion shows the voluntary nature of exercising one's
rights: one can have a right without exercising it, and it is not
self-contradictory and probably true to hold that in certain circumstances a person may be wrong in exercising his right. He
may, for example, have a right to say anything he pleases short
of libel, slander, or incitement to riot, and yet be wrong to
exercise that right by telling his grandmother that her new hat
is ugly. But the consequent of the second criterion again
shows that it is wrong for anyone to try to prevent his exercising his right, whether or not he is correct in choosing to exercise it. It may seem unusual to speak of exercising certain passive or negative rights, such as the right not to be treated
cruelly; for all rights, the presumption is that the person who
has them desires and ought to have them honored, unless he
has expressly waived or forfeited them.

The "others" referred to in the second clause may be
specific individuals or society at large, depending upon the
right in question, and they may be required either to take
positive actions to enable the right holder to have x or do y,
such as granting him a job, or simply to refrain from preventing this. A further distinction is made in addition to whether
the rights hold against specific individuals or society at large.
That is, certain rights ought to be recognized simply by virtue
of their potential possessors' being human or having interests,
while others arise consequent upon individuals' satisfying certain social rules or entering into certain specific relations with
others governed by those rules. Generally, these distinctions
are connected, in that those general rights that arise from having interests, which often constitute prerequisites for having
other rights recognized, generally hold against all individuals,
while those that arise from special relations or satisfaction of

specific rules generally hold only against certain individuals. But this connection does not always hold. My right to parts of my property derives from my having acquired them in a way that accords with specific rules for property acquisition in my society, and yet it holds against everyone.

Finally, the third clause shows that the right holder's being permitted to hold x or do y is important enough to warrant protection. Not all actions that are wrong ought to be prohibited by law, and not all actions that are right ought to be so guaranteed. It may be wrong for me to tell my grandmother that her new hat is ugly but I ought not to be prohibited from doing so; and it may be right for me to keep such opinions to myself, but I ought not to be forced to do so. On the other hand, my right to say what I please ought to be protected by definition if it is a right, and others ought to be prevented from stopping me. The mention of society here indicates that rights arise in a social context, with the formation of a moral community. But the use of "ought" indicates that we are speaking of moral rights, and that not all moral rights are translated into legal ones, although they ought to be.

What is the value or purpose of recognizing rights within a moral or social system? This question, invariably raised in philosophical discussions of rights, is pertinent to our specific task of relating them to utilities in deciding the justice of reverse discrimination. For the first purpose of recognizing rights is to protect certain interests of individuals against utility maximizing or additive calculations regarding (other) interests of others. For example, if we recognize a right to property, this means that if I have acquired something in a manner that is legitimized in the stipulation of the right, I am entitled to continue to hold it in spite of the greater need of others for that sort of object or the greater utility realized by transferring it to them. If in each instance one had to demonstrate only increased utility, interest, or need satisfaction in order to take any part of another's property, the right to property would vanish. To cite another example, if there is a right to free speech, then I am permitted to make and required to be protected in making certain types of statements no matter how much offense others may take at them. If, in order to silence me, it had only to be shown that others take more offense than I derive satisfaction from making specific statements, the right to free speech would dissolve.

This last example shows that we consider certain interests to be qualitatively more important than others; for example, our interest in being able to say what we please is more valuable in its satisfaction than our interest in not being offended. This ranking holds even though utility may lie occasionally on the side of silencing someone when many others might take offense at what he intends to say and when we are quite certain that no long-range social good will come of his statement. Part of the rationale of recognizing rights is to protect these important interests against being overridden by additions of less important ones.

It seems, then, that we recognize a qualitative twofold distinction between types of interests: some generate rights, others remain mere interests or utilities (when satisfied). We might imagine substituting a complete and transitive ordering of interests for this twofold distinction, and we might imagine that this would be theoretically superior. But besides being false to our ordinary moral consciousness or deliberations, such an ordering would be too prohibitive against adding or balancing certain interests against others. It would eliminate quantitative considerations altogether, when actually they are only to be disallowed when weighing interests in the lower category against those in the upper. In the lower category of mere interests, simple additive calculations are allowed and required in deciding moral judgments or social policy—for example, in weighing sales of wheat to Russia, which increase the income of farmers, help to balance trade deficits, and help to improve relations with that country, but which raise food prices for all consumers. In such cases, where only interests are involved, we simply balance those on one side versus those on the other in deciding the right course of action or policy. (I assume in this example that farmers do not have an absolute moral right to sell to whomever they choose, and I ignore the notorious difficulties of figuring and adding the interests or of devising a social decision procedure that will reflect their relative weights.)

Interests that generate rights, and the class of rights themselves, are generally ordered internally rather than simply totaled against one another. For example, the right to equal opportunity is considered more basic or more important than the right of corporations to disburse their assets as they please; the right to equal use of facilities intended for the public is more important than the right of restaurant owners to serve whom they please; or the right to be free from inhalation of noxious fumes is more important than the right of smokers to light up wherever they please. These orderings are *nonadditive*, in that it makes no difference, for example, how many restaurant owners and potential diners are involved in a given area or how much offense the former take at having to serve certain individuals, as opposed to whether the latter are insulted at being turned away. Even were the former feelings stronger than the latter and more numerous, the priority of the right of the diners to the facilities would still hold.

Therefore, when I speak of maximization of rights satisfaction, I intend the satisfaction of higher-order rights at the expense of lower-order ones, and, regarding the same rights of different individuals, simple maximization of satisfactions. While different rights are ordered in this way rather than added, we do not have and will never have a complete ordering within this class. It seems first of all impossible to specify general types of rights that always take precedence over others, although some libertarians can be interpreted as holding that freedom from harms takes precedence over positive liberties, which in turn take precedence over all other rights or interests. The problem with this attempt lies in the notorious difficulty of objectively defining "harms" and in the fact that protection of certain liberties requires restrictions of others. My liberty to use public facilities restricts restaurant owners' liberty to serve whom they please. While such systematization seems to fail, we can still work out priorities piecemeal and maintain the distinction between rights and mere interests.

In practical life it appears that we often have to deal with conflicts between rights, with certain ones being overridden by others. In an ideal system, however, all priorities will be expressed by exceptive clauses, and no further conflicts will arise. For example, I have a right to smoke where I please *except* in certain designated areas where others will be allowed to breathe. The right to breathe and the right to smoke need no longer be seen to conflict once this priority is recognized.[4] Aside from the fact that we do not have a complete system of orderings as expressed by such exceptive clauses, it is nevertheless useful to continue to speak of rights being overridden by others, in order to remind ourselves that when new exceptive clauses are written into existing rights, compensations may be owed, at least in the short run, for frustrations of expectations and infringements upon goods and liberties formerly enjoyed.

Exceptive clauses may differ in the degree to which they annihilate sections of rights formerly acknowledged. For example, when for the sake of equality of opportunity we recognize that corporations have a right to disburse their assets freely except in the case of hiring, the extension of the former right to that area is held to be illegitimate or simply nonexistent, and we do not feel that any compensation is owed to the corporations when we enforce or point out this limitation. On the other hand, if we justify violating the rights of those most competent to positions in order to further promote equal opportunity for others, we may feel that compensation in the form of special consideration for the former when applying for future jobs should be granted, at least for a fixed time after the initial policy is announced and instituted. Finally, an example at the other extreme would be if a contract had to be broken in order to satisfy some stronger right—for example, if payment for goods or services received had to be withheld to pay hospital bills to save the life of a spouse. Here the right of the contract holder would continue despite the morally justified exception, and compensation would continue to be owed indefinitely (although it might be wrong for the creditor to demand that his right be satisfied). Thus, even though morally acceptable priorities may be recognized through exceptive clauses, those rights with lower priority may still have force in the areas excepted. While I therefore continue to speak of certain rights overriding others, if rights are to exist at all, we cannot allow them to be overridden by interests in the lower category or by all or any additions of utilities when these are unconnected with rights. In relation to our specific issue, if there are rights of most competent individuals to positions, as well as rights to compensation and equal opportunity, then these must take precedence, when they apply, over the utilities mentioned in the previous subsection (if these utilities are themselves unconnected with rights). To allow rights to be overridden by all greater additions of utilities is to trivialize the first two clauses of our definition and destroy the major purpose of recognizing rights.

One purpose then of recognizing rights is to protect certain interests against additions of others whose satisfaction is intrinsically less important or valuable. This cannot explain the recognition of all rights, however, since, for example, a person's interest in the things he owns as property is similar to the interests of others or satisfactions they might derive from holding those goods, and the interest of the person most competent in a prospective job is the same in kind as the interests of other applicants. In these cases it is not a question of protecting certain interests against others intrinsically less important. There must be some other rationale for protecting the good of certain individuals against that of others in these situations. I said in Chapter Two that the reason society would wish the most competent hired as a general rule, as opposed to the adoption of any other general rule, is universal utility. But this explains only why such a rule would be generally enforced, not why we speak of the *right* of a most competent individual to a particular position against a certain organization. We still must explain why we refuse to override his claim when utility might be served in a particular case by doing so—for example, when others might need the job more and when society might be relatively indifferent to the performance of its functions. Why should the satisfaction of the rule generate a right on the part of the individual who satisfies it? The answer lies in the value of stability of expectations, or, to put it more briefly, in the great value of security.

The case of rights to property is instructive here. These do not follow from the fact that the interests of people in the things they possess are intrinsically different from interests others might have in those objects, nor from the fact that the ways in which they acquired them intrinsically bestow relations of ownership to them. Rather, we honor them because a fair and useful stipulation of property rights renders us secure in possessions, and because such security is something we value highly. Similarly, with respect to particular jobs, the interests of those most competent may not differ in kind from the interests of others, and utility may not be maximized by granting them the positions. But stability of expectations requires that people know that satisfying certain general social rules through their own efforts entitles them to expect certain returns as their rights.

Of course, simple act-utilitarians can point out that the disutility of frustrating expectations and the utilities of honoring them, including the incentives such rewards provide to others, must be figured in particular situations. But the point of speaking of rights here is that we do not want such utilities calculated on an even basis against all others. For the sake of security and psychological stability we want the interests of those individuals who satisfy such rules to be protected against such calculations, and hence we grant them rights. Where rights exist, expectations can be formed with knowledge of their future protection. And where rights exist, they are not to be overridden by mere utilities, even where this would be rare and unpublicized enough not to threaten the expectations of others. Thus, even if it were not the case that the satisfaction of some first-order interests is intrinsically more valuable than the satisfaction of others, we would still want to recognize certain rights for the sake of security (our interest in stability of expectations might be termed second order, in contrast with our interests in things that we might have expectations of acquiring). Intrinsic differences among interests simply delimit the domain of certain rights in a totally nonarbitrary way.

A final, much-heralded value in the recognition of rights is their implicit assertion of the dignity or inviolability of the individual, as against the single-minded concentration upon collective interests of a morality without rights. As stated, rights free us from dependence upon the benevolence of others and allow us to assert certain claims on the basis of our humanity, our relations to others, or our achievements. A person with rights can demand satisfaction of certain interests: he is a person to be reckoned with and respected. Hence, if self-esteem is based upon being shown respect by others, it depends in part upon the possibility of asserting one's rights. Besides freeing us from the necessity of pleading for goods, the possession of rights entails, with respect at least to certain interests, that we as individuals will not be sacrificed or treated as means to the satisfaction of the interests of others without our consent. Rights establish an area in which the individual is inviolable, and they do this while protecting the moral equality of all. Within the area in which an individual has rights, he can be certain that he will not be used as a means to the welfare of others (where the latter is not connected with stronger rights).

For all these reasons, then—the intrinsic importance of certain interests, the value of security or stability in expectations, and the assertion of the inviolability of individuals—it is morally desirable to protect certain values against others through the recognition of rights. Before proceeding to apply these claims more specifically to the issue of forward-looking justifications of reverse discrimination, let us field possible objections to the above account. First, is it true that rights may never be overridden by utilities? If counterexamples can be found anywhere, they might be damaging to our dismissal of all mere utilities in the face of rights to various positions for which reverse discrimination is considered.

The place to begin to look for counterexamples might be where freedoms ordinarily called rights appear no more weighty than the merest of utilities and disutilities. It seems that some rights are more trivial than those mentioned above—for example, my right to water my roses, to eat dinner when I like, or to choose to wear a green shirt with an orange tie. Can such trivial rights as these not be overridden by disutilities to others? Suppose, for example, that my eating dinner at four o'clock greatly disrupts the activities of the rest of my family (if we tried to talk of their "right" not to be inconvenienced, talk of rights would lose all meaning). Must my right be honored at their expense? The question is misleading for several reasons. In answering it, we can again appeal to the distinction between having a right and being right or wrong in choosing to exercise it. I can have a right to eat dinner when I like and yet be wrong in choosing to exercise it at times that inconvenience others. The point is that no one has a right to tell me when I must eat, since such an order would represent an unnecessary intrusion upon my freedom of choice. This leads to the second part of our answer: these rights may not seem important in themselves, but, as parts of the general right to do whatever we please that is not morally forbidden or that does not interfere with the rights of others, they represent an extremely important interest. This is our interest in being free from tyrannical interference with the everyday course of our lives, an interest that is more important than the satisfaction of our occasional desires to interfere in the course of others' lives.

While it is impossible to isolate a class of rights too trivial to fit our account, there may still appear to be specific counterexamples to the claim that rights may never be overridden by utilities. A well-worn case is the one in which I borrow a gun and promise to return it at a specific time, but then learn that the owner plans to commit suicide with the gun at that time. Must I honor his right to his own weapon by returning it, when I apparently have no right to keep it? While the answer may be no, this does not show that utility overrides a right here, even if we posit great disutilities consequent upon the suicide. For the answer really depends upon whether we recognize a right to interfere to prevent a suicide, or, on the other hand, whether we grant a right to commit suicide. This of course is not at issue in this book, but if the answer to the former is yes and to the latter no, then the right to interfere will override the owner's right to have his gun returned as promised. Likewise, we would have the right to prevent a potential suicide victim from standing on a ledge, despite his usual right to stand where he pleases. In short, the example turns on rights and not mere utilities.

Still, the dictum "Let justice be done, let rights be honored, come what may" may sound fanatic. It may raise images of keeping trivial promises or of giving people trivial things due them at the expense of lives or important unfulfilled needs. But one who read the above account carefully will quickly recognize these as illusory images, since I have held that the domain of rights is determined in large part by the importance of the interests that generate them. When rights are overridden in order to satisfy important interests or fulfill dire needs, they will have actually encountered other rights.

We can see how this works with another purported counterexample. It seems clear that a person is justified in breaking a promise to keep a luncheon appointment in order to help a motorist stranded on the road or a suffering animal, and this case has been claimed to show that utilities, or here disutilities, can override certain rights.[5] Of course the example presupposes that promises always create rights that they be kept, that the motorist cannot demand help as *his* right, and that animals cannot have rights at all. None of these follows from the above account. First, if the motorist is in real need of assistance, he may have a right to our aid. Such rights constitute a major source of the correlative obligation not to leave the scene of an accident. If he is only inconvenienced by having to wait for the next driver who passes, it may be better to keep the promise, if the appointment is important. Second, although philosophers generally presuppose that promises always create rights, this does not follow from the claim that rights are intended to protect certain interests against others. It is true that promises create obligations to perform what is promised, whether or not the action is itself morally best or utility maximizing, and that the acceptance of such obligations is the purpose of having an institution of promise making. But whether the recipient of the promise can claim a corresponding right depends, I believe, upon the importance of what is promised. This accords with my account, but it is also supported by ordinary language. The person waiting in the restaurant who claimed that his right was violated by my lateness for lunch would probably draw some bewildered looks at best, unless the appointment were extremely important. Important promises do create rights, but such promises are ordinarily termed "contracts," whether verbal or written, and they are protected by society through law. Others create obligations but are too trivial to be claimed as rights by their recipients. Such is the case in the example we are considering. (This distinction between types of promises defeats a possible objection to another point mentioned above: the claim that rights ought to be protected by law. Surely we do not require or desire trivial promises to be enforced by police, but if these do not create rights, then they cannot be protected.) Finally, as to the question of whether animals can have rights, although it is not relevant to our central issue, I shall indicate in a moment that recognition of such rights is not inconsistent and probably warranted in my account. In any case it should now be clear that this example supports the above account of the relation of rights to utilities rather than defeating it.

Let us consider one final example that is more relevant to our specific issue. If, as I argued in the second chapter, individuals acquire rights to positions for which they are most competent, it might nevertheless seem that these can be overridden by real utilities or disutilities to the hiring corporations. Suppose that a business with a position open is operating with an unsatisfactory rate of profit. Would it not be justified, in an attempt to cut costs, to hire the first reasonably qualified candidate that comes along rather than spending the expense and time to advertise, recruit, and find the most qualified candidate possible?[6] The question is again somewhat misleading. For the average position in a business that it calls to mind is probably one that requires only a fixed level of competence, beyond which it becomes meaningless to speak of more or better qualifications. For such positions a first-come-first-acquire basis for hiring those qualified is probably fairest anyway. Positions ought to be advertised, but where this is demanded, low-cost or free means of advertising ought to be afforded. Competence rights of specific individuals, on the other hand, obtain where positions call for open-ended degrees of excellence achievable through prior efforts, such as positions in professional schools or in the professions themselves. In these cases, failure to admit or appoint those who have become most qualified through their efforts is not justified on cost-reducing grounds, although again recruitment avenues ought to be provided by the public, since it insists upon enforcement of the rule. If for some reason recruitment is expensive and an institution is at the brink of financial disaster, it may be justified in reducing costs in this and other ways so as to be able to offer positions at all in the future. But this could be taken as an unusual exceptive clause to the rights of the most competent, and in any case the institution would have an obligation to admit or hire the most competent individuals it could afford to find. Again, this case does not show that utilities can legitimately override rights.

The above argument is nevertheless not meant to imply that justice ought never to be tempered by mercy or a sensitive concern for the feelings of others. Usually, when we encounter cases in which giving the upper hand to mercy is laudable, these are situations in which an individual deserves punishment from a retributive point of view, but in which a lightened sentence would seem to maximize future utility. Such cases are irrelevant here, since no one but a die-hard Hegelian would speak of a right to be punished being overridden. But there are rare occasions on which we might ignore a right of one person out of compassion or feeling for another, occasions in which this may not be just, but in which a sympathetic person would not blame us for doing so. A person may have a right against me that I ignore in order to perform a service for another who cannot claim it as his right but who wants or benefits from it (I exclude real needs, as these create rights). I might, for example, take my little boy to the ball game he has wanted to see all year when I ought to be in class, thereby violating the rights of my students to have me there, rights created when I signed my contract and they paid for my services. Such cases may be touching, but we must remember that they are exceptions, and necessarily so, or they would be built into the recognition of rights. They occur because the latter can state only general orderings, and the play of individual human interests and emotions is sometimes too complex to fit general schemes.

But in addition to recognizing that such occurrences are exceptions, we should be careful not to underestimate the interests and feelings of those who have the relevant rights. And in designing guidelines for social policy, the best we can do in any case is to order the relevant general principles. When policies are implemented for whole populations, such orderings must be followed, and justice must have absolute priority. This will result in a maximization of rights satisfaction, which at this level of generality ought by definition to take priority over mere utilities. (When here and elsewhere I speak of certain moral claims following from the definition of rights, this is not meant to impute a moral force to a definition in itself. Our recognition and definition of rights follows from the moral desirability of protecting certain interests against others, and this in turn is dependent upon the empirical distinctions regarding strengths or importance of certain interests as opposed to others. Reference to the definition makes clear that *if* we recognize rights, then we must accept certain priorities among moral claims.)

Having decided general priorities between rights and utilities, it remains to make explicit again which rights are relevant to the issue of reverse discrimination, and, very important here, to determine which of the above-mentioned utilities are connected with or germane to the generation of these rights. Those that are not connected can then be dismissed as at most secondary considerations. In achieving this clarity regarding the specific rights and utilities at issue, we might first consider what has been implied so far concerning the origins of rights in general, since certain utilities can be seen to enter at that more basic level in regard to certain rights (and specifically, the right of those most competent to positions). I have been presupposing, and it follows from a contractarian moral framework, that rights are generated from interests, or from interests of a certain type or order. From an alternative framework we might recognize a person's right to have or do something in virtue of the nature of the person or of the object or action itself. But regarding the latter alternatives, if no one were interested in having these objects or doing these actions, the recognition of rights to them would remain irrelevant to the human condition. (The former alternative will be further discussed below.)

From a contractarian viewpoint, most rights are recognized because it is in the interest of all to protect certain interests against others, either because of their intrinsic importance or because of the stability of expectations guaranteed through their recognition. Other rights are more basic, their recognition being presupposed in the applicability of a contractarian framework itself as a reconstruction of moral consciousness, in the adoption of any moral point of view, or in the recognition of any other rights. The most fundamental of these is the right to have one's interests considered on the same scale as the interests of others. I have argued before the Kantian claim that the adoption of a moral point of view demands recognition of the moral equality of others. This means that if any moral rights are to be recognized, the right to have one's interest considered equally must be granted universally.[7] That it is granted in the contractarian framework is reflected by the stipulation that all must agree to the recognition of any rights. In the context of original contracts, no one would accept an obligation to respect the right of another unless he were granted the same protection himself and unless he had an interest in being so protected. Having moral obligations is thus a sufficient condition for having rights. Certain other rights will follow directly from this most fundamental one, thus being themselves more basic than specific rights, which require separate agreements. With regard to our topic, one right that is implied by the right to have one's interests considered equally is the right to an equal opportunity to satisfy those interests. To have one's interests considered or recognized is in part to have one's right to try to satisfy them recognized as well. It also follows from this most fundamental right that others will be recognized only if they are generated from interests that are in some sense shared, not from those that arise from special and exclusive positions.

One potential problem for a contractarian framework as a reconstruction of recognized rights, and hence as a guide for deciding which problematic rights or priorities among them ought to be recognized, is that it seems from this point of view that rights can be possessed *only* by those capable of also bearing obligations. For the hypothetical contractor, the purpose of granting rights to others is that they accept the correlative obligations toward him. And yet we do and seemingly should recognize rights of those who cannot accept or meet obligations. We allow dependents into the moral community—for example, children, the mentally impaired, and perhaps even animals. Does this nullify the contractarian framework as a guide to ordering rights and utilities in relation to our issues? Rights for children are actually quite easy to explain within this framework, since parents take an interest in their children or identify with their interests, and hence want them protected—against cruel treatment from others, for example. As long as certain full-fledged parties to the contracts have important interests in dependents, granting rights to the latter can be explained. In the case of the mentally impaired, contractors might wish to guarantee maintenance of rights should they be unfortunate enough to be in that state in the future. While these rights are recognized mainly out of benevolence (we need not impute an artificial, narrowly egoistic psychology to the contractors), once they are granted, their satisfaction can be demanded rather than begged for, although it can usually be demanded only by proxies for the dependents. What cannot be asked from a contractarian viewpoint is whether dependents ought to have rights recognized independently of the interests that others have in them, or independently of feelings of sympathy and identification. But from this viewpoint it is impossible to answer any questions about what ought to be the case apart from the interests that humans in fact have and share.

We may now proceed from this abstract defense of the contractarian framework, with its implication that rights are generated from interests, to see how the specific rights and utilities involved in reverse discrimination are to be ordered from the contractarian viewpoint. I have indicated at various places throughout this study how the relevant rights originate and how they are to be ordered in relation to one another. A brief review may be helpful before we consider their relations to utilities and disutilities. The right to equal opportunity was claimed to follow from the most fundamental right to have one's interests considered equally with those of others. The rule for hiring the most competent was justified as part of a right to equal opportunity to succeed through socially productive effort, and on grounds of increased welfare for all members of society. Since it is justified in relation to a right to equal opportunity, and since application of the rule may simply compound injustices when opportunities are unequal elsewhere in the system, the creation of more equal opportunities takes precedence when in conflict with this rule for awarding positions. Thus short-run violations of the rule are justified to create a more just distribution of benefits by applying the rule itself in future years.

The rights of victims of injustice to compensation was said to follow from the adoption of any distributive rules creating any other rights. To create or recognize a right in relation to the satisfaction of some distributive rule without at the same time recognizing rights of compensation for those denied the original right is to imply that the latter can be freely canceled in being violated, which is inconsistent. The right to compensation by reverse discrimination was also said to take precedence in application over rights of those most competent, in order to keep distributions of benefits approximating over time to those that are just according to the stipulation of the distributive rule itself. Since the right to compensation arises directly from this logical connection with all other rights, it is not dependent for its recognition upon any specific utilities or upon those mentioned in connection with reverse discrimination. We therefore need not consider further the possible connection of the latter with at least this right, being confident of its priority.

The main complication here occurs in relation to the rights of those most competent to positions for which they apply, since these rights are themselves recognized partially out of concern for certain utilities. In one sense it can be claimed that existence or rights in general to jobs is independent of the specific rule for hiring adopted. It can be first agreed by original contractors to establish such rights in relation to the satisfaction of *some* social rule in order to create stability in expectations for these important social goods. But the specific rule for rewarding competence is adopted because it tends to result in more and better goods and services for all, that is, in the name of universal utility. Since competence is defined in terms of the ability to satisfy social demand in the performance of one's job and is thus relative to the utilities attached to its performance, the problem becomes one of limiting in advance those utilities that can be legitimately incorporated into the stipulation of competence qualifications. While rights are designed to override utilities, the distinction vanishes in relation to a particular right if all utility considerations are allowed to decide its application. If any purpose that can be filled by granting a position to a particular individual can be incorporated into consideration of his qualifications for the position, talk of rights becomes indistinguishable from talk of utilities, and, according to my account, it is no longer meaningful to speak of rights at all in this context. And if we cannot speak of a right of one most competent to a position, as opposed to all the utilities and disutilities that might be involved in awarding the position, we can no longer speak clearly of discrimination or reverse discrimination either. For we will have to consider the (biased) feelings of those doing the hiring as well as of others involved in estimating the total utilities. The protection of equal opportunity and the stability in expectations that the recognition of rights in this area is meant to ensure will disintegrate.

Is there then any nonarbitrary way to limit utilities to which the rights of the most competent are relative? Which of the utilities mentioned in the previous section can be incorporated into the concept of social demand? I dealt with these questions briefly in the earlier section on qualifications. There I relied heavily upon the reversal test to indicate our intuitive reaction against building in utilities that call for consideration of race or sex as competence qualifications. For example, if we accept that minority clients feel more comfortable with lawyers of their own race, or students with teachers of their own sex, as justification for hiring blacks and women, are we also prepared to accept the biased feelings of white males as reason for allowing only white males to defend or teach them? Are we prepared to accept similar biases on the part of members of all other groups? Distribution of jobs on a strict group percentage basis is the logical outcome of counting such feelings and their satisfaction.

Having expanded upon the nature of rights and their generation, I can now explain why the reversal test brings out this intuitive aversion to consideration of race or sex as competence qualifications, even though competence is defined in relation to certain utilities and some people may derive utility or disutility from having others of a given race or sex in certain positions. We can also see more clearly why the reversal test is applicable or fitting as a test of the justice or injustice of a proposed policy. Subjecting judgments to switches of roles among individuals involved points out that, to be just or moral, we must honor the fundamental right of all to have their interests considered equally. We must not allow interests that arise or relate to particular exclusive positions or nonuniversal inborn traits to enter prominently into the recognition of differential rights, since this amounts to relegating the interests of some to a secondary status. Parties to an original contract would not agree to such reduced status, even occasional reduced status, to accommodate the feelings of others, and therefore they would not accept obligations to respect the differential rights of others so stipulated. Nor would it be prudent in the long run for some individuals to deny equal rights to others on the basis of inborn traits, since that would imply that the latter class of individuals has no obligations to respect the rights of the former. It is prudent to include as many bearers of obligations in the original contract as possible, in order to avoid future harm and conflict.

It is true that if *all* hiring were done on a strict group percentage basis, this would not relegate members of any specific group per se to a secondary status; but such a rule would be rejected by contractors because of the universal disutilities involved (and for other reasons to be explained in the next section). Thus all those utilities that, if built into considerations of competence, would call for recognition of race or sex as qualifications, and would therefore be germane in generating rights of particular individuals to positions, must remain in fact unrelated to competence rights and hence be overridden by them. While the need for Spanish-speaking or ghetto-serving professionals, for example, may be construed as a normal part of social demand, utilities consequent upon hiring or admitting by race or sex must be discounted. Examples would be utilities gained from mixed classrooms in higher levels of education (at lower levels they may be necessary to ensure equal opportunity) or those presumed to follow from having teachers of a certain race or sex. Fortunately, the utilities claimed, even if correctly assessed, are generally temporary and founded upon biases and misperceptions, rather than being those universal and long-range utilities connected with rewarding genuine dimensions of competence for providing goods and services.

All members of society possess a fundamental right to have their interests considered equally in the generation of other rights and an immunity from losing this status in order to satisfy the interests of certain other people. This does not imply, however, that rights, even whole classes of them, cannot be forfeited or alienated. Punishment typically, perhaps always, consists in a denial or withdrawal of rights normally enjoyed—for example, the right to move about freely in society. If punishment is ever justified, so is such wholesale withdrawal of rights (some may be inalienable, however, such as the right not to be tortured). What is implied by this fundamental right is only that such forfeiture be the consequence of some *act(s)* of the individual in question, not a function of his inborn characteristics. Conversely, when we make certain rights, such as those of most competent individuals to positions, conditional upon the satisfaction of particular social rules, we ought, within the limits set by universal utility, to make such satisfaction a function of prior actions or efforts. Eliminating completely the advantages of intelligence (to the extent that it is inborn) falls outside those limits; that is, sacrifices in utility to all involved would be too great for contractors to attempt such leveling. But not so with race or sex. What we require are criteria conducive to long-range and universal utility, toward the satisfaction of which individuals can consistently and securely aim their efforts (no one is to gain a benefit from intelligence alone, as opposed to achievement). Such criteria will rule out utilities of the type indicated above as irrelevant to the award of positions and inconsistent with maximization of rights satisfaction.

Thus, the rights of those most competent to positions continue to override certain utilities claimed for reverse discrimination. Furthermore, these utilities, which call for admitting or hiring of minority-group members or women per se, are not to be construed as generating competence qualifications themselves. I admitted above that the rights in question apply most obviously to positions requiring open-ended degrees of excellence. In the case of jobs requiring only a fixed level of competence, persons with equal qualifications are more likely to apply for the same job. We might imagine that where such ties occur, that is, where individuals therefore have equal rights to the position in question, or no rights in relation to one another, we can justifiably allow utilities to enter as tie-breaking considerations. In general, it certainly seems that when consideration of rights does not settle a moral decision, we ought to proceed to consider utilities. The problem with that precept here is that when individuals have equal rights through competence to a position, they may also have rights to equal chances at that position or to some random process like first-apply-first-acquire for deciding the recipient. This would be the case where utilities, if considered, would consistently work in favor of certain individuals and against others, as they would when related to race or sex. A person who is denied a single position for reasons of utility, when as qualified as the person to whom it is given, perhaps has little complaint that the process of selection was not random. But if we imagine his applying for ten positions for which he is qualified, all of which are decided against him on grounds of the same utilities, such as utilities linked to considerations of race, he will clearly lose out in comparison with use of a random process.[8] If an equal right to each position implies an equal chance to acquire one, he can complain of injustice if denied position after position on grounds of utility. Thus utilities that are linked to preference for race or sex must be discounted in the face of rights of those most competent to positions, and we might well be required to ignore such interests in cases of applicants with equal qualifications.

One final complication regarding rights and the above-mentioned utilities relates not to the rights of those most competent but to the concept of equality of opportunity. Some of the arguments phrased in terms of utility could perhaps be worded more strongly in terms of necessary conditions for honoring the right to equal opportunity or for creating greater equality of opportunity in the future. This translation certainly seems possible for the argument concerning the integration of the racially imbalanced chronic poor into the mainstream of the economic life of the nation. The reduction of poverty or extreme chronic differences in wealth and living conditions, advocated in the name of social harmony, is called for with equal or greater moral force out of concern for equal opportunity, especially for children in such conditions. Is the availability of role models or of professionals of a certain race or sex also to be construed as a necessary ingredient in equal opportunity? Might not the lessening of racial tensions and biases or the increased social harmony envisaged as a utility result in fewer violations of rights in the future, and the means to it be justified on those grounds?

Equality of Opportunity

In this section we must choose among rival possible principles of equal opportunity, for the concept of equality of opportunity has been variously interpreted at different times by different people, all of whom endorse one version or another.[9] In its most conservative form it can excuse great inequalities in the status quo distribution of goods, while at the other end of the scale it is radically egalitarian, a call for perfectly equal chances at goods or advantages. Such widespread endorsement, as in other cases involving broad, emotively loaded social concepts, indicates little more than radical ambiguity in the concept involved. I shall first try to distinguish different senses or dimensions of the concept of equal opportunity from political right to left, and then make more precise the particular concept or principle from which we can derive further inferences regarding justified reverse discrimination.

The Principle of Equal Opportunity

Equality of opportunity becomes an important social concept when inequalities in the distributions of benefits are held to be

EQUAL OPPORTUNITY AND THE FUTURE

justifiable. If shares are to be unequal, opportunities for attaining them ought not to be limited or fixed arbitrarily. At worst, equal opportunity is appealed to in order to excuse otherwise unjustified inequalities in distributions: the myth of free and equal competition becomes an apology for the results of Social Darwinism. Given that the inequalities are not only large but also handed down intact from one generation to the next, belief that the survivors in such unregulated systems are the fittest is obviously false (even if such an outcome were moral). We may then accept that application of the concept cannot in itself legitimize otherwise unjustified inequalities in benefits. The criterion for its own legitimate use is when these inequalities in distributions are justified on other grounds. When they are so acceptable, they will generally be more just if opportunities to acquire the fatter shares are not arbitrarily limited. Let us turn to the various senses in which opportunities can plausibly be considered open.

The first and minimal sense is that in which positions or other goods are to be allotted only according to performance or predicted performance along some socially useful (nonarbitrary) scale. This means that they are not to be allotted according to race, sex, national origin, or social position or background. Jobs, for example, are to be formally open to all strictly according to competence qualifications. Enforcement of such provisions can be seen to be morally insufficient, however, unless all people are given equal chances to acquire such qualifications or develop their potential abilities. We therefore move to a second sense of equality of opportunity, according to which individuals should be afforded the means of fulfilling their natural capacities. The social system assumes responsibility for overcoming initial disadvantages that have social causes—for example, disadvantages owing to low income or social class of one's parents. Individuals from all economic and social classes should be able to achieve those skills they are naturally suited for achieving. Thus, with respect to the award of jobs or socially desirable positions, the concept of equality of opportunity, in its first sense, requires only that irrelevent inborn traits and initial social positions be ignored; in its second sense, it demands correction for socially relative disadvantages.

Historically, the first step toward the realization of equal opportunity in this latter sense was the provision of free public schooling with a common curriculum for students of different backgrounds. Combined with nondiscrimination at the hiring level, the common curriculum and testing procedures would render initial social positions irrelevant as the educational system came to serve the educationally superfluous but socially useful function of sorting people for later careers. One problem with this (aside from overt discrimination against members of certain groups in the educational system itself and in hiring) was the continued ability of upper-class parents to buy superior private educations for their children at all levels. Prestigious universities, whose degrees were tickets to desirable jobs, not only were prohibitively expensive but also showed consistent preference for applicants from exclusive private secondary schools. In recent years mobility among high schools, colleges, and universities has increased. But a second, more subtle and difficult problem with the availability of education as the sole means of achieving equality of opportunity for children of different backgrounds was the burden this placed upon the students to avail themselves of it. Opportunities were there but had to be seized and pursued through long years of study. Children without the motivation and support at home quickly dropped out or remained at the bottom of the social ladder.

The realization that motivation itself is predominantly a function of social and economic class seemed to require more active efforts by the educational system if it was to achieve correction for socially induced initial disadvantages. The connection between motivation and social or family environment is not difficult to explain, although it was long in being recognized or admitted. Motivations are influenced by expectations about the future, and these in turn are governed by what children see on the streets and in their homes. A child is motivated to achieve what he has hopes of achieving, and his hopes are formed in relation to the achievements of those close to him. There are also more direct educational influences of enriched as opposed to deprived intellectual home environments—books, conversations, explanations, etc.—all of which are functions of the degree of education of the parents. Finally, for older children there is often the burden of having to help with family support by taking menial after-school jobs that cut into time and energy for school work. For these direct and more subtle reasons it became obvious that the schools had to attempt more active correction for initial socially relative disadvantages if they were to equalize unequal opportunities. Resources had to be directed disproportionately and selectively to schools in areas where most children come from deprived home environments.

But even where this shift in emphasis from passive provision of facilities to selective, active attempts to motivate and train through special programs has occurred, it seems to have failed to correct for disadvantages. Recent studies indicate that socially induced inequalities in opportunities cannot be corrected in school alone.[10] It was found that differentials in school resources have little effect upon the cognitive achievements of their pupils. In addition, the quality of education (especially at the lower and middle levels), as opposed to the length of time one stays in school, seems to remain unrelated to the type of job one ends up with, while the length of time a child stays in school, as well as the degree of cognitive achievement, seem directly related to home environment or family social background.

The indications, backed by statistical studies, that the educational system in itself cannot create equal opportunity in the second sense, even when it actively attempts to do so, has obvious implications for additional justification of reverse discrimination. In the last chapter I discussed compensatory policies for discrimination in school or for inferior education, arguing that remediation by the school system is the fairest means of providing such compensation. The problem here, however, is the opposite and looks to the future rather than to the past. Not only are nondiscrimination and equal facilities insufficient to ensure equal opportunity for the socially and economically deprived, but even weighing educational resources in their favor fails to overcome or appreciably affect their disadvantages. In addition to the statistical studies, it has been apparent to many teachers for some time that the educational system fails even when seemingly fairest (I speak here from the personal experience of my wife in the New York City school system). For those who mold the environment for such children, reverse discrimination seems a first step toward breaking the circle of deprivation by beginning to improve their home conditions.

Before spelling out in more detail the implications for our topic of the attempts to achieve equal opportunity in the second sense of the concept, we should indicate a third sense and specify and locate our principle more precisely on the complete map of the various concepts. Resuming the logical progression to the left, the obvious next step is to attempt to correct not only for initial social disadvantages but also for natural disabilities. While at the second level the principle of equal opportunity calls for affording equal means to all for developing their natural potentials for socially productive functions, we may exceed this demand by attempting to correct for natural differences in potential, thereby creating really equal chances for goods. The rationale for moving to this yet more egalitarian version, as briefly indicated in the second chapter, is that individuals no more deserve their natural than their social advantages: both types are equally arbitrary from a moral point of view. But the attempt to correct for all natural as well as social initial disadvantages reduces to a demand for completely equal chances at positions and other benefits. If we count all differences in final achievements or distributions as attributable to differences in motivation or natural talent, and all these as deserving elimination, we arrive at the ultimate call for fully equal opportunities. Probably the simplest way to achieve this, if we are not to redistribute arms, legs, and parts of brains or keep gifted children locked at home or out of school, is through fair lotteries for jobs, an alternative argued against at length in the second chapter.

Employing the claims made in Chapter Two, as well as our account of the derivation of rights in the previous section, we may proceed to choose from the point of view of hypothetical contractors a principle of equal opportunity to govern recognition of this right. First, we might review again the reasons for having such a principle at all. While inequalities in distribu-

tive shares render the question of equal opportunity important, we must look deeper for the value of equality in itself.
The central claim here was that part of what we mean by the
assumption of a moral point of view is that one recognize the
moral equality of others. Although the adoption of a moral
point of view can show us what we ought to do, there may be
no answer from a prudential or self-interested viewpoint as to
why one ought to assume a moral stance at all. Here, for once,
it is proper to stop at a definition, being satisfied to find out
what being moral involves.

The granting of an equal status to others is part of what it
means to be moral, but how is this to be spelled out in more
concrete terms? One way is to attempt to live by rules that
could be willed by all or adopted by contractors in an initial
position of equality. One implication of this framework is the
recognition of a basic right of all to have their interests considered equally in the recognition of all other rights. Given a presumption of wants or interests of roughly equal intensity, at
least in regard to basic material goods, this right generates a
presumption or priority of an equal distribution of goods. The
logical priority of equality follows directly from first moral
principles, in fact from the definition of what it means to be
moral (combined with some very general facts about the
human condition). Deviations from equality must be justified,
since it is the morally preferred distribution ceteris paribus.
Where deviations can be justified within a contractarian
framework—for example, for reasons of universal utility (when
resultant distributions provide more goods for all)—we retreat
to slightly weaker demands for equality. What remains is, first
of all, a right of all persons simply by virtue of their humanity
to have basic needs fulfilled (the list of basic needs being
somewhat relative to the affluence of the society in question,
although we can also admit rights that in circumstances, such
as that of extreme scarcity, cannot be met). What remains as
well is the principle of equality of opportunity for acquiring
the unequal shares or final distributive benefits.

How far does the right to equal opportunity extend? Is it
sufficient for society to require only that positions be open to
competents; must we in addition attempt to correct for socially

induced initial disadvantages; and if so, do we compensate natural inequalities as well? The proper principle, the one that would be chosen by rational and equal contractors (contractors who grant equality to others), I believe is the following: (1) *Consistent with limits set by universal utility, we should refuse to allot goods, advantages, resources or positions on the basis of inborn traits*; and (2) *we should attempt to correct for socially relative initial disadvantages*. Again, the radical egalitarian will find our principle too weak because of its refusal to allot resources so as to attack natural as well as socially induced disadvantages, while the libertarian will probably refuse to enforce the first clause, although he might find it morally acceptable as a rule of thumb, and will find the second in violation of other rights and liberties. We may briefly answer each in turn, keeping in mind earlier arguments.

I have already countered the libertarian's reasons for refusing to enforce rules (for hiring) protecting equal opportunity as stated in the first clause, and I shall not repeat those arguments here. We might imagine certain counterexamples to the first clause, however, in which there seems to be a right to award positions on the basis of race or sex—acting roles, for example. We might simply admit such cases and still maintain the general principle; or we could plausibly argue that even in these cases, race or sex should not be considered qualifications in themselves. Regarding acting roles, the sole criterion for awarding positions should be ability to personify the character in question, although it is a very reliable rule of thumb that actors will be more convincing when playing characters of their own race or sex (the "Africans" in Jungle Jim movies and Judith Anderson's Hamlet being no exceptions).

The libertarian has additional reasons for rejecting the second clause. He would claim that a child who begins with social and monetary advantages is entitled to them, even if he cannot be said to deserve them in terms of any actions for which he can claim responsibility.[11] The reasoning is as follows. The parents of such children are entitled to what they have legitimately earned and hence to spend or give their earnings to others, including their children, as they please. If parents are free to give or buy goods for their children, the latter must be entitled to receive them and derive the advantages. The right to give money to another amounts to no right at all if the money is confiscated or its advantages annulled as soon as it is given. Hence it is a denial of the rights or recognized liberties of parents to attempt to remove the advantages that they have worked to acquire for their children. To refuse to allow parents to purchase relative benefits for their children is to reduce substantially the value of what they have earned by unfairly restricting the goods for which it can be exchanged.

My earlier arguments on the rights of corporations to disburse jobs have parallels here in reply to these reasons against correcting for socially relative initial inequalities. First, rights to buy various things are already limited by exceptive clauses for protection of more important rights of others. I cannot freely buy dangerous explosives, for example. Similarly, the right to give things to others is limited by their rights to receive them: I cannot give a gun to an occupant of the local jail. The question here is whether children have the right to receive from their parents uncompensated advantages, which give them important headstarts toward desirable positions, or whether their doing so violates the rights of other children to equal opportunity. The priority of equality in distributions and of equal opportunity when inequalities are justified has been established as basic to a moral social system. I am not advocating taking from parents the right to buy their children goods that make their lives more comfortable and enjoyable. The principle calls only for allocating a certain portion of funds from taxes or directing certain public resources for public goods differentially toward the elimination of disadvantages in competing for future positions. This much seems a minimal embodiment of the moral value of equality in a system of distributions.

The ethical priority of equality was derived above from first principles of morality, from the definition of a moral point of view. It can also be defended in terms of its connection with other values, such as liberty and fraternity. While total equality in all goods is inimical to diversity and liberty, extreme inequalities in opportunities encroach upon the realization of the latter value in society as well. Those who start with nothing but disadvantages will most likely never enjoy the most fundamental and important liberty of formulating long-range plans and pursuing what is to them valuable. Poverty and social deprivation are enslaving in a not very metaphorical sense of that term. Thus, from this direction as well, the libertarian seems misguided or inconsistent in refusing to recognize a right to equal opportunity as stipulated in our principle. We will maximize liberty as well as equality and fraternity in the long run by adopting policies designed to eliminate large initial inequalities for children that result from the unequal social and economic positions of their parents.

Once again, the arguments of the more radical egalitarian are, if anything, more difficult to handle than those of our opponents to the right. The thoroughgoing egalitarian will demand justification for attacking only socially induced initial inequalities and not natural differences, both of which appear to him equally arbitrary from a moral point of view.[12] To him the prohibition against making inborn traits the basis of rewards, especially with its initial rider, appears too weak and, in fact, inconsistent with the elimination of social inequalities in the second clause. He will maintain that if we attack only initial social differences, we will in fact be making inborn traits the basis of future social rewards, since the attainment of competence in many fields is relative to the possession of such native characteristics as intelligence, physical coordination, talents, etc. Thus the first clause of our principle is held to be contradicted in practice by the implication of the second. Is there any sound moral reason for drawing the line as I do in the principle, or is the choice simply arbitrary or, worse, inconsistent?

Part of the reason for refusing to attack certain natural differences that give individuals advantages in pursuing certain positions is universal utility: everyone will benefit in the long run if people are encouraged to develop their socially productive potentials to the fullest. Of course the award of positions is not to be on the basis of a purely inborn trait like native intelligence but on the basis of actual competence, which will have resulted as well from socially productive effort. (While elimination of all advantages gained from intelligence would be a

universal disutility, the award of positions on grounds of race
or sex could never be universally beneficial, although it might
be preferable on grounds of overall utility in certain conditions.) It is hard to see how original contractors can resist
genuine appeal to universal utility to justify choices of principles, since each will be maximizing his own self-interest by
opting for such rules (I ignore envy here, for reasons to be explained in the next paragraph). On the other hand, this cannot
be the complete answer, for we do not allow the same appeal
in relation to our second clause. At least we must be careful
there of appeals to utility in too narrow a sense. Even if society
as a whole would advance, say materially or culturally, from a
social caste system, I do not believe that such a system would
be just or chosen by originally equal contractors.

Part of the reason for the difference here has to do with the
value of self-respect.[13] Individuals are not in general so naturally different that some do not have potential for competence
or at least above-average grades in some respect (if not for desirable job-related talents, then for personal characteristics
like geniality, generosity, etc.). Self-respect can be attained
through the satisfaction of having realized some such potentials. But when social deprivation is allowed to stand, the minimal necessary conditions for full development of natural potentials and the self-respect that goes with it may be lacking.
Lives will be wasted. Thus it is difficult to see how universal
utility could in fact be served by refusal to enforce the second
clause, once we count as an important part of utility the value
of self-respect. (The attainment of this abstract but important
good may be socially relative, in that members of lower castes
may have achieved some degree of self-respect in other, earlier societies. But at the present stage of social development,
this undoubtedly would be impossible were a new caste system imposed.)

A further reason for drawing the line where I do concerns
the ways in which social as opposed to natural inequalities can
be attacked. I have already argued that the attack on social
disadvantages is demanded by the moral priority of equality
implied in the assumption of a moral point of view; when the
right to equal opportunity is construed in this way, it cannot

plausibly be held to be overridden by other rights. Any real attempt to even out natural potentials, on the other hand, does come into conflict with other more important rights, which morally prevent its accomplishment. Literal redistribution of natural assets or attempts at natural equality through genetic tinkering are prohibited by the right of each person over his own body, a right that might well be the most fundamental of all. Other, less ambitious egalitarian schemes, such as job lotteries, were argued against at length in the second chapter because they conflict with such rights as that of the public to safe and reliable goods and services, and, more important, that of individuals to pursue what they consider to be worthwhile through their own socially productive efforts. While equal opportunity in the sense that I construe it is a necessary condition for maximizing liberty, at its extreme it comes into conflict with this important class of liberties. It was also pointed out in the earlier chapter that artificial lotteries are as arbitrary a means of dividing differential awards of goods as is the natural lottery.

The means of attacking natural inequalities that is most relevant to our immediate discussion is the differential direction of social resources and programs in favor of those less fortunately endowed. Again, this brings us first of all to the matter of (universal) utility. Since different positions require different capacities, and since those positions involving greatest social responsibility require outstanding characteristics, everyone may lose in the long run by not encouraging the development of outstanding individuals. Second, I believe that the rights of each person over his own body and to have his interests considered equally in the choice of policies for allocating goods can be construed as prohibiting the unfair neglect of those better endowed—gifted children for example. It seems that the equal consideration of interests calls for allocating resources for public goods such as education so as to make an equal contribution toward the satisfaction of interests or development of potentials of all individuals.

It could be argued in reply that gifted or naturally fortunate individuals will in all likelihood acquire social rewards later on and therefore can be justifiably neglected at lower levels. But their rewards will be for their socially productive efforts and will not be allocations from public resources of public goods presumably for the benefit of all. It is public resources that should make equal contributions to the satisfaction of different individuals' interests. The boredom and frustration caused by the school system's neglect of the psychological needs of gifted children is unfair in itself, whatever awaits them in the future from the exchange market, assuming that education has intrinsic value and is not simply a training ground. If we think of the entire system of social redistribution, I can find no apparent reason why those naturally less well endowed have rights to contributions from those more intelligent, stronger, etc. (I am speaking here only of individuals within the range of normality, who would be parties to the original contract.) To consider the natural assets of the latter individuals simply as social assets appears to violate their rights over their own bodies (including their brains). When the social system itself creates initial inequalities, on the other hand, it must assume some responsibility to correct for the relative lack of opportunities that results for some individuals.

We might readily think of apparent counterexamples to these arguments. Is it really unfair to fund special programs for the blind, deaf, or otherwise physically or mentally handicapped? If such programs are fair or permissible from the point of view of justice, this would seem to contradict the claim that we cannot attempt to correct for natural inequalities. While we could argue that these are cases in which mercy overrides justice, I do not believe that such an answer is necessitated by my position. Such persons have the status of dependents in the moral community, and our rules are designed in the first place to apply to those who are roughly equal parties to the original contract. We can, as argued earlier, nevertheless recognize rights to special treatment in their behalf, satisfaction of which can then be demanded as just. These rights are recognized partly out of benevolence, partly out of the realization that we would want special treatment if we were in that condition, and partly because the concept of contributing equally to the satisfaction of interests calls for greater-than-average efforts and resources in their case.

Whereas physically and mentally normal people can attain self-respect through the development of some potential with an equal or average contribution from society (once social inequalities have been corrected), these individuals require more help to achieve even a minimal satisfaction of interests or needs. There is also the consideration mentioned earlier that all individuals have rights to the fulfillment of basic needs, and for the handicapped, special programs may be necessary to accomplish even that much.

Although it is an extremely important issue for social philosophy, we need not debate the question of natural inequalities any further here, since the attack upon socially induced initial inequalities affords justification for reverse discrimination for individuals other than those owed compensation, and few would argue for the policy as a means of correcting natural inequalities. As a final qualification to this distinction, however, we must recognize that many differences that appear to be inborn may in fact be socially induced. While the distinction is conceptually clear enough, the recent furor over IQ tests indicates that we may have no reliable means in practice of drawing the line between inequalities that are socially relative and those that are not. It is not a question of inborn differences being those that cannot be changed appreciably. All differences, or at least the practical measurable effects of all differences, can be altered, if not through manipulation of genes, then, say, through simply neglecting naturally intelligent children. In the absence of any other reliable tests for precisely recognizing the distinction, we may in practice have to attack both kinds of inequality to some degree. Especially when we encounter differences in motivation among individuals of different social classes, when the upper- or middle-class child is more highly motivated, we must give the underdog the benefit of the doubt and assume that the difference is socially caused. Where we find children of apparently similar social backgrounds differently motivated, on the other hand, we can justifiably give them only equal attention. We cannot reasonably expect or demand all to make the same effort in school, if for no other reason than that to some individuals it may not appear worthwhile in terms of their ultimate goals.

As stated, our principle is designed to give individuals equal chances at goods through their socially productive efforts. While the emphasis on competence in awarding jobs gives social productivity priority over effort, the two clauses taken together ensure that the satisfaction of competence requirements is as much under the individual's own control as is consistent with the demands of universal utility. The principle chosen, motivated by this individualist-oriented aim, is very different from the alternative view of equal opportunity that calls for proportionate representation of each major social or ethnic group within the desirable job categories. [14] One might think that in practice this principle would work out to be similar to the one I have advocated, and that the satisfaction of the former might be a measure of the satisfaction of the latter. The idea behind this equation would be the claim that once socially relative disadvantages were eliminated, major statistical differences among groups would disappear. This might be true of major across-the-board differences, but, as a social goal in itself, exact proportionate representation not only lacks positive rationale, but would also involve serious injustices to individuals if it were enforced. We should not expect the division of the population into even randomly formed groups to result in statistical congruence within different job categories, especially if the groups are divided along cultural lines that incline their members toward different preferences. Given differences among groups that do not result from social injustice, proportioning jobs by innate characteristics or group membership would limit the opportunities of individuals to achieve positions through effort and accomplishment. First, how hard one would have to work and what level of qualification he would have to achieve in order to obtain a particular position would depend upon the group in which he were a member. Second, once the group quota were filled for a particular type of position, even if by older members of his group with whom he had no opportunity of competing, he would be barred from any competition for those positions. Thus the principle of group proportionment narrows opportunities and renders them unequal among individuals, rather than equalizing them. (This is not to say that present vast differences between races and sexes in various types of positions is not the result of social injustice and itself evidence of this injustice.)

While our goal is to give each individual an equal chance to develop qualifications and achieve positions, an all-out attack upon natural differences is prohibited by both utility and the honoring of rights. There are also limits to the degree to which we can justifiably eliminate socially induced inequalities of opportunity. The most prominent among these is respect for the family as a viable social unit. Socially relative early differences cannot be totally eliminated without breaking up families by removing children from their parents and giving them common upbringings. Although achievement of socially equal opportunities would not require total equality of parental income, it would require removal of children from parents even if incomes were substantially equalized, since the influence of parents is pervasive and relative to their social and educational backgrounds as well. I presume that we are not willing to destroy the family and that there are sound psychological reasons for avoiding this drastic step. Equal opportunity is central to a moral social system and related to other values within it, but it must be balanced against other values as well and limited by them.

On the other hand, the closeness of families also means that we can positively affect the opportunities of children by improving the positions of their parents and others around them. We cannot forcibly remove their children from them, but we can offer them decent jobs that they can voluntarily accept. Reverse discrimination appears to be a first step, in addition to efforts within the schools to break the progression of generations of chronically poor and socially deprived, which is often linked to racial injustice. It cannot be a quick solution, since the middle class perpetuates itself by handing down attitudes as well as money, and these may take longer to acquire. Furthermore, many deprived home environments in ghetto communities result from broken families, in which employment of the mothers would leave children with even less adult supervision than at present. Nevertheless, improving employment opportunities greatly for all members of such communities might alter their general atmosphere, making less inevitable the prospect of a life of crime, drugs, and violence for children in these communities. The lack of just means to equalize all opportunities immediately should not prevent the necessary first steps from being taken. Clearly, the preferential provision of decent jobs to those from deprived social backgrounds is one step toward eliminating the great social disadvantages acquired at birth in these environments.

In reaction to the recognized perpetuation of middle-class attitudes and to the fact that length of time spent in school seems to be a function of these socially relative attitudes, another suggested step is to end reliance on quality or quantity of schooling as a measure of credentials for desirable positions. In support of this position it has been maintained that liberal arts subjects bear little relation to later tasks performed on the job—in business, for example. This may be true, but I believe we should be wary of discarding the ideal of the liberal arts education—even though it was perhaps exaggerated in the last generation—in part because we have not devised any more reliable tests for success at these positions. While skills learned in school may be unrelated in themselves to those required for most jobs, the sense of discipline and achievement acquired in many years of school may be as relevant as anything else. More important is the brief chance that a liberal arts education affords individuals to enrich their future lives by adding other dimensions of appreciation to later technologically oriented tasks. Future technological development points to further shifts from productive to service-oriented fields like education, and we should not underestimate the service rendered. For all these reasons, then, while we should perhaps not push all students in the direction of liberal arts, neither should we penalize those who pursue education for not having technical skills acquired as easily on the job or in later training programs.

To return to more acceptable ways of equalizing opportunities, as argued above, the fact that we cannot hope in the near future to see the average achievements or final positions of individuals from lower-class backgrounds equal that of those with greater social advantages should not prevent us from taking the first steps through reverse discrimination toward equalizing opportunities as demanded by justice. Such equalization should begin to be reflected in these averages. In speaking of averages of final positions, we come to a distinction drawn earlier here and in the second chapter, one that should be recalled and sharpened in ending this subsection on social theory. The distinction is that between actual patterns of distributions on the one hand, and opportunities for acquiring goods on the other. Within the former category, we may further distinguish between actual distributions of wealth at a given time and distributions of jobs with their differential pay scales. Corresponding to this now threefold distinction are three different ways to attack inequality in our society, three areas on which the social reforming egalitarian can focus his attention. He can attempt to move toward greater equality through direct redistribution of income, through equalization of pay scales for different jobs, or through creation of more uniform opportunities for acquiring the larger shares or rewards. These goals should be kept conceptually distinct. The first method, while the fastest way of meeting immediate needs, is inefficient as a long-range policy because of the vast intermediary bureaucracy required. Welfare programs financed with money from general taxes are notoriously inefficient and corrupt. The third method, the one being discussed in this section, is not really a move toward equality at all in the usual sense (except possibly regarding group averages), but a means of making inequalities somewhat fairer.

While these means of equalization should be kept conceptually distinct in designing social policy, it is also important to recognize the relationships among them. We saw above that the issue of equal opportunity becomes more pressing the greater the inequalities in distributions allowed. The converse is also clear: if pay scales were substantially more equal, inequalities in opportunities would be less unfair (they would also tend to diminish with class distinctions). Some inequalities in rewards for different positions are necessary to create incentives, to direct personnel into those areas in which they are most needed, and to allocate capital to those best able to use it productively. But given that working at an intrinsically enjoyable job is also a strong incentive, it is obvious that our society has opted for much larger income differentials than are necessary for this purpose. Without doubt, different people would still be attracted to positions for which they are competent, even if pay scales were practically uniform. In fact, if we accept the "Peter Principle," current pay incentives simply attract people to rise beyond levels at which they are comfortable and competent. Long-range equalization of income differentials would render the equalization of educational opportunities important mainly in relation to the value of education itself, rather than as an absolute prerequisite for a just social system.

A final conceptual relation between patterns of distribution of jobs and wealth and the opportunities for acquiring differential shares concerns ways in which we can measure equality of opportunity. While differences in distributive shares among individuals are of course inevitable, given differences in types of jobs and their pay scales, marked statistical differences among groups—for example, blacks as opposed to whites or those from lower-class backgrounds in comparison with others—constitutes strong evidence that discrimination has occurred against some of their members, or at least that opportunities for them in the present are not equal. Barring genetic differences among groups, some discrepancies may still owe to statistical accident and some to freedom of choice, if there are alternatives to work available to group members, say, women, that could be considered equally as attractive. We must nevertheless take such statistical evidence seriously and at face value, since there is in fact no other way, short of detailed personal histories, to collect initial evidence on inequalities of opportunity. (This point will be reiterated when we come to evaluate sections of affirmative action programs.) Whenever a group is defined according to some characteristic that should be irrelevant to acquiring positions in relation to fair distributive rules, and yet we find a marked absence of members of the group in all desirable positions, even among those members who pursue them, we have strong evidence of either discrimination or at least unequal opportunity. In these cases there are grounds for looking into personal histories of representative members. Where suspicions of injustice are supported by such further investigation, corrective social policies are called for. These policies do not amount, however, to an attempt to proportion positions by race or sex alone, as we may now argue more specifically.

Groups or Individuals?

In the previous subsection I claimed that the attempt to create equality of opportunity justifies reverse discrimination for individuals in addition to those actually discriminated against in the past. We now may examine more closely this justification and the individuals to whom it applies. The central question again is whether this additional justification warrants preferential policies directed indiscriminately toward minority groups as a whole. And again, the answer is that it does not.

Before turning to the positive future-looking justification that is implied in the concept of equal opportunity presented in the previous subsection, we can answer some questions left over from the earlier section on rights and utilities regarding the right to equal opportunity. While I have denied that proportioning positions by group membership amounts in itself to equalizing opportunities, it still could be argued that in the present context and in the short run, proportionate representation of minority groups in various job categories must be seen as a necessary condition for equality of opportunity for their members. I dealt in the previous section with the egalitarian's claim that by correcting *only* for socially relative initial disadvantages, we violate the first clause of our principle and reward inborn traits; here it is claimed that in order to satisfy the second clause and remove social disadvantages, we must violate the first clause by awarding positions according to race or sex until reasonably proportionate representation is achieved. (It can be argued that being a member of a socially disadvantaged group *is* a socially relative rather than a native trait, although one acquires this trait at birth.[15] But from my point of view the crucial fact is that possession of this trait does not result from an individual's action or reflect his deserts. Nor does it entail that he himself or his family is disadvantaged.) We must examine whether this claim is reasonable, and also whether such representation needs to be achieved through reverse discrimination in favor of the groups as wholes. The question is whether arguments stated in the prior section in terms of utilities can be successfully reformulated in terms of satisfying rights to equal opportunity.

One argument, which we have already encountered in other contexts, invokes the concept of role models as an essential catalyst for motivating younger members of minorities. I have maintained that motivation is of central concern in attempting to remove socially induced disadvantages. And given that children are often motivated through identification with some adult in a position of respect, the role model argument has some plausibility when stated in terms of equal opportunity rather than simple utility. Role models may be equally central to breaking social stereotypes in the minds of those with power to award positions. But even if we accept the truth of these claims for the sake of argument (it may be that direct advertisement of positions, combined with recruitment and guidance, can accomplish at least the motivational goal equally well), it is nevertheless clear that reverse discrimination is an improper means in terms of the rationale of these very arguments for placing role models in their positions. To break stereotyping and encourage imitation, those minority-group members in positions of responsibility must be free from the burden of suspicion of lower than maximal competence or qualifications. And to achieve just these purposes, it seems worthwhile to trade short-term quantity for assured quality by avoiding reverse discrimination as a means to place model minority-group members.

A second argument for proportionate representation in various job categories as a necessary condition of equal opportunity for minority-group members appeals to the character of our political system. Being a member of some group with political muscle, it is claimed, is necessary in order to have one's interests represented equally in our society. One goal of reverse discrimination, according to this position, is to give those groups that have not been adequately represented before a fair share in the power structure. This is held to be a necessary condition for equal opportunity among individuals, because in our society individuals can communicate their interests in a socially effective way only through the mediation of some group with the power to influence the establishment. Women have interests different from those of men, and blacks' concerns differ from those of whites. The interests of members of these and other groups will not be adequately expressed until they have a proportionate share of the economic power structure, and this means proportional representation in various prestigious job categories.

This argument has some merit in relation to our social structure, but it also exhibits several weaknesses. In addition, its merits must be balanced against the injustices involved in reverse discrimination. In order to bring out the weaknesses in the argument, we may use women and the pressure they have exerted for passage of the Equal Rights Amendment as an illustration.[16] The recent history of this political battle has shown that, given the sharp political divisions among women concerning issues most vital to them, they do not form a corporate group with uniform interests. Furthermore, it is doubtful whether those women who acquire positions through reverse discrimination will form a corporate body capable of speaking for any common interests. Granted that some will speak for the interests of a group of women, we may also ask whether awarding them jobs in this way is necessary to achieve adequate political representation for them. Two considerations are relevant. First, given an end to first-order discrimination and given women's ability to compete, representation in various career areas should be achieved (I take up the claim that first-order discrimination cannot be stopped without its reverse in the next section). Second, the impetus behind ERA also illustrates another obvious oversight in the above account of political influence, namely, that large numbers of people, with some organization among them, can by themselves effectively exert political pressure. Spokesmen need not be of the same sex or have the same native interests, since large numbers in themselves represent votes and money.

Of course women are *not* a minority, and that makes this last point less convincing with respect to blacks and other genuine minorities of smaller proportions. Should we therefore say that such groups have a right to proportionate representation in various job categories, as part of their members' rights to equal opportunity? One problem with recognizing this right, even given the accuracy of the account of political representation upon which it is based, is that of drawing the boundaries around its alleged domain. Just what is to constitute proportionate representation, and, more important, what is to constitute a minority group deserving of this right? The logical outcome of its recognition would be allotment of positions on a group percentage basis. We have already seen that initially equal contractors would refuse such a scheme— because of the universal disutility it would involve as opposed to hiring by competence, because it would ignore socially productive effort as a basis for social rewards, and because it would render opportunities for acquiring positions on the basis of personal achievement unequal.

To be sure, certain individuals who are members of minority groups are powerless to make their interests felt (except through violence), and this is a serious injustice. But the most underrepresented group in our society is not defined by racial characteristics per se: it is simply the poor, and especially the chronically poor. The most undemocratic feature of our political system, aside from first-order discrimination (which I am here assuming can be substantially ended without reverse discrimination), is that money stands for political power far in excess of the votes of the individuals who possess it. But reverse discrimination is justified as a partial means to end the situation in which the chronically poor are locked. It is also true that preferential programs aimed at all candidates whose family income is below a certain level would probably not help to advance blacks and other disadvantaged minorities. But there is a crucial distinction here between those who are temporarily low on the economic ladder and the chronically disadvantaged, who are likely to remain so without special treatment. This distinction relates precisely to chronic lack of motivation, the factor that justifies this form of reverse discrimination. Programs designed to correct for this factor need not employ purely economic criteria for qualification but can be aimed at those from chronically deprived communities and backgrounds. Since blacks and members of other minorities are disproportionately represented in this unfortunate group, preferential policies to achieve this purpose will mainly help them in any case. But it will help them in a way that accords with rather than violates the principle of equal opportunity. And it will help those minority-group members who need help most rather than least.

A claim made above in regard to equal opportunity for women might be challenged in another argument for future-looking group reverse discrimination. I held that to end first-order discrimination is all that is necessary to create equal opportunity for them for the most part (I do not mean to imply that this will be an easy task, or that it is just a matter of fair hiring). It could be replied that while equal opportunity entails an equal chance to achieve any position through effort, prestigious and otherwise high-ranking positions require years of experience in the lower ranks before one can even apply for them. Women have not worked their way up through the ranks in various fields simply because they have not been permitted to do so. Thus, because of previous first-order discrimination, they do not have equal opportunity for most desirable positions at present. Even with an immediate halt to that invidious treatment, without reverse discrimination to accelerate the progress, it would take generations for women to have real equality of opportunity for important jobs. Such delay can no longer be tolerated.[17]

Whatever facts may motivate this argument, it is overstated in that it commits the by now familiar fallacy of substituting (racial or sexual) group statistics for actual individual cases. What truth there is has been covered by my conclusion in Chapter Three that those individuals who were discriminated against at lower levels in various job categories are owed not only jobs similar to those formerly refused, but also back pay and credit toward (accelerated) promotion. If all those individuals owed jobs from previous discrimination were now granted accelerated promotions, the kind of equality referred to would not be so long in coming for them. Younger women applying for their first positions have equal opportunity as soon as they are considered fairly for those positions, however long it takes for statistics regarding percentages of women in different fields to even out. Again, different women, especially of different age groups, constitute different cases, and statistics indicate little save patterns of previous discrimination against specific individuals.

The rate of improvement in group statistics in a given field will be a function of factors other than the creation of equal opportunity in the present. Among these factors will be the rate of turnover for the positions (in graduate schools, percentages should even out within a few years) and the type of positions at issue. For example, statistical balance with regard to jobs requiring a fixed level of competence, which involve fewer variables regarding applicants than do those requiring open-ended degrees of excellence, can be more confidently expected (as new positions open up) once first-order discrimination is brought to an end. (This distinction does not impute a competitive inferiority to women applying for jobs that require excellence, but points only to the number of variables that could affect the statistical sample.) Once again we should see the danger in thinking of statistical balances among groups as good or evil in themselves, rather than as one type of evidence of individual injustices.

Perhaps the strongest argument of the type being considered here is the claim that the reduction of racial antagonisms and of racial and sexual biases—which is to be accomplished as the result of the rapid integration of these groups into the mainstream through preferential policies, and which was formerly held to be a utilitarian benefit—will result as well in fewer violations of rights in the future.[18] A proponent would argue that we are justified in violating the rights of those most competent to positions in the present in order to minimize discriminatory violations in the future, violations that will diminish with diminishing racial and sexual divisions in our society. Accordingly, the most rapid means of lessening these divisions is called for, precisely in order to maximize the satisfaction of rights, and group-oriented preferential policies constitute those means. Can we consistently advocate overriding rights of those most competent in order to create more equal opportunities for the chronically deprived and yet not accept this line of reasoning, which also appeals to minimizing future violations of minority-group members' rights to equal opportunity?

In fact, distinctions must be made among these cases, and this final argument is again suspect on both moral and empirical grounds. First, a point from moral theory. There is an asymmetry relevant here between violating rights ourselves and not preventing violations by others. The asymmetry exists when the rights in question are the same (as when we are to violate rights of those presently most competent so that most competent minority-group members will not be denied in the future). As noted in the section on rights and utilities, rights are generally ordered nonadditively, so that numbers of individuals on opposing sides is not crucial, except in extreme cases. For example, if someone were to take two hostages and threaten to kill them unless we killed his enemy, I take it that we would not be justified in capitulating (and not simply to discourage similar acts in the future). In general, it is problematic to claim that we must violate rights in order to prevent violations of the same rights in the future. The case is different when we are forced to choose among rights, only some of which can be honored by us at a given time. This is the case when we override rights of those most competent in order to create equal opportunities for the chronically deprived, since in the absence of equal opportunity for them, we ourselves enforce injustice in continuing to apply the distributive rule for awarding positions by qualifications alone. Second, it is empirically questionable whether tensions and biases will be ended most effectively and quickly by group-oriented reverse discrimination. I have argued that the enforcement of general nondiscrimination, together with compensation in kind for those previously discriminated against and preferential treatment for those from deprived social backgrounds, are alternative ways to place members of disadvantaged groups in positions, ways that will sooner dispel prejudices by dispelling suspicions that those who obtain these positions do not personally deserve or merit them.

It should by now be clear that any reason we may give in favor of reverse discrimination for whole minority groups, whether as compensation for past harm or in order to create future equality of opportunity, will also constitute a reason for specifying the group to be preferred differently and more narrowly than by race or sex. If we are to grant preferential treatment to compensate for past discrimination, then we should prefer those individuals actually discriminated against in the past; if we are to give decent jobs in order to break the continuous deprivation from generation to generation of the chronically poor, then we ought to design hiring policies to benefit individuals who are and have been chronically poor. There seems to be little distinction in this regard between the backward- and forward-looking justifications of preferential policies. The effect of the market factor cited in the previous chapter as additional support for my position operates here as well. As the market in various job categories works to select the most competent individuals within the minority groups specified for preference, and as the individuals selected will tend to be those who have been discriminated against least in the past, so for the same reason they will tend to be the least socially and economically deprived. The class of individuals who were discriminated against in the past and the class of those who are socially and economically deprived and whose children lack equal opportunities are not extensionally equivalent. Some persons begin and remain in the class of the chronically poor not because of discrimination against them, but because of unjust treatment of their parents or ancestors, or, in rarer cases, simply through the neglect or competitive inferiority of the latter. But there is significant overlap between groups of individuals for whom reverse discrimination is justified on backward- and future-looking grounds, and also significant overlap between the intersection of these classes and certain minority groups, especially blacks, Spanish-speaking Americans, and Indians. But to specify reverse discrimination in favor of such racial or national groups is to slant benefits toward some individuals who have escaped these overlaps. Such a policy is as arbitrary in relation to future-looking justifications as it is in relation to compensatory justifications.

The reader may still feel that future-looking considerations constitute stronger reasons for preferential policies favoring

whole minority groups than do considerations of compensation. This feeling may be bolstered by hypothetical reasoning
of the following form. Imagine two groups, we may call them
A and B, the first of which has been systematically discriminated against and persecuted in the past, but whose members
have managed to overcome this treatment and achieve a relatively favorable social position in the present. While members
of B have not been consciously or systematically persecuted,
through no genetic handicap or fault of their own they have
fallen far below the mean in social position, income, power,
etc. It seems intuitive that we should in the present favor or
adopt preferential social policies for members of B rather than
A. Rather than push members of A even higher on the social
ladder, it seems we should attempt to relieve hardships for
members of B and establish future equality of opportunity for
them and their children.[19] Our sympathies would certainly
seem to lie more with members of B, and this appears to give
future-looking arguments in favor of reverse discrimination for
certain minority groups more force than their counterparts in
the area of compensation.

A closer scrutiny reveals no adequate justification for group
reverse discrimination in the above argument, although interesting comparisons between backward- and forward-looking
justifications emerge from it. In the first place, to the degree
that we eliminate past discrimination, fault of members, or
genetic handicaps as causes for the presently low social position among most members of group B, we relegate their status
to the realm of statistical accident (unless all resided in a particular area hit by natural disaster, a possibility irrelevant to
the argument here). Certainly we would not institute special
programs for arbitrarily defined groups that happen to reflect
such statistical averages. Imagine for example that the group
of left-handed redheads were found to average low on the social and economic scale. If the statistics were significant
enough, we might be motivated to inquire into causes, and we
might suspect prior injustice in the form of subtle discrimination against some members of the group. But if research failed
to support this inference, we would stop there. There would
be no question of supporting a preferential policy that bene-

fited those left-handed redheads who were already well off, just because they were members of a group with a low average. That support for such a policy would be absurd shows that future-looking considerations in themselves go no farther toward justifying group reverse discrimination based upon statistical correlation with deprivation than do considerations that look to past injustice. It also demonstrates again that statistical underrepresentation of some group on the upper rungs of the social ladder or within some job category, relative to its percentage in the general population, or even relative to availability of its members in the work pool for that category, is not itself an injustice necessarily to be remedied. It is at most evidence of injustice or unequal opportunity for certain individuals. Statistical balancing may further *violate* rather than simply further the demands of justice, depending again upon the individuals who benefit.

I do not mean to imply that we should not help those members in group B or those left-handed redheads who are economically deprived. But we should help them because they are in need and in order to create equality of opportunity for their children, not because they are members of some other group statistically correlated with economic deprivation. The argument for preferential treatment based on future considerations works for one group only—the class of socially and economically deprived individuals—just as the argument in favor of compensation for past injustice works only for the class of individuals formerly treated unjustly. Persons who belong to a group that has generally been treated unjustly but who have themselves not been mistreated deserve no compensation; likewise, individuals who belong to a group that is statistically low on the economic scale but who are not themselves deprived should receive no preferential treatment. Even if all members of a group are relatively deprived, degrees of deprivation can still be determined, and equal opportunity or justice calls for helping those on the bottom first rather than last (as occurs if left to the market).

The future-looking argument calls upon us to help such individuals: first, because poverty entails suffering amidst general affluence, and because they have rights to the fulfillment

of basic needs; and second, because the children of these individuals suffer problems of resources and motivation amounting to denial of equality of opportunity. Whereas direct redistribution of wealth may be the fastest and most effective
means of meeting basic needs in the short run, providing decent jobs seems more essential as at least part of a policy aimed
at correcting the second type of injustice.

The element of truth in the initial argument on the hypothetical case derives from the fact that our duty to alleviate
present suffering, and perhaps our duty to create more equal
opportunities, is stronger than that to compensate past injustice in certain circumstances. This may be especially true
when, as in the example, the injustice seems to have left no
serious social scars. For injustice to be compensable by present benefits to particular individuals, they must show that
their positions are presently worse than they would have been
otherwise. This requirement is most applicable in cases involving injustice that occurred in the distant past. Compensation is sometimes demanded on the basis of injustice toward
ancestors of those in the present generations.[20] But according
to the reasoning that present harm must have accrued from
past injustice for it to be compensable, we must measure such
claims in relation to present need. We must assume that if effects remain at all, those presently worse off have been
harmed more by distant injustices, since we have no other way
of tracing the effects. In this case future-looking considerations
take precedence over attempts to look exclusively at the past.
On the other hand, the final argument presented in the previous chapter regarding those who lose through policies involving reverse discrimination is not available here. We cannot say
that since those individuals formerly denied positions ought to
have been occupying them from the beginning we should not
consider the positions at issue to be open in the present, because we are not necessarily dealing in this case with individuals who have themselves been discriminated against in the
past. What we must say to the majority of applicants here is
that hiring by competence (or on a first-apply-first-acquire
basis for positions involving fixed levels of competence) is not
completely just until equality of opportunity has been

achieved. We are therefore justified in regretfully violating the distributive rule in the short run in order to make its application fairer in the long run.

It may appear that there is another limitation upon the future-looking argument, one having to do with its relativity to economic conditions. It could be argued that when there are not enough decent jobs to go around, it makes no sense to give preference to those presently worst off, since this will only cause others not independently wealthy to fall into that deprived condition when they are refused jobs. If the preferential policy causes losses in efficiency by placing less competent people in productive jobs, we might further expect this policy in the long run to produce an even more impoverished class, given lower aggregates of goods. It certainly seems to make little sense to exchange one class of poor for another, even if there are no losses in efficiency, and it therefore appears that in this respect the future-looking justification of reverse discrimination is more limited than the backward-looking one. Compensation for past unjust denials that continue in the present should not be made relative in this way to economic conditions. A person unjustly denied a job in the past deserves that job now, whether others need it more or not. To deny that is, as pointed out in the previous chapter, to imply that rights can be canceled through their violation.

While I would admit that the future-looking justifications are somewhat relative to economic conditions, in that there is little point in giving anyone preference in periods of extreme scarcity, they are not as completely relative as the previous paragraph suggests. Reverse discrimination for future-looking reasons can be justified in periods of moderate unemployment, and not only when there are enough decent jobs for all who want them. For there is again an important distinction between the chronically poor and others who may be temporarily unemployed in moderately hard times. As pointed out in another context, the difference relates to the lack of equal opportunity for the children of the former. Poverty tends to perpetuate itself when locked within the same group of people over generations, even if it is not caused by discrimination. Although the temporarily unemployed will not necessarily pass down defeatist attitudes to their children, this seems inevitable among the chronically poor, who envisage little else. Thus creation of equal opportunity, which is central to our future-looking justification of preferential policies, justifies granting preference for jobs to those who have been chronically poor, even when this results in short-term deprivation for others. Since poverty and chronic deprivation are generally located in small geographic pockets, the types of policies suggested by the above reasoning would include community business and employment projects that give preference to local employees. Where preference is not justified for residents of such communities on grounds of equal opportunity for their children, it will most likely be justified on compensatory grounds anyway. If this criterion of community dwelling is somewhat rough, it is certainly far more refined than that of many current programs, which grant preference to anyone who happens to be black or female and thus benefit those who are already privileged. Policies following the guidelines suggested here are at least sure of granting benefits to those who need them.

Affirmative Action

It is time to turn directly and in more detail to current programs. The arguments, now complete, concerning justified and unjustified reverse discrimination in the abstract have laid the necessary groundwork for intelligent appraisal of specific present policies. It is to be hoped that they may also serve as guidelines to support improved ones in the future that will provide greater benefits for those who deserve them and violate fewer rights in the process.

An evaluation of affirmative action belongs in this chapter on future-looking considerations not only because it had to await the development of abstract principles and their application to various alternatives, but also because the avowed purpose of many affirmative action programs (those to be most closely analyzed here) is not to compensate past injustice through present preference, but only to ensure present and future equality of opportunity for women and minority-group members. I have suggested criticisms of these programs at various places earlier in the book. We now require a closer look at their actual features and at their intended, probable, and actual effects. Unfortunately, it is not an obvious and straightforward task to apply the principles already developed to this multifaceted policy, however clear we may have succeeded in making those principles. For the policy, at least in parts, is conceptually ambiguous in its wording and perhaps in its intent. Opposing political pressures upon its framers and administrators have resulted in proliferating directives, which often encourage in practice what they otherwise expressly forbid, and which therefore result in hiring and admissions decisions that violate justice about as frequently as they further it, according to our previous interpretation of what justice demands in this area.

The programs presently grouped under the heading of affirmative action policy vary greatly. Their features depend upon the educational or hiring level at which they are instituted, whether they are voluntary or court imposed, whether they follow previous findings of discrimination by the organization involved, whether their intention is compensatory or to ensure equal opportunity in the present and future. Much also depends upon the organization involved, which normally draws up the program for itself, subject to official approval. Until the *Bakke* decision, some programs in professional schools and employment fixed quotas for minority acceptance, others handicapped minority applications without establishing explicit quotas, and still others called explicitly for nondiscrimination while requiring active recruitment of minority candidates and setting "target goals" for percentages of minority acceptance or employment. The *Bakke* case, together with a later Supreme Court decision to let stand a program at the American Telephone and Telegraph Company, went some way toward resolving the current legal status of these different programs, although in my opinion it in no way established a consistent moral position. The *Bakke* decision, in which Justice Powell was the swing man, prohibits quotas in programs voluntarily adopted by professional schools innocent of prior discrimination. But it permits race to count as a positive factor for admissions to these schools. Since admissions committees can adjust the number of those admitted with less than maximal qualifications simply by adjusting the degree to which race is to count as a factor, this is a distinction without much moral significance. In a later decision the Court refused to review a program at AT&T that sets quotas for minority and female employment, thus granting the program legal respectability (although the fact that the issue could have been moot because the program was to expire soon might have influenced the decision not to grant certiorari. The difference between these cases was apparently that AT&T itself was guilty of discriminatory practices in the past, while the medical school at Davis was not. This distinction, while morally relevant to the question of which organizations should grant positions by preference on compensatory grounds alone, is not morally relevant to the question of who should qualify as beneficiaries of preference, although the Court apparently thought so.[21]

The crucial moral distinction, according to our discussion, has been between programs that grant preference by race or sex alone, and those that grant preference individually on grounds of past harm from discrimination or disadvantage from socially deprived background. That difference has not emerged as a legally crucial factor in the Supreme Court decisions, although it was indicated in several briefs supporting Bakke and was held by the California Supreme Court to be so. Unfortunately, in this legal debate the alternative to preference by race was generally represented as preference on grounds of family income alone, whereas I have called for preference on grounds of prior discrimination or a background of chronic social deprivation. The main argument against the alternative presented here appears to relate to the practical question of how it would work. A start would certainly be to ask applicants for these programs whether they consider themselves to be victims of earlier discrimination in the educational system or in hiring, or whether they grew up in a chronically deprived community, rather than asking only their race or sex. This might be followed by interviews and further sample checks. The principle complaint against it seems to be the administrative difficulty involved and the possibility of falsification on applications. Such complaints appear to me to disguise other political motives. Admissions personnel already require detailed personal histories on applications and routinely review long essays containing such information. Furthermore, the possibility of falsification always exists. Not only in admissions and employment applications, but also in any programs involving special help—for example, those distributing welfare payments—justice is relative to the degree of honesty among applicants and administrators. But given any degree of honesty at all among participants, preferential programs that employ the criteria suggested here would tend to be more just than those that prefer women and minority-group members who are themselves from privileged backgrounds and not appreciably harmed by prior injustice toward others of their race or sex.

One might question why I am willing to trust to the honesty of applicants in these proposed programs, whereas I argued earlier that productivity must be emphasized over effort in distributive rules and that indirect psychological harm cannot be recognized in compensatory rules because such rules could not then be applied fairly and consistently in impersonal social contexts. Is it legitimate to distinguish these cases in terms of trusting first-person claims? The crucial difference is that in the case of criteria for preference, there is in principle the possibility of independent checks upon applicants' educational and employment experiences and community background; programs that use these criteria with any degree of honesty will be more morally consistent and fair than those based exclusively upon race or sex. There is no possibility of independent checks in attempting to measure pure effort or indirect psychological harm, since even sincere first-person appraisals might be comparatively incorrect, and policies that attempted to use these criteria would most likely be less consistent and fair than those that reward productivity and demand proof of direct or material harm as the basis of compensation.

Thus, regarding programs that straightforwardly advocate reverse discrimination for employment or admissions, the recommendation is to personalize criteria so as to make them match the justifying grounds of the policy, whether compensa-

or future looking. At the educational level, I have rec-
ommended remedial programs with adequate support for
those enrolled, or, where such programs are not feasible and
the costs in potential harm to the public are not too great,
handicapping credentials of those who satisfy the relevant
criteria. By far the most difficult programs to evaluate are
those that explicitly advocate nondiscrimination in employment and yet set target goals for percentage of minorities or
women to be employed. Since programs in university employment typify these, and since they constitute the most
difficult cases for the application of principles and arguments
developed earlier, I shall spend the rest of the chapter attempting to draw out the implications of earlier conclusions for
an evaluation of them.

History and Features

The legal requirement for the earliest affirmative action programs can be traced back to Title VII of the Civil Rights Act of
1964, but it derives more specifically from executive orders
regulating the granting of federal contracts. The Civil Rights
Act prohibits discrimination on the basis of race, sex, etc., by
private as well as public employers. It is administered by the
Equal Employment Opportunity Commission, which was
given powers of enforcement under the Equal Employment
Opportunity Act of 1972. An initial exemption for universities
from the terms of Title VII was later eliminated. The immediate source of affirmative action programs of the type we
are considering here is Executive Order 11246, as amended
by Executive Order 11375 and implemented by Revised
Order No. 4, which was issued by the Labor Department.
These executive orders have the force of law and state the
terms under which federal contracts will be granted; their requirements are specified and implemented by regulations of
the Department of Labor. While Executive Order 11246 prohibits discrimination by organizations that receive federal contracts (to which many universities owe their continued existence) and for the first time mentions "affirmative action" to
ensure nondiscrimination, the form of such action is first
specified in Order No. 4.

Among other requirements, the order stipulates that affirmative action be taken in setting "goals" and "timetables" for the employment of women and minority-group members in job categories where they are presently "underutilized." "Underutilization" is defined as having fewer members of the group in the category actually employed than would reasonably be expected from their availability (in universities, from the percentage of available Ph.D.'s in a given field). The goals and timetables set target dates and percentages of group members that the employer is meant to keep in mind in his future hiring decisions. Ultimate goals generally aim at equivalence between percentages of minorities or women in given departments or faculties at the universities in question and percentages in the pool of available candidates. Their purpose seems therefore to increase the percentage of minority employment, although the overall stated goal of the policy is equal opportunity or nondiscrimination. If such statistical deficiencies are not located, written programs not developed, or good faith efforts not made to implement them, the contractor can be found not in compliance with Executive Order 11246 and his contract rescinded. (This has not yet happened in the case of any university, demonstrating lax enforcement as well as efforts at compliance.) Other requirements include public advertisement of jobs and hiring policies and recruitment of minority candidates.

The authority to enforce Order No. 4 in relation to universities was delegated by the Labor Department to the Civil Rights Division of HEW, headed first by J. Stanley Pottinger and later by Peter Holmes. In October 1972, HEW issued its own set of affirmative action guidelines for university programs (each institution was to design its own program in accordance with these guidelines). In accordance with Order No. 4, these indicated that employers, *in addition to* ensuring nondiscrimination, must make "efforts to recruit, employ and promote members of groups formerly excluded, even if that exclusion cannot be traced to particular discriminatory actions on the part of the employer."[22] Goals in this regard are nevertheless to be distinguished from quotas: "while goals are required, quotas are neither required nor permitted." Goals are defined as "indicator[s] of probable compliance." Presumably, an employer is to use them only to measure the effect of his efforts to be nondiscriminatory, if we concentrate upon the actual wording and try to take this distinction seriously. Although he is to pursue the goal (how else can we interpret the notion of a goal?), he is not to do so in violation of standard hiring criteria. For it is also stated that standards should not be eliminated or diluted, and that unqualified candidates should not be hired over qualified ones. Strong reverse discrimination of either form (outright reservations of places or handicapping) is prohibited, although it is admitted that "misunderstanding" already exists in this regard. (This admission was reiterated in 1974.)

In order to emphasize that reverse discrimination is not demanded, HEW allows university departments to approach their ultimate percentage goals by means of three-year interim goals. While the ultimate goals generally call for percentage equivalence between women and minorities on the faculty and those in the total available pool, interim goals can set *future hiring* ratios to equal rather than exceed the availability percentage, in order to approach the ultimate goal gradually. For example, if a faculty had twenty-four men and one woman, and the availability percentage of women with relevant degrees was 20 percent, then an acceptable program could be one that aimed at reaching five women faculty members by hiring one woman out of every five new members in the future. The idea is that the future hiring of women need not exceed what might be expected from fair competition.[23] (This is the idea, but it rests upon faulty assumptions, as I shall argue below.) Other requirements and suggestions of the guidelines include establishing and making available detailed objective criteria for filling jobs, instituting remedial programs where possible and applicable, actively recruiting minority candidates, encouraging child care programs, etc.

Many features of these programs lie outside the realm of serious challenge and debate as far as I am concerned, even though some of them have been disputed by those who wish to dismantle the programs completely. These features include: the compilation of data showing the percentages of minorities in different job categories, with a view to identifying discrimination against them; the removal of handicaps by remedial programs, child care centers, etc.; the establishment of more objective or predictive criteria for hiring, the application of which will be overseen by an impartial body (HEW) with which complaints can be filed as well; the full advertisement of criteria and an end to the "old buddy" system of hiring; and the active recruitment of minority candidates. Many of these features have been endorsed in earlier sections of this book. Full advertisement of positions, pregnancy leaves, child care centers (or child rearing leaves for men and women), and elimination of unpredictive or rigged criteria for hiring constitute only the removal of unfair disadvantages. It is difficult to see how anyone could challenge these on grounds of justice, although in the case of child care centers, their effects upon children as opposed to family rearing have perhaps not been studied thoroughly enough. The general psychological and sociological effects of the achievement of equality or equality of opportunity by women are probably too vast to be fully appreciated in advance. These effects, however they turn out, while legitimately figured in considerations of utility, do not constitute considerations of justice here. For even if equality for women should mark the destruction of the family as a social unit (I do not believe that it will), I do not see how one could deny their right to demand at least equal opportunity and have this demand satisfied. For that reason, these broader sociological questions remain, fortunately, outside the scope of this book.

Active recruitment of minority candidates may be necessary to overcome motivationally based inequalities of opportunity derived from previous first-order discrimination against others; it does not constitute reverse discrimination when standard criteria are used in the actual hiring decisions. For the most part, such recruitment only amounts to full public advertisement of the position in question and announcement that the final decision will be nondiscriminatory. Again, such measures can only further equal opportunity and cannot be seriously challenged. The overseeing of hiring procedures at each step by government officials, while involving much annoying paperwork, is necessary to ensure nondiscrimination, in light of the extent of previous injustice. Some see this as an invasion of privacy and as a proliferation of meddlesome bureaucracy, but history has shown that employers cannot simply be left on their own or trusted to be fairer than they have been before, whatever the law that threatens them in the abstract. Justice must be enforced whatever the short-run costs, until firm habits of fairness have been established as the social norm. Despite charges of unnecessary meddling or invasions of the privacy of academic sanctuaries, legitimate features of affirmative action have not been enforced rigidly enough. The only real objection to the added paperwork can be that it represents merely an empty procedure when unjustified discrimination of either order is not met with severe sanctions. Finally, the establishment of an administrative grievance board to take the complaint mechanism out of the overcrowded courts is necessary to ensure proper redress in case of predictable continued injustice. Administrators with the power of enforcement can at least be expected to reverse unfair hiring decisions, and this they can be expected to do more readily than to impose punitive penalties upon employers.

Nor can the task of compiling data relevant to searching out discrimination be reasonably objected to on the ground that our laws must be "color-blind." The proper reply to this is that color blindness and sex blindness are simply not adequate interpretations of the requirement of "equal protection" or equal opportunity. To be corrected, injustices of discrimination must first be identified, and they cannot be corrected without permitting race and sex categorization in the collection of evidence. I have said that statistical imbalances are not themselves injustices (an exception will be noted below), but I have also maintained that they often constitute evidence of injustices, both past and ongoing. Racial classifications in themselves are not objectionable, although when they are encountered, it is always proper to ask whether they are being used to violate rights. In the previous section we saw that they do violate rights to equal opportunity when made the basis for differential social rewards, whether in favor of or against blacks or other minority-group members. But this claim is perfectly compatible with recognition that categorization by race or sex is necessary in the present social context in order to protect equality of opportunity by identifying areas where injustice is initially to be suspected. Classification by race or sex for the ultimate purpose of ending discrimination is not the same as using these characteristics as a basis for either first-order or reverse discrimination.

Nor can one possibly deny that widespread discrimination has occurred, or that it has occurred in the case of university hiring and promotion, especially against women. Since January 1970, more than 350 complaints have been filed with HEW by women's groups, and their claims of discrimination in pay, promotion, and hiring have generally been borne out. The low percentages of women on faculties and their concentration in the lower ranks up to the time when affirmative action programs began to take effect cannot be passed off as statistical accident or as the result of free choice. Of course, we must start with the assumption that discrimination has occurred in order to have that statistical imbalance between number of women in departments and available Ph.D.'s verify that hypothesis. (A statistically low representation of Italians, Poles, or left-handed redheads does not necessarily show discrimination in hiring, even if we take the class of available Ph.D.'s as our sample, although we could proceed with the collection of initial and verifying evidence in reverse order.) But given the claims made and the firsthand knowledge of some individual cases, this is a reasonable assumption with which to begin.

We might want to have a sharper breakdown of available Ph.D.'s, indicating where they were awarded, so that we could determine whether most of the discrimination has occurred in hiring or earlier in admissions to graduate schools or colleges. This would affect the appropriateness of various types of compensation for individuals affected, as seen in Chapter Three, and would also help to better direct efforts to ensure equality of opportunity. We might also want more information about the concentration of women in the lower ranks and the reasons for this imbalance at specific dates. With the institution of affirmative action programs and their initial effects on the hiring of women who were never previously employed, this percentage may temporarily rise rather than fall. Nevertheless, the measures indicated above seem a minimal appropriate response to a situation in which first-order discrimination would undoubtedly continue without them. They represent the removal of competitive disadvantages without the imposition of new ones on others.

Goals and Quotas

The interesting debate on the issue of affirmative action centers not on the above-mentioned measures, but on whether the goals and timetables for increasing minority-group representation in university faculties constitute racial and sexual quotas, despite official avowals to the contrary. Is there or is there not an internal inconsistency in a policy that requires "goals" but prohibits quotas? An attempt at clarification must distinguish three issues: whether a semantic distinction can be maintained between goals and quotas; whether the goals function in practice to encourage or pressure weak or strong reverse discrimination; and, if they do, whether this might nevertheless be justified in the current social context. I shall consider each question in turn. Our earlier conclusions will provide an answer to the third.

One attempt to distinguish goals from quotas semantically appeals to the difference between positive and negative, inclusory and exclusory aims:

> Quotas are fixed, numerical limits with the discriminatory intent of restricting a specified group from a particular activity. Goals, on the other hand, are numerical target aims which a contractor tries to achieve. The aim is not discriminatory but affirmative in intent: to help increase the number of qualified minority people in the organization. [24]

Thus we have a difference in intent, similar to one we pointed out between first-order and reverse discrimination. Goals are intended to be floors rather than ceilings. But despite the difference in terms and the difference in intent, as an attempt to draw a crucial distinction this seems to be so much sophistry or political jargon: what is positive, what works in favor of members of certain groups, is at the same time negative, for it works to exclude members of other groups. Increasing the percentage of nonwhite males will decrease the percentage of white males, and in a situation of relative scarcity this means that certain white males will be denied jobs that they might otherwise have secured. What is a positive "goal" for one group must be a negative "quota" for its complement; this is simply a logical truth. What is a floor seen from above is a ceiling from below. It is true that these new-style goals are not intended to insult those they may exclude, but only to ensure equal opportunity or perhaps (in the minds of some framers) to compensate past injustice. Yet the intention to insult was not an invariable feature of the old-style quotas either, nor did it constitute their most objectionable element. Reverse discrimination itself never intends directly to exclude or insult those whom it discriminates against, but this does not make it always just or even excusable. Here the question is not yet whether goals are justified, but whether they are quotas; and attempts at distinction along these lines resemble the distinction between our side, which fights to maintain peace, and theirs, which wages war. Such Washington-style newspeak ought to be exposed and then avoided, especially in philosophical contexts.

Yet another attempt at differentiating these numerical goals from quotas consists in pointing out that contracts will not be annulled as long as employers can show "good faith efforts" to meet them, whether they actually meet them or not. With the injunction against diluting hiring standards, these good faith efforts seem to boil down to meeting the other requirements of the affirmative action program, most importantly, establishing and applying nondiscriminatory criteria and recruiting minority candidates. Thus goals are distinguished from "rigid numerical quotas" that must be met literally. It can be replied to this point that there is no difference between this and the justification of any other failure to meet a quota. For example, France's failure to meet its quota of the UN budget will be excused if it can show good faith efforts to meet it that were blocked by clearly overriding needs. [25] As long as there is some proportion of a total reserved for some participant, it seems that we have a quota, whatever the justifications accepted for deviating from it. There is nevertheless an obvious difference between having to meet a quota, come what may, and having to make efforts to meet it within certain limits or restrictions (for example, hiring the most competent). But as another philosopher commenting on the subject has pointed out, if racial quotas or group percentages are not a morally acceptable way of distributing positions (I have argued they are not), then any good faith efforts to distribute positions in this way are not good either. [26] And if the publication and application of objective criteria and the active recruitment of minority candidates—all overseen by neutral government officials who ensure that the criteria really are objectively applied—constitute "good faith efforts," why should quotas be additionally stated at all? Strict enforcement of the other provisions of affirmative action guidelines should in itself force hiring to be nondiscriminatory, and nothing more than nondiscriminatory hiring and promotion is really required according to the letter of the law. It is hard to avoid the conclusion that the additional purpose to be served by the numerical goals is to apply pressure for reverse discrimination, despite official disclaimers of such intent.

There appears to be little doubt that the goals have in practice been felt as such pressure by those with the authority to hire, and that reverse discrimination is the natural response to them. We can quickly pass over those exaggerated extensions of the policy and the confusions that constitute its humorous side. I shall simply mention the letter from the Educational Testing Service requesting that proctors for examinations reflect the ethnic and sexual ratios of those taking the tests. This led one administrator of tests at Smith College to resign because he was not adept at judging ethnic-group membership from lists of names and because he was himself a French Canadian Catholic male. Or we might consider the statement of the mayor of Houston on hearing complaints of reverse discrimination in police hiring: "We are going to hire qualified women regardless of their sex!" Even those who would like to construe affirmative action goals narrowly have seriously misinterpreted those goals. President McGill of Columbia, after initially resisting the policy, sent a memorandum to deans and chairmen asking them to comply:

> The academic and personal qualifications of each individual to whom a Columbia appointment is offered must continue to be the only criteria for selection . . . at the same time, it is my belief that academic excellence is not one-dimensional. An increased number of members of minority groups and women within the instructional ranks will add significantly to the strength and vitality of Columbia University.[27]

Here McGill seems to be suggesting that, in the present context, being a minority-group member or woman should itself be considered a qualification for being a teacher at Columbia (since any factor that adds to the strength and vitality of the university must be considered a positive qualification for being hired). In relation to standard criteria for competence, this constitutes a call for reverse discrimination, a call that McGill was apparently reluctant to make.

The Committee on Academic Nondiscrimination and Integrity, which investigated charges of reverse discrimination as a reaction to affirmative action, "repeatedly encountered the rapidly spreading practice of administrative imposition of overt or covert racial quotas in both admissions and the hiring and promotion of instructors at institutions of higher education."[28] The U.S. Chamber of Commerce, in its amicus brief in the *DeFunis* case, also commented that business employers have found little guidance in interpreting the alleged distinction between goals and quotas, and it suggested that employers see little legal danger and some benefits to themselves in practicing reverse discrimination when faced with the supposedly nondiscriminatory goals.[29] These informal survey findings somewhat confirm what might have been obvious to anyone attending a recent national convention where hiring takes place in some academic discipline. One statistical study indicates that the percentage of women in junior positions in 1974 exceeded by 7 percent the percentage acquiring degrees.[30] Perhaps the entire difference here can be explained by the fact that women have been promoted more slowly than men, often for discriminatory reasons. Given this factor, the statistics themselves do not reveal much reverse discrimination up to that time. Many programs have been instituted since that time, however, and in any case, group statistics can be misleading for another reason. The fact that reverse discrimination is occurring on a group basis does not contradict the equally apparent fact that in other quarters within the same job categories first-order discrimination against women and minority-group members continues as usual in hiring; the two practices tend to balance out in the statistics. I shall argue below, as I have implied above, that this is a case in which two wrongs add up simply to two wrongs, while rendering much of the recent statistical evidence in terms of group percentages morally uninformative.

That goals encourage reverse discrimination on a group basis, despite disclaimers in the guidelines, can be explained by reference to the asymmetries in expected official response when hiring additional men rather than women. While an administrator must show good faith efforts if he fails to meet the minority goal, no such efforts must be demonstrated to HEW if he does meet it. A chairman of an academic department, faced with a dean and a president, as well as with a school affirmative action officer and an HEW official, can therefore lighten his burden by opting for the woman until the stated goals are met or at least approached. In the case of weak reverse discrimination or of handicapping within reasonable limits, he will have nothing to lose by doing so, while the threat of reduced funds lies on the other side. That the "quotas" charge continues to be heard, despite official denials, is evidence that the policy is being misapplied, or, more accurately, that it is inconsistent. It is true that there has not yet been a case in which good faith efforts have not been accepted (although funds are typically withheld until affirmative action programs are drawn up and put into effect when demanded by HEW), but this ignores the cases in which they have been exceeded. And the time-consuming efforts necessary to gather documentation and present arguments to demonstrate good

faith efforts when goals are not met may in themselves motivate reverse discrimination in order to avoid such administrative burdens.

There also seems to be some difference in recognized recourse available to the woman or minority-group member, as
distinguished from the white male who claims (reverse) discrimination. While the EEOC and Civil Rights Division of
HEW were established to handle minority complaints and
thus avoid the long and uncertain path of the overcrowded
courts, the latter avenue of recourse still appears to be the
only one available to males like DeFunis or Bakke. Some
briefs in the *DeFunis* case argued that even the courts should
take minority complaints more seriously, reasoning that the
majority can work through the legislative process to make
their interests felt, while the insular minorities need the protection of the courts in a majoritarian system. This is true, and
the danger of the tyranny of the majority is real in any democratic system. On the other hand, the argument in this context
oversimplifies again the distinctions among groups and group
memberships involved. A white male job applicant is not
necessarily a member of any relevant majority on this issue,
since his interests differ from those of both the minority applicant *and* the person with the power to grant the position.
Those in the latter category, entrenched in their positions,
have nothing to lose and at least temporary peace of mind to
gain by yielding to the political pressure exerted by an alliance
of various groups for meeting the minority goals. Clearly, the
courts as well as those administrative bodies established for
the purpose ought to protect equally the rights of all involved.
That there exists this distinction in recourse at present (not a
recognized legal distinction to be sure) again partially explains
how the goals can operate to pressure reverse discrimination.

Reverse discrimination is prohibited in its strong version by
the HEW guidelines. However, weak reverse discrimination,
that is, preference for minority candidates as qualified as all
others, is not prohibited there or in the orders, and it is
specifically called for in some affirmative action programs in
universities as a means to achieve the minority goals. (Under
the guidelines, each institution draws up its own program,

again sometimes adding to the ambiguity.) If the purpose of university employment programs is simply to end discrimination and provide equality of opportunity in the present, target goals seem suspect. The legitimate function claimed for them is not to correct statistical imbalances, but rather to shift the burden of proof of nondiscrimination onto the employer. The charge is made that without this feature of the policy, nondiscrimination will once more be left to the good will of hiring officers, and the future of women and minorities will inevitably resemble their past. In view of the long history of discrimination and the difficulty of breaking bad habits and ingrained attitudes, the necessity of shifting this burden is clear, as is that of taking the grievance mechanism out of the courts. Furthermore, if it is true that the injustice of discrimination will not be ended even in the long run without the adoption of numerical target goals, then the benefits of their adoption seem to outweigh any transient injustice to white males on grounds of maximizing satisfaction of rights among which we must choose. But the claim that first-order discrimination cannot be so ended is open to question.

No arguments presented in this section, nor in any previous ones for that matter, should be taken as defenses of the status quo prior to affirmative action. I have assumed in earlier chapters that first-order discrimination can be halted at least to a significant degree through measures short of, or at least independent of, reverse discrimination. It was against that background assumption that I limited the legitimate functions of preferential hiring and admissions to those of compensating specific past injustices and creating equal opportunity for the chronically poor and economically deprived. Some, however, support affirmative action and its numerical goals on the grounds that this kind of pressure is the only way to begin the end of first-order discrimination against blacks and women. While these supporters stop short of advocating reverse discrimination as a means to that end, they frankly admit that the only policy that might work in the current context is one that leans far enough in that direction to result in occasional acknowledged injustices to white males.[31] The argument holds that just this much pressure upon hiring officers is necessary to force them to be fair, and it is the one argument that straightforwardly supports the existing policy while admitting its inherent ambiguities.

The major premise of this position must appeal to the pervasive and fundamental nature of the invidious attitudes that underlie first-order discrimination. It seems true that discriminatory social attitudes that have developed over centuries cannot be altered overnight through half-hearted policies. Nevertheless, I can see four questions relevant to movement from this admission to endorsement of a policy that in practice encourages reverse discrimination: How deeply entrenched are the attitudes of those with power to grant positions? Will these attitudes change when faced with pressure for reverse discrimination? Can they be overridden in actual hiring decisions by pressure for reverse discrimination? Can they be countered by pressures short of the numerical goals?

The first question is perhaps the most difficult to answer and would require extensive psychological research, which I have not undertaken. However, I believe intuitively (and perhaps naively) that the strength of these invidious attitudes may vary somewhat inversely with degree of education (perhaps only the willingness to express them vocally and blatantly so varies). At least in regard to chairmen of academic departments in the humanities, a small sampling of whom constitutes my only firsthand evidence, I suspect that most simply go along with current hiring practices. They would be susceptible to enforced pressures to be fair, as they have been susceptible to pressures from a policy that many of them take to exceed the requirements of fairness.

The second question is slightly more relevant to an evaluation of the complete argument than is the first. There is no reason to suspect that attitudes themselves will change because of threats of sanctions against unfair hiring practice. I stated in the first section of this chapter why they might in fact be exacerbated by policies involving or encouraging reverse discrimination. First, there is simple backlash resentment, which is more applicable, however, to those who are refused jobs than to those who do the hiring. But second, paternalistic attitudes will be further fostered by the implication that blacks and women, even those given equal opportunities, cannot make it on their own and will tend to be less qualified and competent on average than their white male counterparts. Most role models hired on a preferential basis will do little to dispel this belief.

The last two questions are far and away the most important in the context of this argument for the present policy. We may provide answers to both by means of the distinction between the strength of the requirements in the statement of the policy and the degree of enforcement of its provisions. It seems that strict enforcement of the other provisions of the program, which demand objective hiring criteria, nondiscrimination in their application, and minority recruitment, would be sufficient to achieve the stated purposes of the policy. The numerical goals presumably add no new purposes, but only additional means of achieving those stated elsewhere in the policy. The reasoning must be that inclusion of this stronger provision, which can encourage reverse discrimination by certain hiring officers, makes up for somewhat lax enforcement of the requirements to be nondiscriminatory. I want to emphasize that this belief is false and could only arise from concentration exclusively upon percentages of minorities hired.

Lax enforcement of the existing policy, with its provisions that not only demand an end to first-order discrimination but also encourage its reverse in practice, will result in both types of injustice (I call the reverse discrimination involved here unjust, assuming from earlier arguments that those who benefit from it will tend not to be those who deserve to do so). Strong enforcement of the requirements to be nondiscriminatory would result in hiring by competence. While the percentages of minorities hired might be nearly equal under these two alternatives, the statistics will only conceal the double injustice involved in the former, where the effects of reverse discrimination tend to be balanced by the continuation of first-order discrimination elsewhere. The statistical equivalence of these two outcomes shows the danger of relying upon statistics alone to measure the effectiveness or justice of a program or policy. What I am calling for, on the other hand, is stricter enforcement of the provisions of affirmative action policies, short of quotas (or goals), together with reverse discrimination where justified by earlier arguments. (Another sense in which current programs are too weak is in not requiring preference where deserved—for example, preference in promotion for those women faculty formerly unjustly denied it.)

The problem with the argument for affirmative action goals is that it ignores all the other features of these programs, features to which good faith efforts to meet numerical quotas reduce if made according to the letter of the law. The HEW guidelines encourage this narrow emphasis by representing the choice as that between the target goals or a "benign neutrality" that tends to "perpetuate the status quo ante indefinitely." This is a misleading effort to gain acceptance for the goals. The active recruitment of minority candidates, the removal of handicaps from minority candidates, and, most important, the advertisement and application of nondiscriminatory hiring criteria—all overseen and ensured by neutral government officials, who also serve as a sympathetic and prompt acting grievance board with powers of enforcement—seem enough to guarantee equal treatment for new candidates applying for new positions (the stated purpose of affirmative action in university hiring). That such measures in themselves, with proper enforcement, could not end discriminatory treatment at the level of hiring to the same degree as the present policy, with its contradictory prohibitions and pressures, is an untested empirical hypothesis. We should at least attempt to enforce a justice-maximizing policy first, before moving to a stronger one (which in some respects is also weaker).

Thus, if the aim of affirmative action programs is current impartiality toward all who apply for jobs, as is implied in the wording of the guidelines, and not compensation for past injustice through correcting statistical imbalances by the imposition of numerical quotas, then the goals and timetables seem inconsistent in concept and even more so in practice. In fact, if the other features of affirmative action programs are not officially enforced for an indefinite period regardless of percentages of males and females hired in the short run, it will tend to be discriminatory in effect as well. To argue that an end of numerical goals means an end of affirmative action may well hasten its end, given the injustice of the type of reverse discrimination encouraged by the goals and the resulting resistance to them.

It might still be argued that the only presupposition that could underlie an assumption that fair competition would not result in meeting goals, or in an approximate percentage equivalence between women or minority members obtaining jobs and those in the availability pools, would be an invidious suspicion of the real inferiority of members of these groups, even of those with Ph.D.'s. Barring any such assumption, it might be held that goals, certainly interim goals, would naturally tend to be met, and, if interpreted properly, would therefore simply function as further checks that competition was being kept fair. (Remember that interim goals need only set percentages of minorities to be hired in the future to equal percentages available, although the ultimate goal is to match percentages in positions with those of available candidates.) Any such checks, in view of the limited staffs of HEW and the Labor Department and the difficulty of their monitoring jobs, might be argued to serve a useful and just purpose. Even if correct, this argument is of limited applicability in light of the claim that goals are not being interpreted according to the letter of the guidelines. But neither is the argument sound in itself: its first premise is logically (inductively) faulty. Reasons other than competitive inferiority show why percentages as stipulated in specific affirmative action programs should *not* be expected to be met consistently. One is that the programs are drawn up and the goals applied on an institution-by-institution basis. When the availability pool considered is national, the statistical samples represented by the goals, taken individually, are too small in relation to the whole market to expect them to match one another and the overall ratio of minority-group candidates to all candidates in each case. The availability pool for academic jobs is generally figured nationally (although it might be permitted in some cases to figure it locally), but the target goals are set separately for each university. Numerous variables could therefore affect the statistics from sample to sample. These variables, together with the difference in response to hiring women as opposed to men, explain the pressure for preference inherent in even apparently neutral goals.

One variable factor in the case of universities derives from the heterogeneity in both the labor force and hiring institutions. Where a labor force is homogeneous, and where only widely possessed minimal qualifications are necessary for the type of job in question, and where in addition the hiring institutions are concentrated in one area and resemble one another closely, there is more reason to believe that nondiscrimination will result in statistical equivalence from sample to sample (even in this case there will be random variance). But where there are criteria of relative excellence, such that it is doubtful that any two candidates will be exactly equally qualified, where a merit system of hiring is required, as in universities, and where the hiring institutions differ greatly in location and desirability, there are additional reasons not to expect statistical uniformity from sample to sample. Since these considerations show the irrationality of expecting numerical goals for universities to be uniformly met in fair competition, even where the goals call only for hiring ratios in the future to match availability percentages of minorities, they also show why efforts to meet them tend toward reverse discrimination. This counterargument applies, as indicated, mainly to the case of university programs, where it cannot be claimed that fair competition will tend to result in meeting goals in each case. In local blue-collar industries, for example, goals may have more validity as measuring devices.

Finally, to the charge that an assumption of inferiority must underlie the expectation that goals would not be met given nondiscrimination, the converse can be claimed, at least again in relation to university hiring. With the tendency of the numerical goals to pressure reverse discrimination, only an assumption of inferiority can justify an insistence upon their adoption or continuation. If it is assumed that reverse discrimination is required to achieve numerical representation in the whole job population (as opposed to such representation on an institution-by-institution basis), then this must be because it is believed that such an average will not come about through fair competition. And this presupposes competitive inferiority on the part of women or minority-group members. (I argued above that fair competition can be guaranteed as far as possible by law without moving to reverse discrimination.) If we figure the percentages on a national basis, we should not require reverse discrimination on a direct group basis to achieve minority representation. If we figure on an institution-by-institution basis, we cannot achieve such representation uniformly without reverse discrimination. But if reverse discrimination is directed toward groups as a whole, with an eye only toward meeting the numerical goals, it will be unjust.

Sometimes, in order to justify an assumption of de facto present competitive disadvantage without implying genetic inferiority, an appeal is made to motivational handicaps or disadvantages from discrimination earlier in the educational system. Several difficulties are involved in such an appeal in the context of these affirmative action programs, however. First, the reference class that the numerical goals are designed to reflect in various academic departments is generally taken as the class of available Ph.D.'s in the fields. Certainly no motivational deficiencies are present in general among members of that class; if anything, motives had to be stronger than average to achieve membership. Second, these affirmative action programs are not designed to compensate past injustice, but only to ensure present equal opportunity for those applying for positions at all levels. Third, while I argued that those discriminated against in the educational system are owed compensation, reverse discrimination at the hiring level is not the preferred means of compensating them. Other, more indirect motivational harms I held to be noncompensable.

Thus support of numerical quotas solely for the purpose of creating fair competition, nondiscrimination, or equality of opportunity for available Ph.D.'s or others with professional degrees seems unfounded, barring any assumption of inferiority. The goals encourage group reverse discrimination in practice, even though the guidelines prohibit it in principle. Such inconsistency in national policy seems intolerable, especially at a time when honesty and forthrightness from Washington are to be most highly valued and demanded. On the utilitarian side, to continue a policy that often results in reverse discrimination, with its tacit presupposition that minorities or women cannot compete, is perhaps to perpetuate the myth of female and minority inferiority in the minds of those who award and those who are awarded the jobs.

We can now move from the questions of whether affirmative action programs in fact function to encourage reverse discrimination, and whether that is necessary to achieve the limited goal of ending first-order discrimination and establishing fair competition in the present, to an entirely different issue, namely, whether that limited goal is sufficient from a moral point of view, or from the viewpoint of rights and justice, in the current social circumstances. If, in addition to ending discrimination, reverse discrimination of the type encouraged by affirmative action programs is justified, then while the policy might be criticized for its ambiguity, inconsistency, or hypocrisy for advocating one policy in writing and encouraging another in practice, it could not be condemned for its social effect, which is the most important consideration. Here three questions must be distinguished: Are compensatory measures justified in addition to simply ending discrimination? Is reverse discrimination a proper means of compensation? Is reverse discrimination of the type encouraged by affirmative action programs the proper means of compensation? We can at this point rely upon all our earlier arguments to provide the answers.

I have argued that compensation in kind is owed to those who were actually discriminated against in the past, and that reverse discrimination is proper to aid the chronically poor as well. In failing to address itself to these problems, the policy of affirmative action is too weak. As is usual in our political system, the poor and powerless continue to lose out, even when it comes to socially remedial policies, in the face of stronger and better organized pressure groups. With regard to victims of past discrimination, present policy has somewhat alleviated the difficulty of obtaining just redress by allowing circumvention of the court system. But in encouraging reverse discrimination directed toward those most competent within minority groups (by aiming at statistical balances), the policy is not only inconsistent, but also doubly unjust. As we have seen, a program of this type tends to provide the most benefit to those within minorities who deserve it least on compensatory grounds, and it tends to place the entire burden on those least responsible for past injustice.

While these considerations of injustice involving continued violation of rights should be paramount in an evaluation of the policy, most of the uproar has centered around another claim, namely, that standards of hiring, and hence excellence of performance, in various academic categories will be lowered by affirmative action. In my view this is a purely utilitarian, and hence secondary, consideration in relation to the rights involved (not, however, if we think that students have rights to have the best teachers possible). While it is true that these utilities figure in the recognition of the rights in question in the first place, as those considered earlier in this chapter do not, once the rights have been recognized, they are to take absolute precedence in our moral calculations. Even though this is then a relatively minor point if true, I shall comment upon it briefly in closing this subsection. First, it is clear that without numerical goals or quotas, other features of affirmative action designed to remove handicaps and ensure fair competition on a merit basis must in the long run improve efficiency by broadening and stiffening competition. Second, even weak reverse discrimination, according to which a woman or minority-group member is automatically chosen if as (but no more) qualified than the best white male candidate, cannot lower efficiency, although it may be unfair on other grounds. But reverse discrimination of either strong type—that is, handicapping at the hiring level or simply reserving a position for the best woman or black—must, it seems, lower efficiency or academic excellence at least in the short run, and if the precedent continues, in the long run as well.

This reasoning has been disputed by an argument involving a fallacy that by now should be perfectly familiar. It is claimed that since underutilization of women and minorities has been inefficient (since maximally qualified candidates have been denied positions because of race or sex), bringing these groups up to full utilization, which numerical goals represent, will increase efficiency or raise standards in the long run. Again we have an attempt, whether conscious or not, to mask both injustice and inefficiency by substituting a group statistic for reference to a different class of individuals. Inefficiency lies in denying jobs to most qualified candidates, and it will certainly only be increased by further violations of merit criteria. It will be erased by broadening and stiffening the competition through fair application of those criteria. In the long run, nondiscrimination will raise both representation of women and minorities and standards of hiring and performance.

A Final Comparison

Before summarizing my conclusions, I believe I can bring the position on affirmative action defended here into sharper focus by means of a comparison with another issue that may appear to be completely analogous. I am speaking of the case of segregated schools, which may well have been in the minds of the framers of the target goals feature of affirmative action. The parallel that would be drawn by supporters of numerical goals points to the move from outlawing racial assignment to schools to requiring racial assignment as the sole means of ending segregation.[32] It became clear soon after *Brown* v. *Board of Education* that integration would not be achieved by the repeal of segregation laws and the demand that students be assigned by nonracial criteria (for example, districts with natural boundaries). Such assignment was quickly seen to result in de facto segregation. The controversial busing orders were therefore handed down to achieve racial mix in the elementary and secondary schools, amounting to forced integration until racial quotas were met.[33]

The move from outlawing racial assignment to requiring integration is logical and demanded by considerations of justice. First of all, neighborhoods themselves are segregated, at least in part because of clearly unjust discrimination in housing. And second, there cannot really be "separate but equal" schools, because resources tend to be allocated unequally to segregated schools, and because the learning experience itself and the motivation necessary to it require diversity in the classroom at lower levels (given the history of segregation at all levels in education). Segregated schools deny equal opportunity to black children even when adequately funded. Young children placed in segregated classrooms naturally view this as a stigma and a sign that they are not accepted in white society. Motivational problems are likely to arise at this basic level within a segregated situation, and therefore integration is demanded as a necessary condition of equality of opportunity, at least in the short run. This is not because racial diversity per se is beneficial in the classroom, but rather because even de facto segregation of low-income black children tends to result in motivational deprivations.

It appears easy at first glance to draw analogies between this case and the move from the demand that first-order discrimination in hiring be ended to the call for numerical goals to eliminate the vestiges of such discrimination. Just as elimination of overt racial assignment to schools could not appreciably change the situation of black children, so it could be argued that ending overt discrimination in hiring cannot appreciably alter the status of women and minorities at that level, given the degree of discrimination that has occurred in the educational system as well. In both cases, it could be argued, we are justified in moving beyond nondiscrimination to achieve integration, that is, proportionate representation of minorities. The goal in both cases is an integrated society in which race or sex will then fade as invidious criteria for filling positions.

Several difficulties with this analogy as a support for numerical goals in affirmative action programs were indicated above. First, it was pointed out than an appeal to lower-level discrimination is irrelevant in the context of affirmative action at the hiring level, since those who will benefit from the policy by being awarded jobs—those with Ph.D.'s applying for university jobs, for example—are not those members of the groups in question who have been appreciably harmed by such discrimination. An even more fundamental disanalogy was indicated in the previous sections. In the case of schools, segregation itself is an injustice amounting to inequality of opportunity that calls for correction (given the falsity of the "separate but equal" doctrine). In the case of academic departments or other job categories, however, statistical imbalance with regard to different racial, ethnic, or sexual groups is not itself an injustice, but at most is evidence supporting the thesis that unjust discrimination toward certain individuals has occurred in the past. This was implied first by the claim that underrepresentation of a particular group (say, Italians or Jews) is no argument for affirmative action in their favor without other evidence of discrimination against them. To argue that statistical imbalances in job categories are themselves unjust amounts to a call for awarding a percentage of positions on the basis of race or sex, which is itself unjust and in violation of equality of opportunity. At the higher level it is no longer a case of distributing opportunities to those at an impressionable age; rather, it is one of distributing goods to those who have used their opportunities to acquire relative qualifications for them. Thus, while integration is demanded at the lower level as a necessary condition of equal opportunity, forced integration to achieve statistical balance in job categories violates our principle of equality of opportunity.

In fact, at closer view few parallels exist between the two cases. First, there is no injustice in the affirmative action area over and above the total amount of actual discrimination that has occurred in hiring and earlier in the educational system. In the school case, segregation is unjust whatever its causes. Second, it was argued above that reverse discrimination on a group basis does not seem necessary to achieve statistical balance, given that fair competition can be achieved without it, that there are available candidates (as there are at least in the case of women), and that those discriminated against in the past are now compensated with jobs. Third, and most important, not only is group reverse discrimination not necessary to achieve the stated purpose of affirmative action, but it also cannot constitute reasonable compensation for past injustices toward members of minority groups or women. This is because the numerical goals of these programs are specified in terms of the groups as a whole, while they nevertheless function to benefit specific members of these groups; and, as pointed out several times, the members they benefit (women just coming out of graduate schools with Ph.D.'s) are generally those who have suffered least from prior discrimination. This situation is again to be distinguished from the school case, in which integration is not only the proper but also the only remedy for segregation, the injustice to be corrected.

We come to a final disanalogy with the segregated school case, namely, the injustice to the most qualified white male applicant when reverse discrimination is unjustifiably practiced. In the case of jobs, I have argued that the male who has successfully met the requirement of society through his efforts to attain maximal competence for a position attains some right to that position. For society to thwart his expectations after suggesting to him the social task and requiring his efforts to achieve it seems unjust. As he has probably not partaken in or benefited from previous injustice, neither has he forfeited this right, which can therefore only be overridden by stronger rights of specific individuals. Again, there is no parallel in the school case: while there may be some inconvenience to children bused to the far end of a district, despite all the uproar, no one is being denied his right. There may be a right to an equal education, but there is no right to attend a school within a certain fixed distance from one's home. (On the other hand, unnecessary hardships to parents and children should of course be avoided.)

I do not mean here to underestimate the frustration of parents who work hard and save money to buy a house in a nice neighborhood partly in order to have their children enrolled in superior schools, only to see them bused to other areas. But the frustration of every expectation cannot be held unjust—only of those that arise in relation to just standing rules. In order to preserve or create equality of opportunity it is reasonable to limit the rights of parents to buy their children such advantages, which entail the injustice of segregation for other children (just as we limit the rights of corporations to hire whom they please for the same reason). Rational contractors from an initial position of equality would agree to hiring by competence but not to a strict neighborhood school rule, when this would result in inferior opportunities for some children throughout their lives. Thus rights are ignored in the type of reverse discrimination encouraged by affirmative action goals, but not in the demand for integration of lower-level schools.

The general conclusion of this brief final comparison is that neither group reverse discrimination to achieve statistical representation for minorities, nor affirmative action quotas that encourage it, can draw support from the school desegregation case. Regarding the former, as opposed to the latter, the goal can be achieved in other ways, the means proposed are inappropriate on compensatory and future-looking grounds, and rights are violated by their continued enforcement.

FIVE

Conclusion

Our initial conclusion was that those most competent to positions acquire rights to those positions. Such rights are recognized (or would be by rational contractors) in the name of universal utility and protection of equal opportunity. Their recognition limits the rights of corporations to hire whom they please, which, if permitted in a context of irrational biases, would result in losses in public welfare and unjust denial of equal opportunities. Hiring by competence was held preferable to such egalitarian alternatives as random lotteries for filling positions both on grounds of utility and in terms of rewarding effort.

Those unjustly denied positions in the past that they deserved according to this distributive rule now deserve positions as compensation in kind. Strong reverse discrimination is justified for such individuals according to the precept that the principle of compensation is to take precedence over further applications of the distributive rule. The idea is to keep distributions approximating over time to those that would have obtained in the absence of violations. Those white males who are presently most qualified cannot complain of injustice when those discriminated against in the past are now preferred, since the latter should already occupy the positions in question, which therefore should not be considered open.

Strong reverse discrimination was also held justified for the chronically poor. Here the justification rests on the claim that measures designed to create future equality of opportunity for individuals who would otherwise be socially disadvantaged may also take precedence over applications of the distributive rule for hiring the competent, since that rule is the more just as the opportunities for acquiring competence are the more equal. Preferential admission and hiring for these individuals constitutes one step in the attempt to break the seemingly endless cycle of social and economic deprivation for those in certain geographic areas, and it is a necessary step in light of the failure of the educational system to correct for socially induced initial disadvantages.

Preferential treatment was held unjustified when directed indiscriminately toward members of groups defined only by race or sex. It was pointed out that when such policies are applied, the market operates to select members of such groups who are least deserving of preference on the two grounds mentioned above. For this reason, neither administrative ease nor other supposed political or utilitarian advantages could justify stating criteria for preference so broadly. Utilitarian advantages, dubious in any case, are permitted no weight in relation to the goal of maximizing satisfaction of rights. Group-oriented policies tend to violate rights of individuals in three categories: the chronically poor and those discriminated against in the past, who tend to be passed over; presently most qualified white males, who are not liable for past injustices; and the public at large, who pay for such policies not only with funds for those who administer them, but also with losses in efficiency in various job categories. Thus, while racial and sexual classifications are to be permitted in collecting evidence of first-order discrimination against individuals, they are not to be made the bases for present awards of positions.

Preferential policies administered on just grounds will tend to benefit only members of minorities in any case. It is a question of *which* members of such groups are to be preferred, that is, whether we want a policy that inverts the ratio of desert to benefit. We may combine our justificatory criteria either disjunctively or conjunctively. If resources for corrective policies (for example, jobs) are extremely scarce, we might insist that an individual meet both criteria in order to qualify for preference. I do not believe that to be necessary in our present social context, and I would recommend policies that accept either ground. These might amount to large-scale projects involving community employment in depressed areas, for example, or the establishment of local administrative boards to process complaints of discrimination by individuals against specific institutions or corporations, along with strict enforcement of nondiscriminatory regulations.

Such policies bear little resemblance to present affirmative action programs, which are primarily the products of that type of "group think" condemned in this book. They tend to throw into the same categories poor and middle-class blacks, deprived women and those not deprived, young white males and those already entrenched in their positions. They ignore the fact that these individuals are members of more narrowly defined groups, and that neither interests nor deserts divide along simple racial or sexual lines. More specifically, even the weakest programs are too strong in encouraging group reverse discrimination by their numerical goals; many are too weak in failing to provide preference for those who really deserve or need it, and too weak as well in enforcing their justified provisions regarding nondiscrimination.

All of the above conclusions lie in the area of applied social philosophy and are intended as suggestions for future policy. I hope that those more interested in pure philosophy will have found some interest in the more theoretical sections of the book, especially those on the principle of compensation, on rights and utilities, and on equality of opportunity. The first and last are still relatively uncharted territory in philosophical literature. There has not been much debate, for example, on where to draw the line in correcting for inequalities of opportunity (I suggested drawing it at socially induced initial disadvantages). Nor has a principle of compensation been articulated from a philosophical viewpoint that could apply to the various types of cases for which one is required.

I might finally mention, since the reader will have surmised it anyway, that I am a white male, under thirty-five, Jewish, and married. Lest these facts arouse a variety of ad hominem dismissals, let me add that I consider myself among those already entrenched in their positions. I cannot claim that none of my arguments were motivated by initial gut reactions to current policies, but I do not believe that moral argument can ever free itself from the influence of such attitudes. What we should demand is that judgments be defended by analogies or principles, and that attitudes be modified where called for in light of moral theory, so that we may be at least coherent and consistent. Having kept these demands in mind, I hope, if not to have convinced those in power to change their minds, at least to have clarified the issues and introduced the necessary distinctions for understanding a complex problem that is easily oversimplified.

My conclusions may be distasteful to activist leaders among women and minority groups, as well as to conservatives on the issue. In regard to the latter, I certainly have not argued that reverse discrimination is never justified as social policy, or that it is always equivalent in its injustice to first-order discrimination. This book advocates widespread use of preferential policy as a means to compensate past injustice and create equality of opportunity for the chronically deprived. But regarding the former, I have argued that the groups they claim to represent are not the proper kinds of groups to qualify as beneficiaries of a justly administered policy.

Spectacular philosophizing often occurs at the extremes in social and moral stances (along with much bad argument). It is the less spectacular lot of some of us, especially when we attempt to apply philosophy intelligently to specific and pressing social issues, to point out that truth or rightness lie somewhere between.

NOTES

Chapter One. Introduction

1. Some authors use the term *reverse discrimination* only as a pejorative, reserving the more neutral *preferential treatment* to refer to a policy that one might accept. By employing the former term here, I do not mean to imply that the policy to which it refers is never justified; indeed, I shall advocate reverse discrimination as a social policy in certain contexts. I do use this term, however, to indicate the prima facie injustice of the practice in relation to generally acceptable distributive principles and to imply that there must be strong overriding considerations to justify the practice.

2. Regents of the University of California v. Bakke, *New York Law Journal*, June 29, 1978.

3. See, for example, John Rawls, *A Theory of Justice* (Cambridge, Mass.: Harvard University Press, 1971), pp. 20, 48-51.

4. This is the criterion of Rawls, *ibid*.

5. For a defense and elaboration of this position, see Robert Nozick, *Anarchy, State, and Utopia* (New York: Basic Books, 1974), Part II.

Chapter Two. Awarding Positions by Competence

1. For libertarian arguments, see Nozick, *Anarchy, State, and Utopia*, chaps. 7, 8; also Judith Thomson, "Preferential Hiring," *Philosophy & Public Affairs*, 2 (1973), 364-84. For the egalitarian position, see Thomas Nagel, "Equal Treatment and Compensatory Discrimination," *Philosophy & Public Affairs*, 2 (1973), 348-63; also Rawls, *Theory of Justice*, pp. 75-90.

2. Compare Louis Katzner, "Is the Favoring of Women and Blacks in Employment and Educational Opportunities Justified?" in Joel Feinberg and Hyman Gross, eds., *Philosophy of Law* (Encino, Calif.: Dickenson, 1975), p. 291.

3. Compare J. Sterba, "Justice as Desert," *Social Theory & Practice*, 3 (1974), 101-16.

4. For the justification of inequalities as incentives, see Rawls, *Theory of Justice*, pp. 305-6, 311.

5. Need is of course another criterion of distribution and a basic

source of claims to social goods. But I ignore it here as irrelevant to the award of positions, since persons do not have special needs to occupy specific positions.

6. This argument is found in Gertrude Ezorsky, "It's Mine," *Philosophy & Public Affairs*, 3 (1974), 321-30.

7. The analogy is from Thomson, "Preferential Hiring."

8. Compare Nicholas Rescher, *Distributive Justice* (Indianapolis: Bobbs-Merrill, 1966), pp. 90-93.

9. Joel Feinberg makes this comparison in "Justice and Personal Desert," in his *Doing and Deserving* (Princeton: Princeton University Press, 1970). Much of the following discussion draws from his illuminating chapter.

10. See, for example, the testimony of Millard Ruud in the *DeFunis* case as to the success of CLEO program graduates in law schools. This is reproduced in Ann F. Ginger, ed., *DeFunis versus Odegaard and The University of Washington*, 3 vols. (New York: Oceana, 1974), I, 68.

11. Helen S. Astin, *The Woman Doctorate in America* (New York: Russell Sage Foundation, 1969), p. 85.

Chapter Three. Compensation and the Past

1. Some ideas for the following section were derived from unpublished papers by Hugo Bedau, "Compensatory Justice," and James Nickel, "Justice in Compensation."

2. This wording, typical in legal contexts, is from Harold Grilliot, *Introduction to Law and the Legal System* (Boston: Houghton Mifflin, 1975), p. 174.

3. Nickel makes a similar point in "Justice in Compensation."

4. James Nickel, "Discrimination and Morally Relevant Characteristics," *Analysis*, 32 (1972), 113-14.

5. J. L. Cowan, "Inverse Discrimination," *Analysis*, 33 (1972), 10-12.

6. Paul Taylor, "Reverse Discrimination and Compensatory Justice," *Analysis*, 33 (1973), 177-82.

7. This qualification was pointed out to me by Hugo Bedau.

8. The example is from Sidney Hook in an editorial in the *New York Times*, Nov. 12, 1974.

9. Contrast Bernard Boxill, "The Morality of Preferential Hiring," *Philosophy & Public Affairs*, 7 (1978), 249.

10. See, for example, A. L. Bertrand, *Basic Sociology* (New York: Appleton-Century-Crofts, 1967), pp. 146-49, and F. L. Bates, "A

Conceptual Analysis of Group Structure," *Social Forces*, 36 (1957), 103-11.

11. For legal arguments to this effect, see Boris Bittker, *The Case For Black Reparations* (New York: Random House, 1973); for moral arguments, see Hugo Bedau, "Compensatory Justice and the Black Manifesto," *The Monist*, 56 (1972), 20-42.

12. For a defense of this weaker criterion, see Lawrence Crocker, "Preferential Treatment," in Mary Vetterling-Braggin, Frederick Elliston, and Jane English, eds., *Feminism and Philosophy* (Totowa, N.J.: Littlefield, Adams, 1977).

13. See Boxill, "Morality of Preferential Hiring."

14. Crocker agrees, "Preferential Treatment," p. 198.

15. The argument is from Nickel, "Should Reparations be to Individuals or to Groups?" *Analysis*, 34 (1974), 154-60. See also his "Preferential Policies in Hiring and Admissions: A Jurisprudential Approach," *Columbia Law Review*, 75 (1975), 534-58.

16. Nickel draws this distinction in "Should Reparations be to Individuals or to Groups?"

17. This point is made by Boxill, "Morality of Preferential Hiring."

18. Cf. Nickel, "Preferential Policies in Hiring and Admissions," p. 551.

19. These three examples, although not the full arguments here concerning them, are found in Robert Simon, "Statistical Justifications of Discrimination," *Analysis*, 38 (1978), 37-42.

20. The discussion in this subsection benefited from Joel Feinberg's essay, "Collective Responsibility," in his *Doing and Deserving*, and also from all of the essays in Peter French, ed., *Individual and Collective Responsibility: The Massacre at My Lai* (Cambridge, Mass.: Schenkman, 1972).

21. See Virginia Held, "Moral Responsibility and Collective Action," in French, ed., *Individual and Collective Responsibility*, pp. 101-18.

22. The example is from Joel Feinberg, "Collective Responsibility," pp. 241-42.

23. The term is from Irving Thalberg, "Visceral Racism," *The Monist*, 56 (1972), 43-63.

24. This argument is from George Sher, "Justifying Reverse Discrimination in Employment," *Philosophy & Public Affairs*, 4 (1975), 164.

25. Amicus brief of Harvard College, in Ginger, ed., *DeFunis versus Odegaard*, I, 881. The example is from Paul Freund, *On Law and Justice* (Cambridge, Mass.: Harvard University Press, 1968).

26. This is argued by Robert Fullinwinder, "On Preferential Hiring," in Vetterling-Braggin et al., eds., *Feminism and Philosophy*, pp. 210-24.

Chapter Four. Equal Opportunity and the Future

1. James A. McPherson, "The Black Law Student," *Atlantic*, 225 (1970), 99.

2. Thomas Sowell, *Black Education: Myths and Tragedies* (New York: McKay, 1972), p. 292.

3. Compare, for example, Carl Wellman, *Morals and Ethics* (Glenview, Ill.: Scott, Foresman, 1975), p. 252.

4. For a discussion of conflicts among rights, see Joel Feinberg, *Social Philosophy* (Englewood Cliffs, N.J.: Prentice-Hall, 1973), Chap. 5.

5. The example is from A. I. Melden, "The Play of Rights," *The Monist*, 56 (1972), 497.

6. The example is from James Nickel, "Preferential Policies," p. 546.

7. I speak of a fundamental right to have one's interests considered equally, rather than an equal right to freedom, as does H.L.A. Hart, since I think that all rights can be construed as freedoms only by a very stretched concept of the latter. Cf. Hart, "Are there Any Natural Rights?" in A. I. Melden, ed., *Human Rights* (Belmont, Calif.: Wadsworth, 1970).

8. This was pointed out to me by Everett Traverso.

9. Compare Charles Frankel, "Equality of Opportunity," *Ethics*, 81 (1971), 192.

10. Christopher Jencks et al., *Inequality: A Reassessment of the Effect of Family and Schooling in America* (New York: Basic Books, 1972). See also the follow-up essays in D. M. Levine and M. J. Bane, eds., *The "Inequality" Controversy: Schooling and Distributive Justice* (New York: Basic Books, 1975).

11. See Nozick, *Anarchy, State, and Utopia*, Part II.

12. See Rawls, *Theory of Justice*, pp. 73-74.

13. Rawls sees this as the most important good, *ibid.*, pp. 440-46.

14. See Onora O'Neill, "How Do We Know When Opportunities Are Equal?" in Vetterling-Braggin et al., eds., *Feminism and Philosophy*, pp. 177-89.

15. Thomas Nagel pointed this out to me.

16. I am in favor of passage of this amendment, which is, however, irrelevant to the discussion which follows.

17. This argument derives from Virginia Held, "Reasonable Progress and Self Respect," *The Monist*, 57 (1973), 12-27.

18. See Lawrence Crocker, "Preferential Treatment."

19. The argument is from Irving Thalberg, "Reverse Discrimination and the Future," *Philosophical Forum*, 5 (1973-1974), 268-82.

20. See Hugo Bedau, "Compensatory Justice and the Black Manifesto."

21. Another distinction crucial in earlier court decisions in this area is that between classifications requiring only a "rational basis" and those considered "inherently suspect"; the latter demand "strict scrutiny" and require a "compelling state interest" for justification. See McLaughlin v. Florida, 379 U.S. 184, 191-93 (1964); Dunn v. Blumstein, 405 U.S. 330, 342 (1972); and San Antonio Independent School District v. Rodriguez, 411 U.S. 1, 40 (1973). This legal distinction again seems blurred by Justice Powell's position in the *Bakke* case, that race is a suspect classification requiring "compelling state interest," but that achieving diversity in professional school classrooms could be considered such an interest! My position here is that classifications by race or sex are in violations of rights to equal opportunity when these alone are made the bases for social rewards, but that they are unobjectionable when used in gathering evidence of discrimination.

22. The guidelines are reprinted in John J. Ross, *Equal Employment Opportunities Compliance—2d* (New York: Practising Law Institute, 1973).

23. This feature of the revised guidelines of 1975 is emphasized by Gertrude Ezorsky in "Hiring Women Faculty," *Philosophy & Public Affairs*, 7 (1978), 82-91. She takes this to ensure that the goals operate in a nondiscriminatory way.

24. Bernice Sandler, in a letter to *Commentary*, 53 (1972), 14-16.

25. Example from Paul Seabury, "HEW and the Universities," *Commentary*, 53 (1972), 38-44.

26. Cf. Sidney Hook, editorial in the *New York Times*, Nov. 12, 1974.

27. As quoted in *Commentary*, 53 (1972), 11.

28. Amicus brief of the Committee on Academic Nondiscrimination, in Ginger, ed., *DeFunis versus Odegaard*, I, 407.

29. Amicus brief of the Chamber of Commerce of the United States of America, in *ibid.*, pp. 363-97.

30. Scientific Manpower Commission, *Professional Women and Minorities: A Manpower Data Resource Service* (Washington, D.C., 1975), pp. 152, 142. Cited in Ezorsky, "Hiring Woman Faculty," p. 88.

31. This position is represented in an unpublished article by Tom Beauchamp, "The Justification of Reverse Discrimination."

32. For a discussion of this distinction and the historical sequence of cases, see Owen M. Fiss, "School Desegregation: The Uncertain Path of the Law," *Philosophy and Public Affairs*, 4 (1975), 3-39.

33. Quotas were held to be only "points of departure," much as in affirmative action; but as in the latter case, once every departure from them must be justified, there is little distinction to be drawn.

SELECTED BIBLIOGRAPHY

Astin, Helen. *The Woman Doctorate in America*. New York: Russell Sage Foundation, 1969.

Barasch, Frances. "HEW, the Universities, and Women." *Dissent*, 20 (1973), 332-40.

Bates, F. L. "A Conceptual Analysis of Group Structure." *Social Forces*, 36 (1957), 103-11.

Bayles, Michael. "Compensatory Reverse Discrimination in Hiring." *Social Theory and Practice*, 2 (1973), 301-12.

————. "Reparations to Wronged Groups." *Analysis*, 33 (1973), 182-84.

Beauchamp, Tom. "The Justification of Reverse Discrimination." Unpublished.

Bedau, Hugo. "Compensatory Justice." Unpublished.

————. "Compensatory Justice and the Black Manifesto." *The Monist*, 56 (1972), 20-42.

Bertrand, A. L. *Basic Sociology*. New York: Appleton-Century-Crofts, 1967.

Bittker, Boris. *The Case for Black Reparations*. New York: Random House, 1973.

Black, Virginia. "The Erosion of Legal Principles in the Creation of Legal Policies." *Ethics*, 84 (1974), 93-115.

Blackstone, William. "Reverse Discrimination and Compensatory Justice." *Social Theory and Practice*, 3 (1975), 253-88.

————, and Heslep, Robert, eds. *Social Justice and Preferential Treatment*. Athens: University of Georgia Press, 1977.

Boxill, Bernard. "The Morality of Preferential Hiring." *Philosophy & Public Affairs*, 7 (1978), 246-68.

————. "The Morality of Reparation." *Social Theory and Practice*, 2 (1972), 113-24.

Cohen, M., Nagel, T., and Scanlon, T., eds. *Equality and Preferential Treatment*. Princeton: Princeton University Press, 1977.

Coleman, Jules. "Justice and Preferential Hiring." *Journal of Critical Analysis*, 5 (1973), 27-29.

Cowan, J. L. "Inverse Discrimination." *Analysis*, 33 (1972), 10-12.

Crocker, Lawrence. "Preferential Treatment." In Vetterling-Braggin et al., eds., *Feminism and Philosophy*, pp. 190-209.

Daniels, Norman. "Merit and Meritocracy." *Philosophy & Public Affairs*, 7 (1978), 206-23.

Dunn v. Blumstein, 405 U.S. 330, 342 (1972).

Dworkin, Ronald. "The Bakke Decision." *New York Review of Books*, August 17, 1978, pp. 20-25.

————. "The DeFunis Case: The Right to Go to Law School." *New York Review of Books*, February 5, 1976, pp. 29-33.

————. "DeFunis v. Sweatt." In Cohen et al., eds., *Equality and Preferential Treatment*, pp. 63-83.

————. "Why Bakke Has No Case." *New York Review of Books*, November 10, 1977, pp. 11-15.

Ezorsky, Gertrude. "Hiring Women Faculty." *Philosophy & Public Affairs*, 7 (1978), 82-91.

————. "It's Mine." *Philosophy & Public Affairs*, 3 (1974), 321-30.

Feinberg, Joel. *Doing and Deserving*. Princeton: Princeton University Press, 1970.

————, and Gross, Hyman, eds. *Philosophy of Law*. Encino, Calif.: Dickenson, 1975.

————. *Social Philosophy*. Englewood Cliffs, N.J.: Prentice-Hall, 1973.

Fiss, Owen. "Groups and the Equal Protection Clause." *Philosophy & Public Affairs*, 5 (1976), 107-77.

————. "School Desegregation: The Uncertain Path of the Law." *Philosophy & Public Affairs*, 4 (1975), 3-39.

Frankel, Charles. "Equality of Opportunity." *Ethics*, 81 (1971), 191-211.

French, Peter, ed. *Individual and Collective Responsibility: The Massacre at My Lai*. Cambridge, Mass.: Schenkman, 1972.

Freund, Paul. *On Law and Justice*. Cambridge, Mass.: Harvard University Press, 1968.

Fried, Marlene. "In Defense of Preferential Hiring." *Philosophical Forum*, 5 (1973-1974), 283-93.

Fullinwinder, Robert. "On Preferential Hiring." In Vetterling-Braggin et al., eds., *Feminism and Philosophy*, pp. 210-24.

————. "Preferential Hiring and Compensation." *Social Theory and Practice*, 3 (1975), 307-20.

Ginger, Ann, ed. *DeFunis versus Odegaard and The University of Washington*. 3 vols. New York: Oceana, 1974.

Glazer, Nathan. *Affirmative Discrimination*. New York: Basic Books, 1975.

Grilliot, Harold. *Introduction to Law and the Legal System*. Boston: Houghton Mifflin, 1975.

Gross, Barry, ed. *Reverse Discrimination*. Buffalo: Prometheus, 1976.

Held, Virginia. "Reasonable Progress and Self Respect." *The Monist*, 57 (1973), 12-27.

Hill, Jim. "What Justice Requires: Some Comments on Professor Schoeman's Views on Compensatory Justice." *The Personalist*, 56 (1975), 96-100.

Jaggar, Alison. "Relaxing the Limits on Preferential Treatment." *Social Theory and Practice*, 4 (1977), 227-35.

Jencks, Christopher, et al. *Inequality: A Reassessment of the Effect of Family and Schooling in America*. New York: Basic Books, 1972.

Jones, Hardy. "Fairness, Meritocracy, and Reverse Discrimination." *Social Theory and Practice*, 4 (1977), 211-26.

Katzner, Louis. "Is the Favoring of Women and Blacks in Employment and Educational Opportunities Justified?" In Feinberg and Gross, eds., *Philosophy of Law*, pp. 291-96.

Lester, Richard. *Anti-Bias Regulation of Universities*. New York: McGraw-Hill, 1974.

Levine, D. M., and Bane, M. J., eds. *The "Inequality" Controversy: Schooling and Distributive Justice*. New York: Basic Books, 1975.

McGary, Howard, "Reparations and Inverse Discrimination." *Dialogue*, 17 (1974), 8-10.

McLaughlin v. Florida, 379 U.S. 184, 191-93 (1964).

McPherson, James A. "The Black Law Student." *Atlantic*, 225 (1970), 93-100.

Martin, Michael. "Pedagogical Arguments for Preferential Hiring and Tenuring of Women Teachers in the University." *Philosophical Forum*, 5 (1973-1974), 299-307.

Melden, A. I., ed. *Human Rights*. Belmont, Calif.: Wadsworth, 1970.

———. "The Play of Rights." *The Monist*, 56 (1972), 479-502.

Nagel, Thomas. "Equal Treatment and Compensatory Discrimination." *Philosophy & Public Affairs*, 2 (1973), 348-63.

Newton, Lisa. "Reverse Discrimination as Unjustified." *Ethics*, 83 (1973), 308-12.

Nickel, James. "Classification by Race in Compensatory Programs." *Ethics*, 84 (1974), 146-50.

———. "Discrimination and Morally Relevant Characteristics." *Analysis*, 32 (1972), 113-14.

———. "Justice in Compensation." Unpublished.

———. "Preferential Policies in Hiring and Admissions: A Jurisprudential Approach." *Columbia Law Review*, 75 (1975), 534-58.

———. "Should Reparations be to Individuals or to Groups?" *Analysis*, 34 (1974), 154-60.

Nozick, Robert. *Anarchy, State, and Utopia*. New York: Basic Books, 1974.

Nunn, William. "Reverse Discrimination." *Analysis*, 34 (1974), 151-54.

O'Neil, Robert. *Discriminating Against Discrimination*. Bloomington: Indiana University Press, 1975.

O'Neill, Onora. "How Do We Know When Opportunities Are Equal?" In Vetterling-Braggin et al., eds., *Feminism and Philosophy*, pp. 177-89.

Rawls, John. *A Theory of Justice*. Cambridge, Mass.: Harvard University Press, 1971.

Regents of the University of California v. Bakke. *New York Law Journal*, June 29, 1978.

Rescher, Nicholas. *Distributive Justice*. Indianapolis: Bobbs-Merrill, 1966.

Ross, John. *Equal Employment Opportunities Compliance—2d*. New York: Practising Law Institute, 1973.

San Antonio Independent School District v. Rodriguez, 411 U.S. 1, 40 (1973).

Sandler, Bernice. Letter to *Commentary*, 53 (1972), 14-16.

Schucter, Arnold. *Reparations*. Philadelphia: Lippincott, 1970.

Scientific Manpower Commission. *Professional Women and Minorities: A Manpower Data Resource Service*. Washington, D.C., 1975.

Seabury, Paul. "HEW and the Universities." *Commentary*, 53 (1972), 38-44.

Sher, George. "Justifying Reverse Discrimination in Employment." *Philosophy & Public Affairs*, 4 (1975), 159-70.

Shiner, Roger. "Individuals, Groups and Inverse Discrimination." *Analysis*, 33 (1973), 185-87.

Silvestri, Philip. "The Justification of Inverse Discrimination." *Analysis*, 34 (1973), 31-32.

Simon, Robert. "Preferential Hiring." *Philosophy & Public Affairs*, 3 (1974), 312-20.

————. "Statistical Justifications of Discrimination." *Analysis*, 38 (1978), 37-42.

Sowell, Thomas. *Black Education: Myths and Tragedies*. New York: McKay, 1972.

Sterba, J. "Justice as Desert." *Social Theory and Practice*, 3 (1974), 101-16.

Taylor, Paul. "Reverse Discrimination and Compensatory Justice." *Analysis*, 33 (1973), 177-82.

Thalberg, Irving. "Reverse Discrimination and the Future." *Philosophical Forum*, 5 (1973-1974), 268-82.

————. "Visceral Racism." *The Monist*, 56 (1972), 43-63.

Thomson, Judith. "Preferential Hiring." *Philosophy & Public Affairs*, 2 (1973), 364-84.

Vetterling, Mary. "Some Common Sense Notes on Preferential Hiring." *Philosophical Forum*, 5 (1973-1974), 294-98.

Vetterling-Braggin, Mary, Elliston, Frederick, and English, Jane, eds. *Feminism and Philosophy*. Totowa, N.J.: Littlefield, Adams, 1977.

Wasserstrom, Richard. "The University and the Case for Preferential Treatment." *American Philosophical Quarterly*, 13 (1976), 165-70.

Wellman, Carl. *Morals and Ethics*. Glenview, Ill.: Scott, Foresman, 1975.

INDEX

administrative efficiency in preferential programs, 8, 94-102, 140, 202-3

affirmative action, 93, 99, 187; ambiguities of, 200-201, 219, 222-23; enforcement of, 218, 232; features, 201, 204-8, 215, 218-19; history, 201, 204-6; legal status of, 5, 201-2; as pressuring reverse discrimination, 22, 212-15, 218-23, 227, 232; target goals and quotas, 22, 201, 205-6, 210-26, 229; utilities of, 224-25

Anglo-Americans. *See* white males

Astin, Helen, 236n

award of positions, 15; by competence, 14-15, 22-48, 55, 62, 65, 117, 123, 155, 160-61, 178; egalitarian principle for, 41-48; libertarian principle for, 23, 35-40

backlash resentment, 144, 146, 148, 217

Bakke, Regents of the University of California v., 4-6, 9, 144, 201-2, 215, 235n, 239n

Bates, F. L., 236n

Beauchamp, Tom, 239n

Bedau, Hugo, 236n, 238n

Bertrand, A. L., 236n

Bittker, Boris, 236n

blacks: equal opportunity for, 17, 190-92, 195, 225-26; injustice toward, 52-53, 59, 74-77, 82, 85-86, 92, 94, 98, 112, 117-18, 184; qualifications for positions, 17, 22, 51, 54-60, 147; recipients of compensation, 75-76, 85-86, 97-98

Boxill, Bernard, 236n, 237n

Brown v. *Board of Education*, 99, 225

busing for integration, 225, 228

Chamber of Commerce, U.S., 213, 239n

chronic social deprivation, 6, 39-40, 61, 170, 177-79, 184, 191-94, 199-200

Civil Rights Act of 1964, 204

Committee on Academic Nondiscrimination and Integrity, 213, 239n

competence. *See* award of positions, by; qualifications for positions

Congress, U.S., 40

consistency. *See* moral reasoning

contractarian framework for morality, 11-16, 70, 162-64, 167, 175, 179, 191, 228; liberal criterion for principles of, 11-15, 18, 24-25, 27, 29; libertarian criterion for principles of, 12-14, 39; strong criterion for principles of, 11-15, 18, 23-24, 29

counterfactuals, 68-69, 129

Cowan, J. L., 236n

credentials for positions, 17, 22, 49-50, 61-62; as discriminatory, 51-54, 58-64; handicapping of, 8-9, 58, 61-63, 115, 128-31, 206

Crocker, Lawrence, 237n, 238n

cultural deprivation, 59. *See also* chronic social deprivation

De Funis v. *Odegaard and The University of Washington*, 9, 118, 130, 144, 213, 215, 236n, 239n

desegregation. *See* integration

political power: for minority groups,
8, 88, 189-90; as pressure for reverse discrimination, 4, 93, 102;
redistribution of, 4; social benefits
and, 32, 88, 189-90
Pottinger, J. Stanley, 205
poverty. *See* chronic social deprivation
Powell, Lewis, 5, 201, 239n
preferential treatment. *See* reverse
discrimination
prejudice, 26, 40, 55, 77, 80, 100,
142, 147, 166, 168, 194; assumption of inferior qualifications for
minority-group members, 59-61,
146, 220-23; as attitude of all white
males, 107-8; equal opportunity
and, 216-17
prima facie rights, 6, 23, 25, 34, 48,
65-69, 117, 120
productivity: as measure of desert,
30-33, 43-46, 63, 68, 130, 140, 203;
as measure of effort, 30-32, 44-45,
56
professional schools, 59-60, 129, 145,
160, 201-2
property. *See* rights to property
proportionate representation of
groups in positions, 8, 46, 81, 93,
113-15, 144-47, 166, 183-84, 189-
93, 197, 224-27
psychological harm. *See* harms;
women
punishment, 72-73, 107, 161, 168

qualifications for positions, 1, 7, 34,
49, 52, 58, 60, 166-67; causal factors
of, 45, 59; credentials and, 50-51,
60-63; defense of, as basis for
awarding positions, 22-48; fixed
level of, 30, 62, 65, 99, 124, 160,
169; membership in minority
group as constituting, 17, 22,
54-58, 61-64, 75, 166-69, 176;
open-ended degrees of, 9, 30, 62,
65, 124, 160
quotas for minorities, 5. *See also*

affirmative action, target goals and
quotas

racism. *See* blacks, injustice toward;
prejudice
rationality, 14, 35
Rawls, John, 12, 26, 235n, 238n
reflective equilibrium, 11. *See also*
moral reasoning
regress argument against reverse
discrimination, 123-25
relativism, 19
remedial programs. *See* educational
system
Rescher, Nicholas, 236n
reversal test, 16-17, 34, 100, 166-67
reverse discrimination: affirmative
action and, 22, 212-15, 218-23,
227, 232; backward-looking arguments for, 4, 9-10, 65-102, 120-40,
195-99; as compensation in kind,
57-58, 71, 74-82, 85-90, 112, 121-
22, 127, 132, 137, 227, 230; defined, 4-8, 23; directed toward
groups, 8, 82, 89-103, 113, 116-17,
140, 142, 188-95; equal opportunity and, 56, 174, 182, 184-97, 230;
evidence for, 49-58, 166, 213-14,
218; future-looking arguments for,
4, 9-10, 55, 141, 195-200; statistical
justification of, 81, 95-97, 101-2;
strong, 8-9, 22, 76, 120-24, 127,
130, 136, 140, 206, 215, 224; utility
of, 141-49, 169; weak, 8-9, 76, 121,
124, 214-15, 224
rights, 13, 87, 95, 180; to award positions without restrictions, 23-24,
35-36, 38, 40-41, 153-54, 230; to
compensation, 16, 69, 88, 95,
110-11, 121-25, 143, 155, 165; defined, 149-51, 162; dignity and, 57,
156-57; to equal opportunity, 16,
26, 28, 38-41, 153, 155, 163-64,
170, 175, 177, 181, 188-89, 194; to
free association, 35-40; interests
and, 36, 151-52, 155-59, 162-64;
ordering of, 37-38, 153-54, 159-61,

Library of Congress Cataloging in Publication Data

Goldman, Alan H.   1945-
  Justice and reverse discrimination.

  Bibliography: p.
  Includes index.
  1.   Affirmative action programs.   2.   Discrimina-
tion.   I.   Title.
HF5549.5.A34G64   331.1'33   78-63595
ISBN 0-691-07233-7
ISBN 0-691-02003-5 pbk.